VOYAGE TO
THE AMOROUS ISLANDS

Captain Wallis meets Purea at the house Agitation. From an engraving in *Hawkesworth's Voyages.*

NEWTON A. ROWE

Voyage to The Amorous Islands

The Discovery of Tahiti

ANDRE DEUTSCH

FIRST PUBLISHED 1955 BY
ANDRE DEUTSCH LIMITED
12–14 CARLISLE STREET SOHO SQUARE
LONDON WI
ALL RIGHTS RESERVED
PRINTED IN GREAT BRITAIN BY
TONBRIDGE PRINTERS LIMITED
TONBRIDGE KENT

FOR
ROSALIND ROWE

CONTENTS

ILLUSTRATIONS

FOREWORD

*

Ruskin has said that 'the only history worth reading is that written at the time of which it treats; the history of what is done and seen, out of the mouths of the men who did and saw it'. While this sweeping statement is not entirely true, there is an element of truth in it, and it seems to me particularly applicable to the history of geographical discoveries. The men who made them did more than fill in blank spaces on the map of the world; sailing out into unknown seas and dropping anchor by unknown shores, they were actively engaged in enlarging the boundaries of human experience and their records have a greater value than belongs simply to the physical facts they interpret, or misinterpret.

This book, therefore, is largely compiled from the actual words of the men who 'did and saw it'. My concern has been to find out and set down what really happened when Captain Samuel Wallis, officer commanding H.M.S. *Dolphin*, discovered the island of Tahiti in 1767.

My sources are described in the Epilogue.

The structure of the book, good or bad, was worked out in the course of many years, and after following many blind alleys, for the subject – within its set limit of introducing no fiction, while providing a reasonably colourful running narrative – is a complicated one. Perhaps I clumsily eliminated every wrong way by trying it. The point is perhaps of interest because it has been suggested recently in *The Times Literary Supplement* that experience seems to show that a book of this nature, dealing with such a voyage, may be technically impossible. It was only at a last attempt, by throwing in everything including the kitchen sink, that it seemed to fuse and work out as I hoped. At any rate, this is precisely the sort of book I was aiming at, and I have no apologies to make on that score, for I believe the technical problem to have been solved.

I would like to thank Sir Harry Luke for his valuable help. He read this book in typescript, taking infinite pains in suggesting ways in which I might improve the presentation of my material. The book owes a great deal to his clear mind and his sense of style.

Others to whom I wish to express my warm thanks are mentioned in the Epilogue.

N. A. R.

AUTHOR'S NOTE

*

I have referred to Francis Wilkinson as a master's mate and an officer. In the *Dolphin's* Muster Book for 1766 (ADM. 36/7580) he is shown as an able seaman aged nineteen and born at Chatham. (It might be remarked that Richard Pickersgill, aged eighteen, began the voyage as an able seaman and acted as master's mate. He is also referred to as a midshipman. He was a clever draughtsman and drew charts of the Straits of Magellan.) There can be no doubt that Wilkinson also had petty officer rank, for in his journal he constantly gives details of latitude and longitude and the distance run daily by the ship, which would not have been available to him otherwise. And on the day of the *Dolphin's* departure from Tahiti he says: 'In the morning when the boats went on shore, manned and armed as commanded, for water, which duty I was charged with . . .' Robertson refers to him on this occasion as 'the officer'.

There is, I think, no doubt that Wilkinson was the hero of the 'handsome little woman' episode, and Robertson then refers to him as 'a gentleman' and 'my freind' and 'my old freind'. Robertson may have lent him his cabin on this occasion. He may have sailed as an able seaman to escape the ban put on officers taking boys as servants. It was the age of privilege.

The subject of the poem written inside the back cover of Wilkinson's journal is the Speed of Sound, and the poem takes the form of a Conundrum on that subject:

> *One evening walking on the sandy shore,*
> *Where shell fish breed and seas for ever roar,*
> *I saw a ship dance on the rouling tide,*
> *With curling smoak advanceing from her side.*
> *Which for some moments my dull sence imploys*
> *Untill I heard the thundering cannon noise.*
> *Then from my fob time's register I drew,*

13

And from her side a second lightning flew.
Full 14 second of swift time expired
Before the thundering noise my listning ears admired.
Now you that time's progressive motions know
My distance from the floating vessell show.

* * *

The answer: 8 miles, 49 yards, 1 foot.

Wilkinson sailed as an able seaman in the *Endeavour*, on Captain Cook's first voyage to the Pacific, shortly after the *Dolphin's* return to England. Within three weeks of sailing – on August 19th, 1768 – he was promoted to Master's Mate.

'Look out tomorrow for the clouds containing a rainbow, and by it will the ship arrive at your shore.'

From an ancient Tahitian legend

VOYAGE TO
THE AMOROUS ISLANDS

CHAPTER I

*

GIANTS IN THE PATH

WHEN Captain the Honourable John Byron – 'Foul Weather Jack' to the members of his Service – who was to be the grandfather of the poet, returned to England in the *Dolphin* in the spring of 1766, he had circumnavigated the globe in the record time of twenty-two months. During this voyage he had discovered, it is true, nothing but a few small, unimportant coral atolls in the Pacific, but he brought back exciting confirmation of the existence of a race of giants on the southern coast of Patagonia in South America. There had been reports to this effect since Magellan's voyage in 1520.

The British Admiralty, less interested in giants than in the Southern Continent, ordered the *Dolphin* to be made ready as fast as possible, so as not to lose the proper season for returning to the Pacific through the Straits of Magellan. It was to be her new task to make discoveries in the southern hemisphere and, if possible, to find the Southern Continent.

Some curious views were then held on this mysterious land. It was generally believed that there was a Southern Continent in the Pacific, an enormous land-mass which geographers thought must lie in the southern hemisphere to balance the northern land-masses; for otherwise, so it was held, the world would turn upside down. It was believed to be a vast inhabited piece of the earth's surface, lying in the temperate zone and destined to equal in gold and other resources the wealth that Cortés and Pizarro drew from Mexico and Peru for the benefit of Spain in the sixteenth century. All the major European Powers, therefore, were interested in it. It had been the fond dream of geographers for centuries, this *Terra Australis Incognita*, not to be confused with Australia, whose existence was already known although its eastern coast had not yet been touched by Europeans.

19

Australia was then called New Holland. Some thought that the north and west coasts of New Zealand, discovered by the Dutchman Tasman in the seventeenth century, were outposts in a silent sea of the Southern Continent. The map of the Southern Pacific – apart possibly from mythological, bestial and fishy drawings, and from the Solomon Islands, which geographers put in where they thought fit or else left out – was an almost complete blank, for ships tended to keep to the northern Spanish trade route, being concerned to reach the East Indies before running out of supplies and losing too many men from scurvy. Anson showed nothing below the equinoctial line but the Solomon Islands, in the position approximately of Tahiti.

So the *Dolphin* was promptly refitted and underwent a thorough repair in Deptford Dock in London. There was considerable secrecy concerning the purpose of the voyage. The French and Spanish Embassies in London were much interested in the *Dolphin's* movements, past and projected. They had been speculating for some time as to what she had been doing.

She was a new ship of 511 tons with a copper bottom, the second ship in the British Navy to be so constructed. She was 130 feet long; and thirty-four at her greatest beam. She had three masts, with a very large fighting-top round the head of each lower mast, and she carried three tiers of sails on her square-rigged fore- and main-masts. She was fore-and-aft rigged on the mizzen. Her quarter-deck was unusually long, fifty-five feet, reaching almost to the main-mast. Her forecastle was the same height as the quarter-deck, and in the low waist between was the gun-deck. The gun-deck also ran under the quarter-deck and forecastle; and there was a lower-deck. Gangways skirted the bulwarks between the fo'c'sle-head and the quarter-deck, so that it was possible to avoid descending unnecessarily to the gun-deck. She had a square forward bulkhead with a beak in front of it – not rounded bows – and a high-jutting bowsprit and jib-boom, with – in addition to the stay and jib sails above – square sails suspended close to the water beneath from sprit-sail yards. She wore flags fore and aft, at a flagpost at the stern and at a small flagstaff on the bowsprit above the upper sprit-sail yard. Long pennants fluttered from the three lofty mast-heads, of which that of the main-mast was much the highest and the mizzen the lowest.

A man-of-war of the sixth rate, a 'true frigate', she carried all her main armament on the gun- or upper-deck and none on the lower-deck, belonging to the class of vessel that had come in during the recently concluded Seven Years' War. Designed for independent cruising at high speed, such ships were intended as the eyes of the fleet. Great Britain was now in command of the sea, and, under the patriotic young King, George III, was turning her attention to a new and scientific era of exploration. The means for determining longitude accurately at sea had only recently been discovered. John Byron had initiated this phase of exploration.

The *Dolphin's* upper-works were painted blue, her sides at the level of the gun-deck canary yellow (with wide black strakes at the water line), her poop above the quarter-deck guns and the tops of her sides red. Inboard she was bright red (and this included the gun carriages and other fittings) so that any blood spilt during an action – when splinters flew with devastating effect – might not contrast too violently with the surrounding paintwork.

It had been found inconvenient to work the cables on the lower-deck, so they were now to work on the upper- or gun-deck; and the capstan was placed on the very long quarter-deck.

The officer appointed to command this ship was one Captain Samuel Wallis, a Cornishman, aged thirty-eight. Wallis was a realistic sort of person, who took a measuring-rod to measure the giants. He, the First-Lieutenant, William Clark, aged thirty, and the Purser, a jovial fellow, were personable-looking men; so was John Hutchinson, the Surgeon. The Second-Lieutenant was one Tobias Furneaux, just over thirty, a good, kind, gentle man, so it was said. The Master, or navigating officer, was George Robertson, aged thirty-five – pleasant but very curious (in the sense of inquisitive) and of exceptional physical strength.

Captain Wallis signed his seamen on in London, but was instructed not to take boys for himself or any of the officers. There was a peculiar system of patronage in the Navy, by which the captain, lieutenants and senior petty officers could take as servants boys –

usually sons of friends – who in due course were eligible for promotion to the quarter-deck. This was not, however, the regular mode of entry to the officer class in the Navy, and the fact that on this occasion it was not allowed, indicated that the voyage was to be an unusual one. Most of the men signing on were healthy and young. The complement was 150, including thirteen marines, who were intended to preserve a balance on the side of authority against the ordinary seamen. There were thirty-seven warrant or petty officers, including the master, doctor or surgeon, gunner, purser, mates, boatswain, carpenter and midshipmen. There were only two commissioned lieutenants.

The seamen were called tars, from the tarpaulin hats which they wore, with the brims tacked up in the shape of a triangular apple pasty. Their hair was worn long and thick, not queued, and some had it cut short on the neck. Their shirts were chequered and their short white trousers tightish fitting. Handkerchiefs tied round their necks fell to a point behind and their short jackets, like modern pilot jackets, were usually worn open with long white waistcoats, either spotted or striped red or blue.

The three commissioned officers wore blue frock-coats with white facings and white stand-up collars and cuffs as part of the coat – Nelson fashion, white breeches and stockings. The warrant and petty officers wore blue breeches, and their blue frock-coats were lined, although not edged, with white. All officers and midshipmen carried blue triangular hats, those of the seniors laced with gold. Most of the officers had white wigs or powdered hair queued with a black ribbon.

It was rumoured that all were to get the same encouragement as had the officers and men on Byron's recent voyage round the world, that is to say double pay and other privileges, if during the voyage they behaved to the captain's satisfaction.

The liquor ration in the Navy was one gallon of beer a day for each man or boy, and it was good beer. The Admiralty had established brew-houses in the naval dockyards because of the rascality of contractors. Beer could not be carried on long voyages, and the ration was then half a pint of spirits or wine. The daily ration of spirits had formerly been issued neat in two lots; but Admiral Vernon, known as 'Old Grog' – in dirty weather he used to wear a hairy grogram coat – had introduced the watering of spirits before issue, wherefore the mixture was called grog. In England the men got beer. Women were allowed aboard the warships when in home ports, for something had to be done about sex. When the *Royal George* sank at her moorings at Spithead, there were aboard five hundred women, who were drowned.

On the 8th July, 1766, the *Dolphin* was hauled out of dock and lashed alongside the sheer hulk – a dismasted ship – to take in her masts and ballast and be rigged. On the 26th she sailed down the Thames for Long Reach, where she took in her guns and gunners' stores. On the 3rd August she anchored at the Nore, where she entered into sea victualling and was got ready for sea. Some astronomical instruments were sent aboard, put up in wooden boxes. It was rumoured that the crew's encouragement would depend entirely on discovering an important place in the South Seas.

Robertson, the master, responsible for all matters concerning the sailing of the ship, thought this was a poor encouragement for so dangerous a voyage. Although for his own part he loved the idea of the voyage, he believed that few on board, if any, would willingly have signed on had they known the uncertain footing on which they were sailing. But it was too late to repine. It was rumoured that Captain Byron had discovered several small islands in the South Seas but no place fit to make a settlement and no anchorage where he could get wood and water; and that it was his positive opinion that the Southern Continent lay not far south of what he called King George's Islands.

The *Dolphin* anchored in Plymouth Sound on the 16th August and was joined in a few hours by the *Prince Frederick*, store-ship, and the *Swallow*, a sloop. The *Swallow* had been refitting at Chatham. Her captain, Philip Carteret, a Channel Islander, had begun the recent voyage with Byron as first lieutenant of the sloop *Tamar*, then transferring to become first lieutenant of the *Dolphin*. Carteret was not informed of the purpose of the forthcoming voyage or its intended destination.

The *Dolphin* was crammed with stores and everything else necessary for a long and dangerous voyage. Even the captain's state, or sleeping, room was stacked with 'portable soup', and the steerage – the officers' central cabin on the lower-deck in the stern, used normally by the officers for writing and recreation – was filled with 'slops': clothing, knives, tobacco and such articles as the crew might wish to buy during the voyage from the purser, who not only kept the books and supervised the issue of stores at sea, but was also paymaster outside home ports, and sold the slops to the crew on a commission basis. His wages also included a percentage on stores passing through his books.

Dr Hutchinson, who had much experience, offered to buy an additional quantity of medical supplies if room could be found to stow them. Captain Wallis gave him leave to put them in his great cabin, the only place in the ship where room could be found for the three large boxes. The captain's cabin was on the gun-deck in the stern, right above, and much larger than, the steerage, being eighteen feet by twenty-two. Its windows, forming a gallery, stretched some fifteen feet across the stern. It lay immediately beneath the poop of the quarter-deck.

The *Dolphin* was victualled for twelve months with what were thought the best provisions that ever went to sea; and the boatswain's, gunner's and carpenter's stores were good and plenty for two years.

But the *Swallow* was supplied only sparsely with common necessities, and the few things for which Carteret applied were refused him. Having been on the recent voyage, he knew that such things as a forge, some iron and a small skiff would be invaluable; but he was refused them. He had not even enough junk, or old cable, to cut up for oakum, for caulking and preventing wear and tear to sails and rigging, a vital necessity on any voyage in a canvas-propelled ship. He was told that enough for both ships had been put aboard the *Dolphin* and that the vessel and her equipment were entirely fit for the service she was to perform. Knowing that the *Swallow* was old (she had been thirty years in the service) and that her slight wooden sheathing was not even studded with nails to keep out the boring-worm – a protective system in vogue since the time of

Charles II – Carteret came to the conclusion that she could not be intended to go further than the Falkland Islands, where was another copper-bottomed frigate, the *Jason*, who might replace her. In these islands a British colony had just been established, Byron having surveyed them for that purpose.

On the 19th August the marine detachment – a sergeant and twelve men – came aboard the *Dolphin*, wearing tall grenadier caps, scarlet frock-coats reaching to the knee, breeches and close-fitting gaiters. The ship completed her stores and was made all clear for sea despite rumours that the voyage would probably be cancelled.

That day, however, Captain Wallis received his sailing orders, with directions to take the *Swallow* and the *Prince Frederick* under his command. He was soon disgusted to find that the *Swallow* sailed extremely badly.

The three ships' companies having received two months' pay from the pay offices ashore, the vessels weighed anchor and sailed from Plymouth on the 22nd August, 1766. Wallis ordered the *Dolphin's* company to be put on three watches. Mr Clarke, the first lieutenant, took the first watch; Mr Furneaux, the second lieutenant, the second; Mr Robertson, the master, the third.

Robertson maintained that this rule should be observed by every commander embarking on desperate ventures such as discovering New Worlds, since success depended on the maintenance of the men's health. If they were distressed with hard labour, had no regular meals and no proper time for rest, it was impossible for them to hold out long. When the ship's company was kept at three watches, they did only four hours' deck duty, followed by eight hours' rest below. When they were kept at watch and watch – four hours off and four hours on – they were tempted to fall asleep on deck and not only neglected their duty but frequently caught severe chills which might cost them their lives.

They anchored off the island of Madeira in the Atlantic, where wine, six live bullocks and a large quantity of onions were brought aboard the *Dolphin*. Carteret, not yet knowing his destination, represented his want of junk in a letter to Wallis, who sent him five hundredweight; a quantity so inadequate that Carteret was soon reduced to cutting off some of his working cables to save his rigging.

Nine of Carteret's best men stripped themselves naked and, each taking only his money in a handkerchief tied round his waist, not worrying about being eaten by sharks or dashed to pieces by surf against the rocks, swam ashore to get a skinful of liquor. They said that they were bound on a long voyage, though they knew not where, and none could tell who might live or who might die. They thought it hard not to have an opportunity to spend their own money.

Having caused astonishment and scandal ashore, they were sent back aboard by the British Consul. Their spokesman stated the facts about their money. He said: 'We hoped to get a skinful of liquor. We never had any intention of deserting the *Swallow*, which we are determined to stand by as long as she can swim. We hoped to have got back before we were missed.' The rest of the ship's company, who stood round them, highly approved this apology.

Carteret replied: 'I am glad to see that you look contrite. With a skinful of liquor you would have been in a bad state to swim back to the ship.' (The men, however, had probably been referring to the island custom of putting up Madeira wine in goat-skins.) 'As I may possibly have need of good swimmers during the voyage, I am very glad to know to whom I may apply. Put on your clothes and get some rest.' A murmur of approval ran through the ship's company – and Carteret was rewarded for his lenity by the example of unfailing zeal and alacrity which the nine men set in all hardships and dangers.

Not until after leaving Madeira was Carteret told the particulars of the voyage by Wallis, who gave him a copy of his instructions: these required the *Swallow*, but not the *Prince Frederick*, to accompany the *Dolphin* in the search for the Southern Continent. The commander appointed a rendezvous in the Straits of Magellan in case they should be separated.

Bullocks were killed from time to time and fresh meat sent aboard the other ships as opportunity offered. The bad sailing qualities of the *Swallow* and the store-ship caused much worry. The weather began to grow cold.

On the 17th December the ships anchored off Cape Virgin Mary
of Patagonia, less than a mile from the shore. Some horsemen came
riding down the cape and dismounted. A few of these approached
close to the shore, hallooed loudly and waved their cloaks. They
were tall, big men, and were supposed to be Byron's giants, who
had spoken to him here. They camped abreast of the ships and made
several large fires, and kept up their hallooing all through the night.
The strange stories so often told about their stature made most of
the seamen fancy that their voices resembled the bellowing of bulls
or the roaring of lions rather than the speech of men. All longed for
the day that they might see for themselves what sort of creatures
the Patagonians were.

The following morning at six o'clock Wallis, Carteret, the
lieutenants, doctor and purser from the *Dolphin* went ashore, with
the party of marines, all armed. Wallis ordered Robertson to bring
the ship's broadside to bear on the shore, to keep the guns loaded
with round-shot and to fire a few shots among the giants should they
prove troublesome.

Wallis measured a number of the people. All were decently clad
and had horses to ride. The eyelids of all the young women were
painted black. He found that the tallest men measured from six feet
five to six feet seven inches, but that most of them ranged from
five feet ten to six feet. Yet Robertson recorded that Wallis found
the full-grown men to measure from six feet to six feet nine inches,
though some appeared to be two or three inches taller. Wallis's
report tended to discredit Byron, who had estimated the height of
the shortest of the people at six feet six inches and bulky in propor-
tion, with many of them over seven feet.

During recent years reports of a race of giants had been eagerly
disputed among all classes in England; indeed, stories to that effect had
been current for more than two centuries. The limping Portuguese
Magellan, then in the service of the King of Spain, had in 1520
passed from the Atlantic to the Pacific through the stormy, narrow
waterway north of Cape Horn that now bears his name; Cape Horn
was then unknown to Europeans. Just before entering the Straits he
captured two gigantic natives and under the pretence of making

them presents, loaded their feet with fetters, giving them to understand that this was the best way of carrying their presents, since their hands were already full. When they were dragged aboard Magellan's ships, the giants in fury cried to their god Setebos, a name adopted by Shakespeare for the god of Caliban's mother. Magellan gave the race the name of Patagones – the clumsy-footed people – either because of their enormous feet or because they wore half boots, open behind and stuffed with straw. They were probably members of the Tehuelche tribe.

Magellan, with his starving crews eating rats and leather from the booms, sailed across the ocean he misnamed the Pacific and discovered the Ladrones (Thieves') and Philippine Islands, where he was killed in an attempt to convert the idolators of the island of Mactan to a higher faith. The object of his voyage had been a misconceived endeavour to prove that the Portuguese Spice Islands of the East Indies – known later as the Dutch East Indies – lay in the western hemisphere; for the Borgia Pope, Alexander VI, of evil memory, had allotted heathen lands in the western hemisphere to his native Spain, all those in the eastern hemisphere to Portugal.

Some sixty years later Drake followed in the tracks of Magellan but gave no account of the giants; his companion, Winter, thought the story a lie. Other Europeans now penetrated to the Pacific, and several gigantic Patagonians were seized, but all of them died. No skeleton was brought to Europe, because of the superstition universal among sailors that compasses would not traverse with a dead body on board.

Certain European navigators had averred that the giants were eleven feet tall and could tear large trees up by the roots without effort. The British had generally been moderate in their claims, some having even denied the giants' existence. But Lord Anson pointed out that, if they had rarely been seen during the last hundred years, it was probably because they feared, like other native races, to be seen by strangers and retired to the mountains.

Wallis brought aboard five Patagonians, singing songs and very merry. Robertson received them at the gangway and shook hands.

They were the colour of North American Indians and seemed to be brave, cheerful men, under no apprehension of danger. The captain showed them down to his cabin, where, like the gentleman he was, he treated them with extreme civility. They ate biscuit and took two glasses of wine each, but preferred Thames water, of which they drank several tumblers. They were not so covetous as most Indians, except for an old man who made signs that he wanted a coat, shoes and stockings. He was given stockings, shoes and buckles, but none of the coats was large enough. An officer put a gold-laced triangular hat on his head, and he began to sing and be merry, but when the officer took back his hat he seemed uneasy and his companions laughed heartily at him. They were given some cigars, which they smoked but did not seem to like. One of the largest men, who was thought to be a warrior, had his face painted with several streaks of red and black; Byron had noted previously that many of the women had their faces hideously painted.

The matter of sexual repression presently began to make itself felt. Sex is usually ignored in accounts of exploration, but it was often an important factor. Who can assess the cruelties to natives that have resulted from such repression, the consequent bloodshed, the harsh treatment and flogging of seamen? Accounts of exploration reek of it.

One of the Patagonians, apparently some eighteen to twenty years of age and six feet tall, was much fairer and smoother-faced than the others and was thought by the officers to be a woman. But when she showed her breasts and nipples, which were both very small for her size and age, opinions divided. Some declared she was a maid; others said it was impossible at her time of life, especially as she was in company with so many fine, strong, healthy, broad-shouldered fellows. She was better dressed than the others: her cloak was richer and better sewn. Robertson inspected the inside and found it of much finer hair, not unlike a tiger skin. The other natives were wearing reddish-brown skins with the hairy side inward which belonged to the guanaco, a wild cousin of the llama.

Seeing his interest, she showed him one side of her cloak open, but carefully concealed that which would soon have ended the

dispute. Her modest behaviour put a stop to the master's investiga-
tions, but the officers began to tell stories of what they had seen in
various parts of the world, accompanied by gestures which made
her laugh heartily. She threw open the other side of her cloak but
still took care to cover herself with the alternate side, so that some
of the officers remained in doubt about the young person.

They were taken out of Wallis's cabin and shown the great guns,
which none appeared to understand. Next, the marines were ordered
to go through a part of their exercise and fire three musket volleys.
Four of the natives seemed much astonished at the first volley and
not to understand the reason for the noise; but, seeing all the officers
merry and none of themselves hurt, they began to be merry too.
But the old man was very serious. The instant the firing stopped he
lay down on the gun-deck, pointed to the muskets and smote his
breast, then lay some time with his eyes shut. Before going ashore
he uttered what appeared to be a long prayer at the companion-
ladder leading to the quarter-deck, frequently lifting his hands and
eyes to heaven while the warrior stood watching him stolidly.

On the same day, the 18th December, the ships entered the
eastern entrance to the Straits of Magellan and Carteret was ordered
to keep ahead to lead the way through the shoals, having been
through the Straits before. But the *Swallow* steered so badly that he
could seldom make her tack without a boat to tow her head round.
They did not reach the entrance to the First Narrows, still in the
country of the Patagonians, until the 23rd December. That day a
cask of beef was opened in the *Dolphin* and was found not only to
be nine pieces short, but to consist of very old, bad, repacked meat:
an act of rascality on the part of the contractors. The general anxiety
was assuaged by the rum and the brandy, which proved sound.

In the First Narrows many sea-lions were seen on a sandy beach
under a high cliff on the north shore, some apparently asleep, others
flopping about like seals. No attempt was made to trade with the
Patagonians for fresh provisions, as the ships were in danger from
the rapidity of the tide.

In the Second Narrows the *Dolphin* anchored on Christmas Day,
as the other ships were a long way astern of her 'and Christmas Day

Tahiti bearing south-east, distant three miles. Engraved from a painting by W. Hodges.

H.M.S. *Dolphin* in Matavai Lagoon. Sketched by Midshipman George Pinnock in 1767.

be ever a time that the most of seamen gets merry on,' as Robertson said. Wallis, Clarke, the doctor and purser went ashore with their muskets and shot several birds. The oyster-catchers made fine eating. The gulls were fishy, but made acceptable Christmas pies. The seamen did much of their own cooking, for they were divided into messes, which were exclusive little clubs, a man from each mess taking it in turn to act as cook for himself and his companions. The official cook and his mate boiled the salt beef and did the bulk-cooking in the coppers. The sick in the *Dolphin* were usually supplied with food from the captain's table or that of the gun-room officers, who had their own supply of livestock.

As the ships proceeded the mountains rose high, and the woods began. Two-thirds of the way up, the mountains were covered with tall trees, then with grass; a few places were covered with snow. It was now midsummer here.

After great labour and risks the ships anchored on Boxing Day in deserted Port Famine about a third of the way through the Straits. The place was so named by Cavendish, who, about one hundred and eighty years before, had found here twenty-four survivors of a Spanish colony of four hundred, established by the ill-fated Sarmiento de Gamboa, to prevent the English using the Straits.

As there was no wind, the *Dolphin's* boats towed the *Swallow* and the *Prince Frederick* into Port Famine, and a camp was established on the banks of a river. The place was beyond the land of the Patagonians.

The seine was hauled every day, and enough fish caught to provide regular fresh meals for all hands. Wild celery and pea-tops were found in plenty and were boiled with dried peas and portable soup; there was a profusion of berries resembling cranberries and the sour but edible leaves of a shrub. Everyone had begun to look pale and thin and many had scurvy; yet in a fortnight there was not a scorbutic person in any of the ships. The men were ordered to eat plenty of vegetables and to wash their clothes and bathe daily in the sea. Wallis and the members of the officers' mess resolved not to kill any of their livestock while in the Straits, but to take their chance of shooting wildfowl to supply their tables.

The *Swallow* and the *Dolphin* set about taking in provisions from the store-ship. All the *Dolphin's* sick now began to recover, though two had to be invalided home in the store-ship. Both had come aboard in England with venereal diseases, which it was thought would cost them their lives. There had been twenty cases when the *Dolphin* left Plymouth, but the surgeon had proved himself very capable, and his humane and friendly way of treating the sick was admired. Those able to walk were now employed in cutting grass and making hay for the livestock, and gathering cranberries, which made excellent pies.

During the second week in January, the *Dolphin's* carpenters returned from the *Swallow*, where they had gone aboard to widen her rudder so as to make her steer better. They now turned to completing their own ship for sea. On the 15th January the *Dolphin* was ready, her decks and sides having been caulked, all the rigging and sails repaired, her water completed and as much firewood taken aboard as the ship could conveniently store.

The *Dolphin* was now very deep in the water and was stowed so full of provisions that the men had to eat their way before they could sit to mess below. Bread and brandy were stowed in every officer's cabin; the captain's state-room was stacked with biscuit and his cabin was so full of provisions that he could scarcely find room for the three officers whom he invited every day.

The empty casks were sent on board the store-ship. Her hold was filled with firewood to supply the warships at the colony of Port Egmont in the Falkland Islands, where there was no timber, and several thousand young trees were taken up by the roots and set or laid in boxes of earth to be delivered to the commanding officer there. The French, too, had been planting a colony in the Falkland Islands as a half-way house to the yet-to-be-discovered Southern Continent. This colony was, in fact, already in being when Byron surveyed the islands, having been established, at his own expense, by Count Bougainville, a former aide-de-camp of Montcalm.

On the 17th January the store-ship sailed for the Falkland Islands, and on the following day the seekers after the Southern Continent continued their westerly navigation of the Straits.

CHAPTER II

*

THE STRAITS TO THE ATOLLS

THE scenery of the Straits was considered horrible and depressing. Grim mountains towered on either side, covered with tall trees that gave way further up to stumps and starveling shrubs, and above these were patches of snow and broken rock. The naked summits pierced the clouds in jagged crags like the ruins of Nature. In that age of that formal landscape gardening, relics of which still beautify the English countryside, mountainous scenery was generally thought to be detestable.

Four of the *Dolphin's* great guns on the fore gun-deck and four of the aftermost had been lowered into the hold at Port Famine to keep the ship from straining her upper-works, indeed from straining her whole frame; a precaution which eased her a lot when she was pitching hard in the bays in which she was to anchor in the Straits.

The most scrupulous attention was paid to cleanliness. The seamen had to bathe and change their clothes frequently. The cook had to report daily to the officer of the watch after his coppers were cleaned. His word was never trusted, for most ships' cooks, if not well-supervised, were thought to be dirty, lazy fellows, so that either the officer of the watch or some midshipman would go forward to the galley and order the first seaman who came to hand to rub the coppers round with a dry, clean cloth. Should the cloth show the least stain the cook and his mate were reprimanded or punished; but they, like the rest of the ship's company, seldom neglected their duty. It was known that if there was any trace of verdigris in their burgoo or peas or other victuals the seamen were sure to be seized with violent sickness or other ill-effects. Burgoo, although now usually taken to mean porridge, was a thin mixture of oatmeal sweetened with molasses – the unpopular breakfast drink

of the Navy, later to be replaced by cocoa. Those employed in extra
duties such as fishing with the seine, cutting firewood, or sounding
and surveying, had a double allowance of good old rum or brandy
grog.

Yet Robertson never saw any man in the least intoxicated when
on duty in the boats. Any who got wet had to strip and put on dry
clothes the instant he came on board, for in order to prevent the
sour unhealthy smell too frequent in ships, no one was allowed to
take any wet clothing below. The fire was kept burning in the
galley from four in the morning until nine at night, which gave
the men an opportunity of drying their clothes in bad weather; the
ship was cleaned above and below every day, and any man of dirty
habits was punished as soon as he was found out. But there were
few 'sluggish, nasty fellows' in her, for the master-at-arms and his
assistants had instituted an efficient spying system on the gun-deck.
Sometimes the two captains went out shooting together and a man
from each mess of both ships was frequently sent ashore to gather
wild celery and mussels from the rocks.

When the ships were half-way through the Straits, the master of
the *Swallow*, Mr Simpson, climbed one of the highest mountains on
the north shore, hoping to see the Pacific; but he found his view
intercepted by higher peaks on the south coast, those of Tierra del
Fuego, the 'Land of Fire', so called by Magellan from the fires of
the natives. On the top of the mountain he built a pyramid, in
which he deposited a bottle containing a shilling and a paper with
his ship's name and the date written on it, a memorial, he thought,
which might possibly remain there as long as the world endured.

At the end of January the 'Canoe Natives' of the Straits – the now
almost extinct tribe of the Yahgano, perhaps the inspiration of
Swift's Yahoos – were encountered for the first time. They had
previously been seen in the distance, and now, as a boat was sent
ashore for water, they came up in three bark canoes, six of them
approached to within a hundred yards, then stopped and called out,
making friendly signs, while the seamen showed them beads and
toys. The natives continued to advance, laughing and hallooing,
and the sailors did likewise until the two parties met and shook

hands. The natives, who were armed with slings and small bows and arrows, wore only a seal-skin which stank intolerably. They were of the same colour as the Patagonians, but the tallest was not more than five feet six. Trade began and presently the mate took three of the natives on board the *Dolphin*, where Wallis gave them food and drink and a few toys. They took a little brandy and, as it warmed their stomachs, they began to talk and sing.

When they were shown a mirror they looked afraid and stared hard at the officers, then peeped behind the glass, as if expecting to see one of themselves. But seeing nothing they began to smile and looked at the glass again. When they saw their friend smiling in the glass, they all laughed heartily and took another peep behind. Finally Wallis and several of the officers went ashore with them. At the watering-place they found several of the wives and children all dressed in filthy seal-skins. They were delighted with the trinkets which the captain gave them, and in return offered some of their arms. They had with them pieces of stinking blubber which they ate and sucked very greedily. Part of this they offered to the officers, who, much to the natives' surprise, declined it. One old woman looked hard at the muskets and made the white men understand that some of her children had been killed by such things. It was supposed that this had been done by the Dutch in 1722, when one of Roggeveen's ships passed through the Straits, for the Dutchmen had mentioned having killed some of these poor creatures as they had also killed people on Easter Island, which they had discovered.

The natives parted with complete indifference. Not one stopped to look back after they set out in their canoes. They hoisted a piece of skin for a sail and steered over to the south shore, where Mr Simpson, when surveying, saw them living in wigwams, which they took very little trouble to make wind- or water-tight. They made a fire in the middle, where they roasted mussels and limpets, and lay round the fire more like pigs than human beings.

In the middle of February the *Dolphin* was rushed by a current towards the south shore. The sails were asleep and the boats all ahead, towing her. But she drove so close to the rock that the boats' oars became entangled in weeds. For three-quarters of an hour she was hurried along, her crew almost in despair, and expecting to be dashed to pieces against the cliff. At length, however, they entered St David's Sound, where a current set them in mid-channel. The *Swallow*, being on the north shore, knew nothing of their danger.

Three days later, at Butler's Bay in what they called York Road (though it figures differently in modern Admiralty charts) there was a gale, with torrential rain and hail. They struck the yards and top-masts, ran out two hawsers to a rock and hove the *Dolphin* up to it with the capstan. The storm increased until evening, when the sea broke clear over the fo'c'sle to the stern, a thing that seemed impossible considering the narrowness of the Straits and the smallness of the bay.

The following morning Wallis sent a boat to the *Swallow* to find out how she had fared. Though she had felt little of the gale, she had been nearly wrecked among the islands two days before owing to the swiftness of the tide, for, in spite of the alteration to her rudder, she was still steering very badly. So now Carteret sent a letter to Wallis asking him to consider whether she should be dismissed or continue the voyage.

Wallis replied that he was not free to alter her destination and she must continue to accompany him. However, he would wait for her, and if any disaster should happen to either ship, the other could assist.

Wallis ordered Robertson to survey all the bays on the south shore to the eastward of Snow Sound. The master landed on Spider Island; and with Midshipman Pickersgill and a seaman climbed to the top of a rocky mountain to get a full view of the Straits and the dismal country.

To the westward lay the entry of Snow Sound, which was as broad as several parts of the Straits and continued so for several leagues into the Tierra del Fuego shore. The south side of this sound had the most dreadful appearance of any place that Robertson believed he could ever set eyes on. There was not a green thing to be seen anywhere on the mountainside. In other places they had come upon the valleys had some vegetation; here they had none, only a deep bed of snow with rivers of frost rather than water tumbling down immense precipices. He thought it would require the pen of Milton or Shakespeare to describe it, and in his opinion the snow which lay on these rocky mountains and valleys had perhaps never been dissolved since Noah's Flood. He questioned whether it had dissolved then, if the world still stood in the same relation to the sun. He had seen most parts of the habitable world but thought he could now say that he had looked on one of its barriers. Since the day they first anchored at York Road they had beheld no human beings, nor any beast on shore; even the fowls of the air had deserted the coast. Only sea-birds remained.

Even the natives had disappeared, although it was what might be considered the summer season. Mr Simpson told Robertson that when he went some leagues up St Jerome's Sound on the north shore, he there saw three canoes full of natives whom he supposed to have left York Road. He made signs to them to come with him to the ships, but they pointed to the tops of the snow-covered mountains and shivered with cold, then pointed to the sun and laughed as they steered in their bark canoes to the northward up this great sound.

The ships continued to navigate the Straits, Carteret being ordered to lead the way. But seeing that the *Swallow* might so delay the *Dolphin* as to make her lose the season for attaining the high southern latitudes of the Pacific, thus defeating the object of the voyage, Carteret proposed to Wallis that he should lay her up in some bay and himself attend and assist the *Dolphin* with her boats until the frigate was through the Straits. He urged Wallis to complete his stock of stores and his company out of the *Swallow* and then send her back to England with such of the *Dolphin's* crew as were unfit for the voyage. He also proposed that on his way home in the *Swallow* he should explore the eastern coast of Patagonia. If his knowledge of the South Seas was thought necessary, he offered to go with Wallis in the *Dolphin* and to give up the sloop to Mr Clarke, whose duties he would perform, if Clarke would take the *Swallow* back to Europe. But Wallis still thought the voyage should be made by both ships together.

The *Swallow* had become so foul by this time that with all sails set she still could not go as fast as the *Dolphin* with only her top-sails with a reef in them; she could not go above two feet to the *Dolphin's* three, and it was sometimes necessary for the *Dolphin* to take her in tow.

On the 2nd March the *Swallow* was anchored in a small cove, while the frigate lay in Good Luck Bay, the modern Valena Cove. All that day and the following night there were hard gales. Next morning the gusts were so violent that it was impossible to stand on the frigate's deck; sheets of water hurled from Cape Notch, a league away, broke over the deck. They lasted not more than a minute, but were so frequent that the cables were kept under constant strain and it was feared they might break. It seemed impossible that the sloop could ride the storm, some of the *Dolphin's* men were so certain of her being lost that they fancied they saw some of her crew coming over the rocks towards them. Oddly enough, the men of the *Swallow* had the same optical illusion regarding those of the *Dolphin*. Until the 7th the weather remained so bad that Wallis could not send a boat across to the sloop; then one was dispatched and returned in twelve hours to say that the *Swallow* was safe but that her crew were terribly fatigued, all hands having been upon deck for nearly three days and nights on end.

The weather was cold, with hail, sleet and snow, and as the men were never dry, Wallis got up eleven bales of Fearnought, thick woollen stuff, provided by the Admiralty, and set the tailors to make jackets, one for every man. He ordered them to be made very large – they were perhaps the first duffle-coats – allowing about three yards of cloth for each one. When they were cut out, his cabin was full of tailors, and every officer who had any space in his cabin took two or three men in to sew, there being no room in any other part of the ship. Seven bales of Fearnought he sent to the *Swallow;* and, with three bales of finer cloth, had jackets made for the officers of both ships.

The men now began to go down fast with colds, but the extraordinary care taken of them by the surgeon and the other officers prevented any serious consequences. The ships having to lie in the same situations for another week, Wallis put both companies on two-thirds allowance of everything but grog. Of this they had their full ration to sustain morale. When on short commons the men were credited by the purser with 'short allowance money'.

On the 15th March the ships were again under way, the *Dolphin's* crew thinking themselves fortunate to have got safely out of Good Luck Bay. On the 17th they took the *Swallow* in tow, but had then to cast her off and tack, for the weather came on very thick with a great swell, and they saw land close under their lee. They were now nearly through the Straits. Carteret advised Wallis to bear away for Upright Bay while he himself went ahead. The boats were ordered to go between him and the shore, and the *Dolphin* followed. At eleven o'clock in the morning they entered a large lagoon and, a current setting strongly into it, the *Swallow* was driven among the breakers close to the lee shore. There being no anchorage, she made signals of distress, and Wallis sent his boats, which took her in tow, but they would have failed if a breeze had not come down from a mountain and wafted her off.

As a heavy swell came on about noon, the ships hauled over to the north shore of the Straits, where they found themselves in a maze of small islands. The fog was so thick they did not know which way to steer and though the boats were sent to cast the lead, they could still find no anchorage. They guessed they were in the Bay of Islands and, if so, would have had no chance to escape shipwreck except by hauling directly out. When after some time the weather cleared for a few moments they saw Cape Upright, for which they steered, and at half-past five both ships anchored in the bay.

Here, two days later, while some seamen were collecting mussels, the cutter brought alongside the *Dolphin* a bark canoe containing a grey-haired old man and apparently three of his sons. Each had a piece of stinking seal-skin around his shoulders, and when they were paddling, threw this off and sat stark naked. Their spears, used for striking seals, fish and penguins, were pointed with bone. All of them smelt offensively and had sore eyes, which the white men attributed to their sitting over the smoke of their fires.

They were cramped with cold and extremely hungry, yet when

they were given some fish, which they ate raw, they took it with as much indifference as a dog would take a bone. A midshipman gave the old man a live fish, one somewhat bigger than a herring, which he instantly killed by giving it a bite near the gills, and then devoured completely bones, fins, scales entrails and all. He was then given some biscuit and a dram of brandy which he seemed to like, for it put him in high spirits and made him chatter to his sons.

A week later, in the same place, the *Dolphin's* main-sail was loosed to air. It was mildewed and mouldy, and it was feared that all the other sails would go rotten; but the weather was so stormy that none of them could be aired for fear of setting the ship adrift. Shortly afterwards all the spare sails were got up to air and were found to be eaten in several places by rats. However, they were repaired, the rat-holes in the sail-room were filled up, and the sails put down again.

Three days later two canoes came alongside the *Dolphin*, with four men and three young children in each. The children, who were much fairer than the men, were naked. An old man, who remained in the canoes, was very careful in handing the children out and in. Wallis gave them all necklaces of beads and put a few strings about their arms, which seemed to please the young ones; but their fathers took little notice of anything except some old clothes.

When the boats were sent for wood and water, the old man looked very attentively at them as they set off from the ship and, the moment he saw them make towards the watering-place, where was gathered a group of the wives, he called loudly to the other natives, who hurried into the canoes and set off paddling at a great rate, hallooing, to alarm their women.

The boats' crews lay on their oars until they came near them. Then one of the seamen pointed out to his companions some heavy smoke, which he supposed to indicate that the women were cooking dinner, and to get a little fun they pulled very fast towards the place. The natives paddled like madmen and roared like wild beasts. When the seamen got near the smoke they saw two of the women gathering mussels among the rocks. They lay on their oars until the men came up, then made signs that they wanted wives. But the natives paddled on and yelled until the two women went out of sight, then shook their paddles, looking very fierce. But the seamen only laughed and rowed in towards the watering-place, having always strict orders not to hurt any of the natives. Nine days earlier there had been a brawl between them and the seamen over the native women.

Three days later two canoes came off, full of men and young children, the only female being a girl of about thirteen. All came aboard except the girl and an old man who sat close by her. The children were given beads and toys, and the men hatchets and old clothes. Robertson looked several times over the ship's side but never saw the girl's face until they were all back in their canoes and paddling off to visit the *Swallow*. Only then did the old fellow allow her to turn round and look at the Europeans. She was much fairer and more decently dressed than any of the others. A gentleman of the *Swallow* told them afterwards that, seeing the young creature much fairer than the rest and not permitted to come on board, he stepped into the canoe and gave her some trinkets. When he saw she was a girl, he tried to get her aboard his ship, but the old man would not allow it and set off for the shore.

On the same occasion, when the natives were aboard the *Dolphin*, one of the oldest men, talking to a companion, was overheard by the captain's personal cook, a Malay, to speak some Malay words. The cook asked him how he came to understand that language, but the old man gave no direct reply. He invited the cook to go ashore in one of the canoes, but the cook answered that he was afraid. The old man told him that nothing should hurt him, but the cook replied that he was busy and could not go, and invited the old man to stay and dine with him. Then the cook was called away to prepare dinner and the conversation ended.

Several seamen and one of the officers had heard the conversation and when the captain and the other officers heard about it the following day, they sent for the cook and he repeated the story, which caused Wallis and some of the others considerable disappointment, for the old man might have told them something well worth their attention. How to account for the native speaking Malay they did not know. Malaya was thousands of miles from the Straits of Magellan, though the language was understood all over the East Indies and the Malays had spread far from their native shores. Sumatra and Java and all the Dutch settlements were full of them. Robertson remarked that if there was any land to the west, no one need be surprised to see the natives of its shore here. If they ever went fishing any distance from land, some of them must certainly be blown off their coast towards this one.

A couple of days later the weather moderated and boats were sent ashore for wood and water, with a man from each mess to gather limpets. A canoe came off to the ship with four men in her. The officers ordered the cook to speak Malay to them, but they stared and made no reply. He listened to them speaking to one another but could not understand their language.

Among them was a smart young fellow whom the seamen clothed in a sailor's dress and a marine's high cap, which delighted him, and he went all round the ship with one of the boatswain's mates. He had no fear and went wherever the boatswain's mate went, including the mast-heads and yard-arms. When the other natives returned to their canoe he ran below among the seamen and was most unwilling to go ashore. The others called to him but he took no notice until they returned and carried him off, much against his will.

The following day the young man returned with the three others. His friend Jones, the boatswain's mate, treated him so well with grog and a hearty dinner that he resolved to stay with the white men. When the natives wished him to go ashore, he hid himself below and would not go near them – until Jones was ordered to hand him over. When the two were parted, it was hard to say which was the more affected. Jones declared that he would willingly spare him a part of his provisions if he were allowed to go with the ship.

* * *

The *Swallow* and the *Dolphin* got under way the following day, the 10th April, 1767. The western exit of the Straits opened out and the Pacific was in sight. Hitherto Carteret had tried to keep the lead according to instructions. But now the *Dolphin*, being nearly abreast of him, set her fore-sail, which soon carried her ahead, and before nine o'clock in the evening, as she showed no lights, he lost sight of her. The sloop had a good breeze from the east, of which she made the best use she could during the night, carrying all her small sails, even to the top-gallant studding-sails, in spite of the danger to which it exposed her. But when day broke the *Dolphin's* top-sails could only just be made out above the horizon. It could be seen, however, that she had studding-sails set – extra sails which appear as wings upon the yard-arms. By nine o'clock she had entirely disappeared and was thought to be clear of the Straits' mouth. The ocean grey-hound was off the leash, with a bone in her teeth. During the nine months they had sailed together none of the commodities intended for the use of both ships, for exchange with the natives – the woollen cloth, linen, beads, toys, scissors, knives and other cutlery had been put on board the *Swallow*, although they had been nearly four months in the Straits.

Carteret now gave up all hope of seeing the *Dolphin* again until arrival in England since no plan of operation had been settled, or rendezvous appointed. But the following day, while he was in his cabin, he heard a shouting and a stampeding on deck, and coming up himself heard his men shouting – 'The *Dolphin!* The *Dolphin!*' in a delirium of surprise and joy. In a few minutes, however, they were convinced that what had been taken for a sail was merely a water-spout, which, through the haze, had a deceptive appearance. For a little while the seamen were dejected, but they soon recovered their usual spirits.

At noon of the 11th April, the day of separation, Robertson climbed to the mast-head and saw the *Swallow* about twelve miles astern. That was the last he saw of her. What orders Wallis had given Carteret – whether to return to England through the Straits or to pursue the voyage in search of the Southern Continent – he did not know. Wallis had consulted Clarke and Furneaux as to the action he was taking. In a sense he was doing what Carteret had suggested. His official excuse for proceeding without the *Swallow* was that he lost touch with her owing to fog. There was certainly a mist and Robertson said that there was a huge swell from the

south-west, which obliged them to carry a lot of sail to keep the
ship easy and prevent her rolling too much in the hollow of the
seas; that was why they were so far ahead of the poor, dull *Swallow*.
Wallis said that the *Dolphin* had to carry the sail in order to clear
the land.

Perhaps the captain thought that Carteret could now use his
discretion. Or could he have wanted to reap alone the honour of the
discovery of the Southern Continent? Or perhaps he feared undue
delay. He might have been just tired of the *Swallow*. Possibly he
avoided putting the extra stores aboard her because the desertion
might then have looked too obvious.

The separation of the two ships resulted in the discovery of
Pitcairn Island, the future home of some of the *Bounty* mutineers,
which Carteret was to pass soon after Wallis reached Tahiti. Carteret
also rediscovered the Solomon Islands. His men suffered terribly
from scurvy and the inadequacy of the ship, many of them dying.

★   ★   ★

During the first part of the day all hands on board the *Dolphin* were
employed securing the guns with ropes and chains, lashing the
water-casks placed between the guns and turning the boats – which
in those days were not hung in davits – upside-down upon the
booms, to prevent their being filled or smashed by the heavy seas
expected outside the Straits, with the swell coming up from beyond
the Cape Horn. The frigate being full of water-casks and provisions
between decks, the carpenters were engaged in shoring them up and
lashing them to permanent stanchions and hollow cleats among the
massive timbering of the frigate's interior.

The weather remained bitterly cold and the men were still on
two-thirds allowance of everything but grog, of which they had the
full ration. There was a nine months' supply of brandy and rum;
ten of biscuit or bread; fifteen of beef, pork, suet, peas, flour, wheat
and oatmeal. Mustard and vinegar were served out every fortnight,
but the pickled cabbage was kept for those with scurvy, which was
again appearing.

Scurvy is caused by the lack of vitamin C, but not much was then known about the disease and nothing about vitamins. In the early stages a man suffered from swollen gums and loosened teeth. When he became really bad his limbs turned black, he could not move without help, and he suffered excruciating pain. The next stage was death.

Wallis now told his principal officers that the object of the voyage was to make new discoveries. Most of them already knew this, but he repeated it so that they might keep a strict look-out night and day. They were now going on an entirely new track that no ship had sailed before, and their books and charts would be of no use. A good look-out was the only thing they could depend on, apart from God's help, which, he said, was never wanting to those who sincerely besought it.

He proposed to carry as much sail during the day as the masts and rigging would bear, and to keep a seaman at the mast-head from sunrise to sunset. A midshipman was to visit the mast-head once an hour. If land or rocks appeared, the officer of the watch, or the master, was to go to the mast-head. At night, when sailing before the wind, they were not to carry more sail than they could haul the wind with immediately; when close by the wind every rope was to be kept ready for tacking at the shortest notice.

There was still a great south-west swell, so the ship was kept a point from the wind that she might run the faster off the land.

Three days after leaving the Straits, in cloudy, hazy weather, many whales were seen. These were yet to be thinned out by the notorious whalermen, who were to find the girls of the Pacific Islands so pleasant. Numbers of birds were about the frigate – gannets, sheerwaters, oyster-catchers and the black and white wandering albatross, which was bigger than a swan. The smaller, bay-coloured albatross – the mollymawks, about the size of a large goose – seemed more inquisitive than any of the others; they frequently flew between the masts and kept soaring over the ship, until several were shot, whereafter they kept their distance. One which fell dead aboard the ship was the fattest bird Robertson ever saw.

Four days later, in stormy weather, heavy seas were shipped and the frigate was pitching so much that it was feared her masts would be carried away. As the water in the casks was used, the casks were knocked down and the staves stored beneath the cable-racks to make more room.

By the 24th April the men began to go down fast with colds and fevers. Their beds and clothes were continually wet, the ship's upper-works being open from the buffeting she had received in the Straits. The doctor feared that if they did not run into better weather soon they would be too short of hands to work the ship. Wallis's secret instructions were to stretch to the westward for a great distance after leaving Cape Horn, without losing southing. He gave a sheep to be killed for the sick and the convalescents. Several men had very bad symptoms of scurvy, particularly those who had had it on former voyages. Those who were fit had enormous appetites and said that they could have eaten more than the full allowance. But all began to be a little weak.

Four days later Wallis wore ship and stood to the northward, being afraid to stand farther west since the weather continued dark and thick. He was a thousand miles to the west of all previous tracks, and had passed over an area where many navigators and geographers believed the Southern Continent to lie.

On the 1st May a large turtle went by the ship. On the 3rd, the topgallant masts and yards – the uppermost – were got up for the first time since leaving the Straits, and the ship steered N.N.E. in the hope of finding Davis Land, usually identified with Easter Island, of the huge, mysterious stone statues. On the 11th the water stored in the hold had to be used, that between decks and between the guns being now exhausted.

Two days later, John Smith, a seaman, threw his own and his messmates' provisions overboard because they had cooked dinner not as he thought best, but in their own way. For that rascally action, as it was termed, he got a dozen lashes on the bare back from each of his messmates. They laid on well and kept him without food until noon next day, but they had their dinner and supper from the food of the captain's table and that of the officers of the gun-room. The gun-room was on the gun-deck, separated from the captain's cabin by two narrow cabins, his state-room and another.

The gun-room, which had great guns at its ports, was not only the gunner's armoury but the living-room of the warrant officers and midshipmen. The gunner, who held second place among the principal warrant officers (the master taking precedence of him), was responsible to some extent for the discipline of the junior officers. The gunner, Mr Harrison, was a good gunner but blunt and cunning. His position differed from that of his colleagues the boatswain and carpenter; they lived forward, their store-rooms being under the fo'c'sle, whereas his was aft, that sacred position where naturally the arms were kept. Robertson, although he had nothing in particular against him, thought him – and indeed gunners generally – unfit to be in charge of the midshipmen, whom he considered very well-mannered young gentlemen.

The next day several porpoises were seen disporting themselves round the *Dolphin*, the first to be encountered since leaving the Straits. The explorers now gave up hope of seeing Davis Land and concluded there was no such place.

During all this time, noted Wallis, they were looking out for the *Swallow*. The following day the man at the mast-head called out 'Land!' and several officers who went up thought they could see high land, but others were doubtful. They bore away for it, steering that course for fifty-four miles, but saw no more than at first. So they hauled their wind to the northward to get into the true south-east trade wind, having found it impossible to get to the westward on the borders of the trades. The false course had taken them away from Easter Island, which actually was not far distant.

About this time a large man-of-war bird (so called because its black plumage resembled the paintwork below a man-of-war's gun-deck, or from its predatory habits) was seen, causing several officers to assume that land was near since seafaring men believed this bird to roost ashore at night.

On the 28th May several flying-fish and some tropical birds were observed, raising the men's hopes that they would soon see some place where rest and food could be had. Tropical birds, or bo'sun birds as they are sometimes called, are of spotless white with long red tail feathers. They fly with a jerky motion or skim over the

surface of the sea and nest, among other places, in the high cliffs of
Tahiti.

The men were now going down fast with scurvy. The captain
and officers spared as much of their livestock as possible for the sick,
but it began to run short. The hay made in the Straits for the sheep
was nearly finished, and very few peas could be spared for them. So
little was given to the hogs that they could not walk the deck
without falling.

Portable or dried soup was boiled in the men's peas and oatmeal;
they had pickled cabbage and as much vinegar and mustard as they
wanted, and wine instead of spirits. As the weather had much
improved some of the canvas hammocks were washed and hauled
up into the rigging to air; and every day the remaining hammocks
were brought on deck at eight o'clock and stored in the boarding-
nettings along the gunwales. Every part of the ship between decks
was frequently swabbed with vinegar.

The things most appreciated were the fine warm weather and the
plentiful supply of water. Any man could drink what he wanted
at the scuttled cask which stood near the main-mast with an armed
marine standing by it day and night. If a man produced tea or coffee,
he was allowed to take a pint of water, as these beverages were
thought beneficial. Several of the men had brought tea and coffee
and had saved it till now. The master said the men's behaviour was
in every way the best he had ever known in a ship's company.

The carpenters meanwhile had been repairing and painting the
boats, which were now fitted for landing and if necessary making a
sudden attack along a coast. The barge, a fine ten-oar cutter, had
four proper swivel-stocks made by the armourer for holding four
musketoons – short, bell-mouthed pieces, of large bore, which threw
a ball weighing from five to seven and a half ounces or a number of
smaller balls. The launch and the cutter each rowed six oars and had
four stocks. The jolly boat, which rowed five oars, was too slight
for swivel-stocks but very handy for rowing between the ship and
other boats with messages or supplies.

All the boats' crews, as well as a few picked hands, and all the
midshipmen, were trained in the use of small-arms. The great guns

were exercised frequently. So the *Dolphin*, the most formidable piece of mechanism all round which had ever entered these seas with the possible exception of Anson's flagship, the *Centurion*, was tuned up as she went driving into the unknown wastes of the South Pacific.

Conversations were mostly on a single theme. All hands wished to come to some well-inhabited country, where they could find what they liked best. As for landing and searching such a country, where there were no firearms, no one anticipated much difficulty in that; they were eager for a chance to try their skill and courage. Some wanted gold or silver, wild game, diamonds, pearls, or fine young women. Some wanted good beef, others sheep, hogs, or fowls. Those sick of the scurvy wanted vegetables, which the doctor told them were the best remedy. But what they all wanted most was a good harbour, where the ship could lie in safety to get wood and water.

On the 31st May several frigate or man-of-war birds came soaring over the ship. Tropical birds, dolphin and flying-fish were also seen, heralding, as all hands were convinced, that land was near.

At sunset the watch on deck shortened sail and the ship ran under the top-sails and fore-sail. At eleven that night the weather appearing threatening, they double-reefed the top-sails. An hour and a half later all sails were taken aback by a hard squall of wind with rain and lightning. The watch close-reefed the top-sails, and the ship lay to under the mizzen and mizzen stay-sail. At one o'clock in the morning the wind blew fresh with heavy rain. All the watch were kept collecting rainwater in spare sails, and saved about a ton.

The ship's company were now afraid of running her during the night, as they expected every minute to see land and began to regret the absence of their poor, dull consort the *Swallow*. Had she been with them they could have run without fear by making her go ahead. And, had she met with some disaster, her boats together with their own, could easily have saved her crew, and the frigate was big enough for both crews without too much overcrowding. The loss of such a ship would have been a small matter compared with men's lives. As it was, the loss of the *Dolphin* would mean not only the loss of their own lives but of any discovery they might make.

Five days later another large turtle passed close by, and also some flocks of spotted tern, making the same shrill cry as gulls in England. Robertson, certain that these birds roosted on shore, was convinced that land must be near. In the afternoon large flocks of grey noddy were flying all round the ship.

At eleven o'clock next morning – about seven weeks after leaving the Straits, a weary length of time to be away from land – Jonathan Puller, a seaman, called out from the mast-head to the delight of all: 'Land in the west-north-west!'

At noon a low, small island could be seen from the deck, and the spirits of everyone, especially the sick, revived. It was Pinaki, an atoll of the Tuamotus – the Far-off Isles and Roggeveen's Pernicious Islands – with an inner lagoon. The first things observed on sighting such atolls are the coconut palms, appearing to grow out of the water: a line of green, tufty trees rising out of the sea and with the shallow lagoons casting opalescent reflections on to the blue sky.

According to a legend which the famous Queen Pomaré related to Pierre Loti, the Tuamotus were the last of the island groups to be inhabited because the water fiends who lived there beat the seas with their monstrous albatross wings and so prevented anyone landing in canoes. But at length the water-fiends were defeated by the god Taaroa – the God of the Universe – and the islands were then colonised by Polynesians.

While the *Dolphin* stood in for the green line of palms and the woods with the diamond surf at their feet, Robertson was at the mast-head. He sighted, lying to leeward, another atoll which, being larger, made everyone hope for something good there. The ship was brought to and soundings were taken, but no ground was found with 130 fathoms of line. From the first atoll two canoes put off with three or four men in each of them and paddled towards the other island. Wallis ordered the barge and cutter to be hoisted out, with Furneaux, the second lieutenant, in command of both, and to land if possible and get provisions. Plenty of coconuts were on the trees, the fruit bunching in ovarian clusters beneath the green, tufty tops. Furneaux was to take possession in the name of George III and call the atoll Whitsun Island, it being Whitsun Eve.

The boats rowed about two miles along the shore, looking for a place to land. The surf ran high all round the island, which was surrounded by a dangerous reef. But the coconuts tempted the lieutenant and some of his men – all were wearing cork jackets – to land at the risk of their lives. They found three small open-walled deserted huts, neatly thatched with palm leaves. In them were a few fish-hooks made of oyster-shell, which they took.

They returned to the ship with plenty of coconuts and scurvy grass – a plant of the mustard family – and purslane, valuable in salads. The boats were hoisted in and the ship stood off and on to the atoll all night, for it was hoped to get more coconuts in the morning.

Wallis ordered the herbs and the coconuts in their shining husks to be divided among the messes. Everyone ate the scurvy grass or cress and purslane eagerly, but saved his coconuts.

At sunrise the frigate was close in to the island and once more the barge and cutter were sent to shore. But the surf now ran so high that it was impossible to land, so they returned to the ship, which bore away for the larger atoll. The barge went ahead to be ready to land.

CHAPTER III

*

THE ATOLLS

THERE was a white coral beach with coconut palms leaning above it towards the sea, their elephant-grey trunks touched with pink lichen, and on their feathery fronds a metallic sheen. A little way inland were the small houses of the natives – thatched brown roofs supported on poles but with no walls. About fifty natives were gathering among the houses as the two boats rowed in towards the village. They were good-looking, copper-coloured people of medium size with some sort of mats tied round their waists and long black hair hanging loose around their shoulders.

They came down to the beach – men, women and children – the young men and women armed with spears from ten to fourteen feet long, tipped with bone. The seamen made signs that they wanted to land, but the natives signalled to them to keep off and return to the ship and advanced, shaking their spears and pointing them towards the boats.

The lieutenant showed them shears, nails and beads, but the natives went on shaking their spears, though they kept their eyes fixed on the trinkets with a kind of wistful curiosity.

Some of the older men and women made fires at places where there was any possibility of landing. It was supposed that they worshipped fire, for they made odd gestures as they circled two or three times round each blaze. The young men and women kept watching those who lit the fires and when the flame sprang up, they advanced another step in the water looking fiercely at the seamen. But the seamen continued to laugh and make friendly signs.

The ship fired a nine-pounder and stood in near the shore. The noise of the great gun and the sight of the gaily-painted vessel standing on startled the natives. The seamen in the boats made signs that they wanted water and coconuts, so some of the native men called to others to bring them. Furneaux indicated that they should lay down their spears and pointed to the seamen putting down their muskets. Most of the natives then threw their spears down on the beach.

Three midshipmen jumped ashore with trinkets and shook hands with the native men, who brought water in polished coconut-shells and about two hundred nuts, from which they stripped the husks – a Polynesian gesture of politeness in giving drinking-nuts – although it was supposed by the seamen that they wanted the husks for fishing-lines and ropes. Signs were made to them to put the nuts in the boats and the midshipmen paid for them with nails, beads and small hatchets, of which the natives seemed to prefer the nails. One of them presently stole a silk handkerchief with some trinkets wrapped up in it and carried it off. The midshipmen, on missing it, made signs that it was stolen, but the natives seemed not to understand the white men and took them by the hand and led them back to the boat, indicating that they should return to the ship. The midshipmen shook hands and they parted good friends. But when they indicated that they would come back in the morning, the natives stared and seemed displeased.

The ship made a snug sail and stood off and on to the atoll all night. Wallis ordered that a coconut should be shared between every two men and that the rest be locked up in a spare cabin for the use of the sick. That night most of the men had violent purging from eating the scurvy grass and purslane, but the green food none the less benefited all who ate it. One or two who had scarcely a well-anchored tooth in their heads from scurvy were able to crack hard biscuits in a few days.

At sunrise two large double-canoes, some thirty feet long, with masts up, were lying before the village. Furneaux with the marines, was ordered to take possession of the atoll and name it Queen Charlotte's Island in honour of the King's consort. (It is now called by the natives Nukutavaka.) At nine o'clock the boats got close to the village, where they now found four large double-canoes, with all the wives and children on board. When they rowed near the canoes the young women jumped overboard and swam ashore to the men, who were drawn up on the beach with their spears; but the men ordered them back to the canoes and made signs for the boats to keep away from the canoes.

Furneaux indicated that he wanted coconuts and water but the men kept shaking their spears and pointing to the ship. He then ordered his men to row in closer, whereupon the natives advanced further into the water, looking very fierce. The women meanwhile had got back into the canoes very frightened.

The seamen lay on their oars. It was thought that the men would go off to their wives and children, but they still seemed determined on the boats withdrawing. So Furneaux caused a musket to be fired along shore that they might see the ball take the water. But it had not the desired effect, so a musketoon was fired near them.

They all seemed afraid and made signs that they would embark with their families and desert the island if the boats would go to leeward and land there. Furneaux complied, and the natives made sail to the west, being joined by another large canoe from the west end of the atoll.

The seamen landed and searched the native houses but the only living creatures they found were rats running about every one – the comparatively harmless, indigenous brown rats of the Pacific Islands, now probably exterminated by foreign rats, which lived mostly on fruit and vegetables and were believed to be the shadows of ghosts. The seamen loaded the boats with coconuts and pandanus nuts, which grow upon a round core and have the appearance, when ripe, of a pineapple. But they found the coconut palms stripped of most of their fruit. Some, which had been laden the previous night, were now denuded.

At noon the boats returned to the ship. They were unloaded and sent ashore for more coconuts, but no pandanus nuts, as the men did not like them. At six o'clock in the evening the boats returned full of coconuts.

Furneaux informed Wallis that he had found three small ponds of good water about a hundred yards from the village. This was better than was expected and gave the more joy since water was running short. It also gave hope of finding more on the next island, for which the natives had steered.

At daylight Mr Gore, one of the master's mates, who had sailed in the *Dolphin* with Byron, was sent with twenty armed men to get water. They had provisions for a week and were ordered to lie ashore all night in one of the houses and keep a sharp look-out. They were not to pull down or injure the huts nor to destroy the palms, which certain men were selected to climb. During the morning they cut down long, feathery palm fronds to lay on the coral rocks so as to make a way for rolling the water-casks.

Wallis was very ill at this time with a bilious disorder but he and the surgeon went ashore with several men who were feeble from scurvy and took a short walk.

Robertson, the inquisitive master, also went ashore to see if he could find anything out of the ordinary. There were some twenty houses in the village, where he saw three partly-built canoes on the stocks. Two he reckoned were of eight to ten tons. The third was larger but had only been framed and had no planks on her. The master could not imagine what trade the natives carried on in such vessels. They were, he felt sure, not built for fishing, but for visiting some distant land. This supposition was correct. The natives were partly migratory among the atolls and sometimes visited even the high volcanic islands.

With one of the midshipmen, Robertson walked across the island and for several miles around it. All over the atoll they found numbers of turtle shells, the backs of which had been burnt and thus a great quantity of fine tortoiseshell spoilt. Nothing in the way of food was seen growing except for palm trees and a little coarse grass in the woods. The natives in fact lived almost entirely on fish and coconuts. At the west end of the atoll they found a village of eight or ten houses, deserted except for rats. Several very tall palms round the village had been stripped of most of their fruit. In two of the houses, apparently used as carpenters' workshops, were several fine pieces of tortoiseshell – used for overlaying the seams of canoes in the Tuamotus – and some large, fresh pearl oyster shells, some of which were fixed in pieces of wood and had been made sharp for cutting.

At each workshop there was a piece of stone in a wooden frame, apparently used as a whetstone for the oyster shells and presumably brought from some distant shore, probably from one of the volcanic islands. For the things he took away, Robertson left two handfuls of nails.

He found two wells of good water near the huts, and two burying-places between the two villages. In the first were two graves, with canopies erected close by them with neatly-woven walls. The doors opened to the middle of the graves, which were raised about two feet. Robertson began to remove the coral rocks of one of the graves but the body stank so abominably that before he could see it he had to stop. These people, like the Tahitians, exposed for a time under these canopies their more distinguished dead, partly mummified by extraction of the viscera and by anointing the corpse with coconut oil before burying the body.

Gore stayed ashore all night and kept a large fire burning. By ten o'clock the following morning eight tons of water had been sent aboard the ship, and the signal was given for the watering-party to return. The British flag was left flying, and an account of taking possession of Whitsun Island and of this one was cut upon a piece of wood and in the bark of several trees. Some hatchets, nails, bottles, shillings, sixpences and halfpennies were left as a present and as compensation for disturbance.

*   *   *

The *Dolphin* now had a fine breeze from the east and followed the course which the natives had steered in the hope that this would bring her speedily to some much finer country.

At one o'clock the man at the mast-head sighted land, and at four the ship was off another atoll with a large oval interior lagoon. As she ran along about six hundred yards from the shore, eight double-canoes with their masts up were seen hauled up on the beach in front of six small houses. There were some eighty people on shore, the women and children near the canoes and the men advancing with spears and firebrands, making much noise and dancing strangely.

When the ship was abreast of them, Wallis had a nine-pounder fired over their heads. They stood still apparently terrified and stared at the shot as it went whistling over and landed in the lagoon. Not one moved as long as they could be seen. It was assumed that these were the people who had deserted Queen Charlotte's Island. This atoll Wallis called Egmont Island, in honour of the Earl of Egmont, the First Lord of the Admiralty. (Its native name is now Vairaatea.)

At six in the evening the ship lay to because of the risk of running ashore or passing some important place during the night. The following day all hands were put on full allowance of provisions, which caused much joy, as most of the men were expecting to be put on half allowance.

In the afternoon they were off the east end of a coral island full of palm trees. Over the middle of it they could see a large cloud of smoke. When they came abreast of this, they fired a nine-pounder. Eighteen natives, armed with spears, then came running along the shore. Every thirty or forty yards one of them lighted a smoky fire. As the ship drew near the west end of the island the captain ordered a nine-pounder to be fired close to where the natives stood, that they might see the ball take the water. They saw the ball strike a long way from the shore, then rise again and lodge near them. Like the natives on Egmont Isle they stood stock-still for a while but soon they made another fire. This island, which had a large lagoon in the middle was Paraoa. Wallis now named it Gloucester Island, in honour of the royal Duke.

The following day another atoll was seen through hazy weather and heavy rain. This was Manuhangi, which the captain renamed Cumberland Island, after another member of the royal family. And a day later a sixth atoll was discovered. Its name, which was Nengo-nengo, was changed to Prince William Henry's Island, after the King's third son, who later became King William IV.

Four days later, in the early morning, land was sighted from the deck in the form of a round, lofty hummock, with what appeared to be very high land lying to the south; but the weather was too thick and hazy for certainty. At noon, when still fifteen miles away Wallis thought it looked like the Mewstone in Plymouth Sound. Other officers likened it to the dome of St Paul's. It was, in fact,

Mehetia, the most easterly of the Society Islands. (This group was named by Captain Cook, then a lieutenant, and in charge of a scientific expedition to Tahiti in 1769 to observe the transit of Venus. By his own account he called the group the Society Islands, as the islands lay adjacent to one another, not, as is usually said, in honour of the Royal Society of London. Tahiti and Mehetia were only later included in the group.) Mehetia, a verdant, extinct volcano, rises solitary from the ocean about sixty miles from Tahiti. Wallis named it Osnaburgh Island after Prince Frederick, who bore the title of a Bishop of that Hanoverian see, partly, perhaps, because of its resemblance in outline to a bishop's mitre. Since it was here that the god Oro first descended to earth in search of a wife, this seems the place to recount the Oro legend.

CHAPTER IV

*

THE ORO STORY

THE Tahitians ascribed the origin of all things to a state of chaos or darkness. Taaroa and other deities of the highest order were said to be born of the night. Taaroa was the first and principal god, and had existed from the beginning, or from the time he emerged from the world of darkness. Known to the Cook Islanders as Tangaroa (to the Samoans as Tangaloa), he was not made by any other god. His consort, Hina-tu-atua, also uncreated, likewise proceeded from the night. Oro, the great national god of Raiatea, Tahiti, Moorea and other islands, was the son of Taaroa and Hina-tu-atua. He was born at Opoa, in Raiatea.

The world, and all adorning or inhabiting it, came from the procreative power of Taaroa, who embraced a rock, the foundation of all things which brought forth the air and the sea. Soon afterwards the heralds of the day, the dark and light blue sky, appeared before Taaroa and solicited a soul for his offspring, the then inanimate universe. Taaroa replied, 'It is done', and directed his son, the sky-producer, to accomplish his will. In obedience to the order his son looked up into the heavens and the heavens received the power to bring forth skies and clouds, sun, moon, and stars, thunder and lightning, wind and rain. He looked downwards, and the unformed mass received the power to bring forth earth, mountains, rocks, trees, herbs and flowers, beasts, birds and insects, fountains, rivers and fish. The sky-producer looked into the abyss and imparted to it the power to bring forth the purple water, rock and coral and all the inhabitants of the ocean.

Some of the gods were procreated by the god Taaroa looking at the goddess his wife, Hina-tu-atua, who became the mother of his children. Raa was among the principal deities, although inferior to

Taaroa and Oro. Tane, the god of the winds and closely concerned with human affairs, the tutelary deity of Huahine, proceeded from the state of night or chaos. His goddess was Tanfairei.

In the heaven above the Society Islands, Oro grew weary of being without love, for he had cast his wife down to the earth, where she had changed into a heap of sand; so he decided to mate among the mortals. He, the warrior god, disguised himself as a young warrior, with a basket-work helmet five feet tall and covered with small shining red feathers, and the long, thin red tail feathers of the tropical bird set in an aureole; his gorget was of oziers covered with dogs' hair and the gleaming black feathers of the man-of-war bird, decorated with sharks' teeth; down his back hung plumes of feathers.

Now he summoned two of his sisters, the goddesses Darkness and Grossness, who dwelt on the summit of Mount Paia in Pora-Pora, one of the most north-westerly islands of the Society Group. His sisters, too, disguised themselves as mortals.

Snatching up a rainbow on which to pass between the islands and over valleys and mountains, they landed on the earth at Mehetia – Wallis's Osnaburgh Island. They searched Mehetia – its thatched houses couched in fragrant woods – but nowhere in the steep and scented island, emerging like a slim, firm breast from the sea, its nipple the rough edge of the crater, did they find the desired woman.

On the curving arc of the rainbow they walked onward for sixty miles to mountainous Tahiti. Far beneath them, like a toy, passed the war-canoe with which communication was kept up between Mehetia and Tahiti; for Mehetia was subject to Vehiatua, the hereditary paramount chief of the eastern province of Tahiti. The great canoe would sail to Mehetia on the north-westerly wind, and return to Tahiti on the prevailing wind from the east. From Mehetia the Tahitians obtained pearls and pearl shell and stools and dishes carved from the hard *tamanu* tree. Sometimes thence they would stand to the north in their canoes to visit the Tuamotus to obtain pearls, pearl shells and red feathers. Oro and his sisters searched the scattered settlements of Little Tahiti and Great Tahiti. Everywhere the glamorous strangers were feasted and made much of; but nowhere could Oro find the woman of his imagination.

By means of the wheeling rainbow, blazing with iridescent colours, they spanned the eight miles of purple sea, passing above foaming coral reefs to land on Moorea. Shaped like a gigantic hollow tooth, Moorea lies off the north-west coast of Tahiti, directly opposite Papeete. They combed the island – its settlements dotted along fragrant lagoons and other dwellings nestling among the warm dark forests of the interior – but nowhere was the woman to be found. Again without success they tried Tapu-a-manu (Sacred-to-the-birds) the small island which lies to the west of Tahiti.

Next the rainbow carried them to mountainous Raiatea, far to the north-west of Tahiti, above whose clouds is situated Rohutu Noa-Noa – Sweet-scented Rohutu. But again, although they were sumptuously entertained and Oro received love, he himself did not love. Now Oro and his sisters went to nearby Huahine, a mountainous mass surrounded by a coral reef and divided down the middle by a long, warm arm of the sea. Its name, Huahine, denotes the sexual organ of a woman, from the physical peculiarity of the land mass. One can imagine the first discoverers sighting it from their canoes and so naming it. The Polynesians do not mince words. The name might have seemed propitious, and the women of Raiatea and Huahine were fairer than the generality of women of Tahiti; but although, as in other islands, in Huahine Oro was loved, again he did not love.

In sight of Raiatea and Huahine is craggy Pora-Pora, the last island of any importance in the Society Group. One of its peaks, the Sea-of-Birds, shattered crater of an extinct volcano, towers abruptly to a height of over two thousand feet, giving it something of the appearance of a medieval castle on the Rhine. Oro and his sisters having searched Huahine in vain, now crossed despondently to Pora-Pora.

Here, in the little emerald lake at Vaitape (Remnant-water) Oro saw bathing a tall and beautiful girl, a *vahine purotu aiai*, a woman possessed of every charm. It was love at first sight. He begged his sisters to intercede for him – in Polynesia wooing is usually done by proxy – and himself climbed to the summit of Mount Paia, which flanks the Sea-of-Birds.

Darkness and Grossness approached Vairaumati, exclaiming aloud at her beauty, then encompassed her with flashes of lightning, making her divine like themselves.

'We are from Avanau,' they said, naming a village of Pora-Pora. 'Will you become our brother's wife?'

Vairaumati eyed the strange women carefully. Her face was as the noontide light; the lustre of her eyes shone forth like stars in the deep-blue sky.

'You are not from Avanau, but that matters not. Is he handsome?'

'Yes!' said the sisters, 'he is handsomer than all the sons of men, and is for ever youthful.'

'If your brother is young and beautiful and a chief, tell him to come, and I will be his wife.'

Hastily the sisters climbed Paia to tell Oro.

He placed the rainbow with one end in the heavens, the other resting at the foot of the Red-Ridged Mountain at Vaitape. When he had emerged from the scintillating mist which surrounded the rainbow like a cloud, he found Vairaumati awaiting him.

Oro spent the night with Vairaumati and in the morning climbed the iridescent rainbow and passed the day on the summit of Paia with its embracing view of blue and green lagoon, coral reef, palm and mangrove, purple ocean and mountainous islands.

The rainbow remained fixed, extending to the heavens. Every evening Oro descended it and spent the night with Vairaumati; every morning, after they had bathed in the caressing waters of the lake, he disappeared from his beloved's sight by climbing the rainbow to rest during the day on the top of Paia.

In due time they had a child named Friend-Sacred-to-the-Heavens, who became a powerful ruler among men. Oro had already three daughters – Axe-with-eyes, Eater-of-summit and Fog-of-many-owners. Eater-of-summit probably means a cloud cutting off the top of a mountain; Fog-of-many-owners, the pearly mists of the Pacific; unless there is a more sinister interpretation.

Oro's absence presently aroused curiosity in heaven. After many months, two of his younger brothers, minor deities called Vain-warrior and Vain-head, assumed human form and set out to find him. One evening they descended the rainbow, and beneath a sacred tree, beside the lake they found Oro seated, talking to Vairaumati.

Her beauty made them marvel. They were ashamed to salute the couple without a present and one changed himself into a sow, the other into a bunch of *ura* – a tuft of red feathers, a valuable offering equivalent to jewels. Then they reassumed their original form and the presents, which remained, they gave to the lovers.

Oro and his bride were delighted, and Oro made Vain-head and Vain-warrior kings and *Ariois*, saying – 'Be you two *Ariois* in this world, that you may enjoy your portion.'

The first of the litter of seven pigs thrown by the sow, Oro named Warrior-of-the-laid-down-spear, meaning that Oro, the God of War, was then a god of peace, whose emblem was a triangle made of spears. He took Warrior-of-the-laid-down-spear to his *marai* or temple named Taputapu-atea at Opoa in Raiatea, about twenty miles away, depositing it there with the words – 'This is the sacred pig. In its blood shall be dyed the race of men who shall spring from me, for I am the Father in this world. These men shall be the *Ariois*.'

★ ★ ★

This temple at Raiatea differed from the *marais* of Tahiti, consisting merely of four walls of coral stones – some of immense size – filled up with smaller stones and embracing an area about seventy-five feet square; the whole was adorned with planks set up on end and carved throughout their entire length. Nearby were altars for offerings, such as pigs, which were left there to decay and to be eaten by birds.

The name of the *marai* meant Sacrifices from Abroad. In early days natives came in canoes from all over the Pacific to Opoa, bringing human sacrifices, meeting at sea, and then approaching the temple in solemn procession. The human victims were called Long-legged Fish. They were strung through the heads with sinnet and suspended alternately with large real fish upon the boughs of the large trees about the *marai*. This was not the conventional method in the Society Islands of offering men in sacrifice. The victims were then buried in a sitting position. The practice ceased many centuries ago.

Because of the sacred pig, Raiatea was of supreme importance in the *Arioi* cult, and the Chief Priest of Raiatea was the principal *Arioi*. Members of the *Arioi* in the Society Islands wandered continually among the various islands of the group as travelling entertainers. Sometimes a small party of dancers and mimes would work their way about a single island; sometimes they travelled in a fleet of as many as seventy canoes. The *Arioi* canoes were decorated with long pennants of many colours. At the tops of the masts were small semi-circular sails of matting tipped with spreading bunches of cock feathers. As the *Ariois* approached the shore in their journeying from island to island, they would begin their performance. With drums and nose-flutes sounding and their faces stained scarlet, some wearing breast-plates of yellow banana leaf shining like golden armour, some hung with garlands of scented flowers and seeds with massed flowers adorning their heads, and with wild vociferation and antic gesture they would appear on stages set upon the forepart of their double-canoes. With the rolling surf booming and breaking on either side its sound mingling with their music and voices, they would pass through the reef-passage into the calm waters of the lagoon, the people ashore flocking eagerly to meet them.

Having beached their canoes, the *Ariois* proceeded to the house of the local chief, where they made him a present of a hog and a bunch of red feathers. But first they would go to the principal *marai*, preferably one of Oro's, to make similar gifts in acknowledgement of their safe passage at sea.

The brothers Vain-head and Vain-warrior were (very significantly) celibate, for which reason – although celibacy was not imposed on them – the *Ariois* were required to destroy their offspring by suffocating them at birth. It seems, in fact, to have been a sort of glorification of birth control and pacifism. Most of the chiefs of the Society Islands were members of the fraternity. As they feared to be known as child-bearing *Arioi*, a derisory term, since these occupied an inferior status and were served at feasts only after the bachelors had been served, they seldom preserved any of their children until the passionate fires of youth were spent. They were aided in this by the fact that on the birth and survival of a son the titles and honours of the father at once devolved upon the infant, so that the father henceforth was no more than the regent, so to speak, for his child. One explanation for the destruction of new-born infants was that without this practice the higher classes would have increased too rapidly to be able to preserve their rank. The Society, as such, never took part in the local wars, and its members might pass freely through a war zone and be well received, even if in enemy territory.

Although a declared apostle of free-love, every *Arioi* had his own wife, who was also a member of the Society. They were so jealous in this respect that improper conduct towards the wife of an *Arioi* was sometimes punished with death. Yet they often changed partners and seldom cohabited with the same one for more than three days. Women prided themselves on the number of their suitors. When a child was born, it was immediately strangled unless a man could be found to sponsor it; but a man usually abandoned a woman as soon as she became pregnant. The *Arioi* women did not object to this, as they thought that nursing children spoilt their beauty and robbed them of the pleasure of having numerous lovers.

The *Ariois*, on their arrival, took up residence at the local guest-house, consisting of a thatched roof supported by pillars. These structures were large and sometimes highly ornamented. In the Faa'a district near Papeete was one 397 feet long and 48 feet wide. It had twenty wooden pillars, each 21 feet high, supporting the roof, and a hundred and twenty-four, each 10 feet high, supporting the sides. The whole place was enclosed beneath the eaves with a low wooden fence to keep out pigs and other animals.

At night in the enormous house illuminated with fires and candle-nut tapers, they began the *Upa-Upa*, an entertainment so pleasurable that even the crickets, it was said, cried for joy. When all was ready, with the spectators watching within the building and outside upon the grass, the chief *Arioi* entered with a strutting gait. Crossing his arms over his breast he would utter a boastful speech beginning with the words: 'Ha, ha, indeed! It is I, I stand,' and after claiming a relationship with the important features in the local scenery would refer to himself as the 'comedian of the land'.

The entertainments that were to follow went on for several days and nights. There was dancing, the dancers' bodies being blackened

C

with charcoal and their faces stained with scarlet dye; there were comic pantomime; sometimes there was wrestling, or a recital of dramatic poetry, or a repetition of the ancient Sayings of the Gods. When the pantomime called for it indecent costumes were assumed. For example, a woman in labour might be represented, provoking immoderate peals of laughter from the spectators. The man who acted this part went through the gestures which the Greeks were wont to admire in the groves of Aphrodite-Ariadne, where the same ceremony was acted in memory of Ariadne, who died in child-bed. A tall stout fellow personated the new-born infant. The audience were particularly delighted with his running about the stage, whilst the rest of the dancers endeavoured to catch him. The ladies were much pleased with this scene, which, according to their natural minds was not in the least indecent. They felt under no obligation, like some European women, to peep through their fans.

The *heiva* dance, usually performed by torchlight, was danced by men and women in separate parties. The women, usually beautiful young girls, not more than four in number, were dressed in long white petticoats bordered with red. A kind of vest or corselet of white or coloured cloth covered the breasts, with bunches of black feathers at the point of each breast and with tassels of the same falling from the waist to the knees. Two or three red or black feathers on each forefinger took the place of rings. On the back, fixed like a fan or furbelow, were two large pieces of neatly-plaited cloth edged with red. (Having seen this dance at night in the forest – the French, it was said, did not allow it to be performed within a mile-and-a-half of Papeete – I venture the opinion that these fans or furbelows were intended to represent wings and that the women were supposed to be butterflies.) Wrapped like turbans round their heads were vast braids of human hair decked with flowers and ornamented with sharks' teeth and sometimes pearls. The drumming was barbaric, vibrant and rapid, yet it sounded melodious and distinct. The women began by advancing sideways, their hips soon began to shake. Sometimes they stood, sometimes sat or rested on their knees and elbows, moving or rather vibrating their fingers with incredible rapidity. Much of the spectators' entertainment derived from the fantastic wantonness of the dancers' attitudes, gestures, grimaces and inarticulate cries.

While the women rested the men acted a kind of interlude in which they spoke or sang as well as danced; or actors performed pantomimes, seizing upon the manners of visitors, which they imitated to perfection not sparing their own chiefs and priests, if who, they were at fault, were sure to be publicly exposed.

A chief could, at the will of the community, be deposed and driven from the district. It is somewhat surprising, therefore, although characteristically Polynesian, that the local chief should always have been eager to detain the *Ariois*, and every day would send servants to ransack the best plantations for gifts. For this reason the *Ariois* were not always popular although regarded by all classes as closely allied to the gods.

During their visit indulgences were permitted to all members of the local community and there was a general loosening of bonds. The women might eat turtle, porpoise, albacore and dolphin, sacred fish normally forbidden to them.

Children could be dedicated at birth, but the fraternity was open at any time to individuals of all classes, provided they were of the necessary standard of good looks. Any man wishing to join went to the *Upa-Upa* in a state of exaltation bordering on madness, his hair anointed with sweetly-scented oil and adorned with fragrant flowers, his forehead decorated with dead coconut leaves, and wearing a loin-cloth of golden leaves of the wild plantain. With staring eyes he would hurl himself through the crowd and leap into the house to join with frantic abandon in the pantomime.

If the candidate was approved, he was appointed to wait as a servant on the principal *Ariois*. At a later meeting of the Order he would be brought forth by the chief *Arioi* and named by another as acceptable to Oro. After repeating an invocation concerning a sacred lake, he completed his initiation by seizing the cloth worn by the chief woman present and thus became a member, one of the eighth or lowest class. He, with any others who were being initiated or promoted, would then be taken to the temple and anointed with scented oil. A sacred pig wrapped in the cloth of the Order made from the bark of the mountain sloe was put in his hands and offered to Oro. If he were already a member of the Order, he was declared to be an *Arioi* of the class to which he was raised. The pig, if dead, was buried in the temple; if it was alive, its ears were ornamented with a sacred tassel of coconut fibre and it was set free to roam the district until it died – presumably representing Warrior-of-the-Laid-Down-Spear.

There would then be a feast and an entertainment lasting for days. The *tabu* which prohibited females, on pain of death, from eating the flesh of animals offered in sacrifice to the gods was removed, and with the men they ate pork and other sacred food. Women could eat pigs in the ordinary way, provided they had not been touched by men. Finally, tattoo-artists imprinted the signs of the different classes to which the various *Ariois* were raised. The highest class had their legs tattooed in chequered patterns. The markings on the lowest class were very slight, but increased stage by stage. (The whole population, both men and women, were tattooed on the loins and buttocks at puberty, the tattoo artists first praying to the god Tohu, painter of the fishes with their beautiful colours and patterns, which were imitated on the human flesh.)

It was not only aspirants to the Order who attached themselves to the *Ariois*. Ordinary men and women sometimes did so to attend them on their journeys, prepare their costumes and share their feasts. These attendants were under no obligation to destroy their infants, unlike the *Arioi* novitiate, who was commanded to kill his at birth.

The funeral rites of an *Arioi* are described in an early account of a burial in Tahiti. The *Arioi's* body was taken, after the lamentation in his house, to the great temple in the district of Pari on the north-west coast in sight of the island of Moorea. This temple, like the one at Opoa, was named Taputapu-atea, and was one of Oro's residences on earth. There an 'effigy' of him was kept – a log of iron-wood about six feet long, decked with sinnet and with red, yellow and black feathers. (Here, too, the coronations of the Tahitian kings took place, at the age of six or seven, and here also their bones were deposited, and, on occasion, the chiefs brought their human sacrifices.)

The dead *Arioi* being taken within the temple, Oro's priest came, and, standing over the body, divested it of all sacred influence. Oro was requested to confer the influence on the spirit and the body was buried as that of a commoner within the precincts of the temple.

Ariois, being rich – for they obtained large presents of cloth, scented oil, red feathers and hogs – were able to secure the services of the priest who had the passport to Rohutu Noa-Noa. He succeeded the priest of Oro, offering his petitions to Urutaetae, the Charon of the local mythology.

Rohutu Noa-Noa – Sweet-scented Rohutu – was near Glorious Temehani, a stupendous mountain near Hamaniino Harbour in Raiatea. The paradise, invisible to mortal eyes, was in the *reva*, the celestial regions. There, every delight was at hand; perpetual banquets of rich and delicious food, handsome youths and women, *purotu anae*, all perfection, flowers of every form and colour, the air was scented with fragrant perfumes and never harsh. These joys were only for the relatives of the privileged who could afford to pay the priests, for the charges were beyond the means of the common people. Those who had been kings or *Ariois* in this world retained their identities in the next world for ever, and there were no children to mar their pleasure.

The *Arioi* Society apparently was an attempt to get rid of war. It was perhaps the first, even the only, effort in history to deal with war – as opposed to waging it – on a psychological basis. A connection between war and sex was recognised, as by some European psychologists. The human obsession with war may be largely due to refusal to face its basic facts. War probably originated, and continued for half a million years when man was in a nomadic ape-like state, and the main reason for fighting within the small groups was probably for the possession of females. This racial memory persists, being the more dangerous for being suppressed and driven into the subconscious. The *Arioi* Society merits close consideration, even if they had hit on the wrong solution.

Captain Wallis was on the eve of meeting some interesting and in some ways advanced people, for it was at Mehetia that Oro, one of the great Archetypes of the subconscious – the god of war who became a god of peace – descended to earth on the eternal quest.

CHAPTER V

*

TO THE LAND OF ILLUSION

THERE was a heavy swell from the south-west. The *Dolphin*, having left the atolls behind her, stood off and on to Mehetia – or as they now called it, Osnaburgh Island – all night. At midnight a large fire sprang up on the east side of the fourteen hundred feet high island; at daybreak it was extinguished. The ship was brought to about two miles to the west of the island, and Furneaux took the barge and cutter to sound for anchorage under its lee side.

Before the boats put off, several canoes with three copper-skinned men in each approached the frigate. They stopped paddling when they got within pistol shot and, although greeted with friendly signs and offered trinkets, they would not come aboard. The boats pulled towards them, but they were frightened and paddled away, shouting to one another. The seamen let them keep the lead, which made the natives happy. They paddled softly, apparently thinking that they could run from the boats when they thought fit.

Thereupon Furneaux ordered his men to pull with all their strength and they soon overtook the canoes and rowed past them laughing. At this the natives became merry in their turn and followed the boats towards the shore. The seamen, getting no soundings, rowed round the cliffs; the island was completely covered with coconut palms and fruit trees. Only one landing-place was seen, guarded by about a hundred men armed with spears and clubs. The women who were drawn up in the background had fine figures and delicate features. They were dressed in graceful loin-cloths like petticoats of a whitish-brown cloth resembling paper, and had short cloaks round their shoulders. The men wore loin-cloths of the same stuff or girdles of green banana leaves. A few grandees had sleeveless tunics of the paperish material, with sashes about their waists.

70

One handsome, middle-aged man in a white turban was clothed better than the others and had a white wand which he used frequently in chastisement; and all appeared to pay respect to what he said. Such supervision and beating by a master of ceremonies acting for the principal chief was a regular feature of ceremonial landings in the Society Islands.

The boats dropped their grapnels and Gore, the master's mate, who was in charge of the cutter, threw a line to the islanders, signing to them to make it fast. They did so and signalled to the white men to land, but Furneaux refused as they were too numerous.

One of them got into a small canoe, and laying hold of the buoy-rope, tried to raise the cutter's grapnel, while the rest stood ready to haul the boat aground. When the fellow began to haul up, Gore fired a musket across his nose, and he jumped overboard and swam to the shore. The rest of the natives were astonished at the noise, but when the man landed – he kept under water until he got close to the rocks – they laughed heartily and again invited the white men to land, pointing to hogs, fowls and fruit which they had collected. But the seamen, although tempted, declined. Instead they showed some toys, indicating that they wished to barter. The women, seeing the toys, rushed down to the beach, but were driven back by the men, at which they seemed disappointed and vexed.

Some of the natives gave fowls, a pig and a few plantains or bananas for some toys, but the others went into the woods and carried away with them the provisions they had brought. Some made signs that they would soon return, but no more was seen of them. It was the hour of their midday sleep.

After waiting for a time, the seamen went back to the ship, where Furneaux reported that the natives seemed too numerous for so small an island. He had noticed some large double-canoes on the beach and thought there must be larger islands not far away, where provisions could be procured more plentifully and, he hoped, with less difficulty. Wallis agreed and decided to run farther west.

The ship sailed at two o'clock in the afternoon, to the general disappointment of her crew. The main hope was the prospect of the high land which was thought to have been seen the day before.

It was the only comfort for departing so soon from Osnaburgh Island, where they had observed plenty of food and natives armed only with clubs and spears.

But at three o'clock that afternoon land was sighted bearing W.½.S. – first what appeared to be an enormous mountain, its summit covered with clouds, and then the tops of several other mountains. All now looked on their troubles as over, believing that what they saw was the long-wished-for Southern Continent. It was Tahiti, warm, sensuous, shrouded in haze and clouds, never before beheld by Europeans.

To prevent the *Dolphin* from being embayed in the recesses of the supposed Southern Continent, Wallis ordered her to be steered for the northernmost land in sight. To the south there was none – an illusion, caused no doubt by clouds and haze, although there is in fact to the extreme south an island where the climate is so temperate that its coconuts are said never to ripen. At sunset Furneaux, Robertson and most of the midshipmen were at the mast-head looking out for shoals. But they saw none, so they risked sailing until ten o'clock at night. The ship was then laid to, with all aboard longing for the new day.

At two o'clock in the warm, tropical night, the weather being very clear, sail was made. At sunrise course was altered and they steered straight in for the land. The atmosphere now became very thick and hazy, with the pearly mists of the Pacific which often presage a day of extreme heat. Nothing could be seen of the land which they thought had been sighted to the south.

At nine o'clock the ship had to lie to, the fog being so thick they could not see even the real land. Everyone was very uneasy lest the ship should strike a shoal, especially as the sea was heard thundering on a reef.

A little later the fog cleared and the easternmost point of Tahiti was seen bearing north at six miles, the high, green land culminating in sharp, needle-like spires. There are some cliffs at the south-east end of the island, and above them The-great-ascent-of-Pai-into-the-Mist, whose summit, called Fare-tua – the Sea-house – rises over 3,000 feet.

More than a hundred canoes lay between the ship and the white curling line of breakers on the reef. They were outriggers – dug-outs with no sails – and each one carried from one to ten men. The natives had put off from the sandy beach of the lagoon, behind which the thatched, barn-like houses were visible among the bread-fruit trees and lofty palms. Many more canoes were drawn up along the sandy beaches.

When they were within pistol shot, the brown-skinned men, who wore only loin-cloths, lay by, looking at the white men with astonishment and conferring with each other.

The Tahitians have various traditions regarding the coming of white men, among them that one day a canoe without an outrigger would bring to their island the children of a glorious princess. Several generations before, during one of the enormous Tahitian festivals at which the people congregated in such vast numbers that it would have seemed to a stranger as if all Tahiti was present, there was feasting, dancing, wrestling and scrambling for hogs and canoes. A priest named Maui who prophesied the appearance of the canoe without an outrigger was scoffed at by the assembled chiefs, for it was thought a canoe must either be double – two canoes lashed together side by side – or have an outrigger, a floating baulk of light timber to hold it upright in the water.

Maui filled the bottom of his wooden feeding bowl with stones and, wading into the blue lagoon, launched it to prove that a canoe without an outrigger could float without overturning. The commoners were impressed but the chiefs were unwilling to believe. Maui thereupon made a prediction even more incredible – that after the canoe without an outrigger would come one without sails and cordage. (His prophesy was fulfilled with the arrival of the first steamship.)

There was also a more recent prophecy. At the great *marai* at Opoa in Raiatea, at one of the vast gatherings for worship, there came at the close of the ceremony a whirlwind which plucked off the head of a tall, spreading *tamanu* tree, named Screen-from-Wind-of-Aggravating-Crime, leaving the bare trunk standing. (*Tamanu* wood is very hard and close-grained, much like walnut.) The awe-struck representatives of each people looked at those of the other in silence, until a priest of Opoa named Vaita – Smitten-water – exclaimed: 'Friends, upon what are you meditating?'

'We are wondering what lies in the breaking of this tree; for such a thing has not happened to our trees from the remotest ages.'

Then Vaita said: 'I see before me the meaning of this strange event! There are coming the glorious children of the Trunk (God), who will see these trees here, in Taputapu-atea. In person they differ from us, yet they are the same as we, from the Trunk, and they will possess this land. There will be an end to our present customs, and the sacred birds of sea and land will come to mourn over what this severed tree teaches.'

The wise men and priests, amazed by this speech, inquired where such people were to be found.

'They are coming in a ship without an outrigger.'

'We have seen ships that men have learned to build from Hiro (a giant and jester, who was supposed to have taught men how to build canoes), but they have outriggers, for without them they would overturn. How, then, can what you say be true?'

Then a high priest of the neighbouring island of Huahine derided Vaita and told him he had gone back to his childhood or was insane, and two other priests of Opoa reasoned with him until they all dispersed.

The chief Tamatoa – Son of the Ironwood Tree – hearing of this, sent for Vaita to come to his house, where his fellow priests and a numerous throng had assembled to hear him.

He was received kindly by the chief, who, however, was doubtful of what he said. Whereupon Vaita, seeing a large wooden trough used for the preparation of food – some of the troughs were large enough to take a whole hog – asked the chief to send some men to fill it with stones and balance it in the sea. This was done and the trough sat upon the waves with no signs of upsetting, amid the applauding shouts of the people, with whom the chief sided. As they parted, the priests swore vengeance upon Vaita should his prediction prove false.

Another prophecy was that of a priest of Raiatea who told

Tamatoa that there would come a time when the restrictions on food for women would cease, and that they would be free to eat turtle and all other food sacred to gods and men. This prediction, too, was received with scoffing.

A later seer named Pau'e, had said: 'There are coming children of the glorious princess, in a canoe without an outrigger, and they will be covered from head to foot.'

The spectators applauded, but three days afterwards Pau'e died.

Pau'e had also said: 'There will come a new king to whom the government will be given, and new manners will be adopted in this land; the *tapa* (bark cloth) and cloth-beating mallet will go out of use in Tahiti, and the people will wear different and strange clothes.'

Such were some of the prophecies made by the priests of Tahiti. It is known that it seemed that one of them at least had come true on the morning that the *Dolphin* appeared.

*   *   *

Wallis, who was still ill, made his feeble way on deck and was surprised to find the ship surrounded by canoes, which seemed to have arrived unseen and unheralded.

The Europeans – 'children of the glorious princess' – made friendly gestures, showing the natives trinkets and inviting them to come aboard. The islanders first drew together in their canoes to confer, then, making signs of friendship by holding up branches of plantain trees, they paddled round the frigate.

One held up a plantain or banana shoot, supposed to be an effigy of their own persons (for which reason a plantain shoot was always presented at the *marai*), and called out the words: '*Ta'ata, o mei'a roa*' – Man, long banana. The native made a speech of great length, then threw the branch into the sea, signifying that their intentions were friendly; for the sea was sacred to all, being regarded as a vast moving *marai*. Polynesians are in their element at ceremonial speech-making, and have a remarkable command of flowery and ceremonial compliments and expressing shades of meaning unknown to ourselves.

The canoes now came nearer the wallowing ship. The natives talked so very fast that the white men were unable to distinguish one word from another, though their speech seemed to resemble that of the Patagonians. To please them the white men too assumed a jovial air and spoke to them in English. There were now fully one hundred and fifty canoes round the ship and more were approaching. The visitors calculated that there must have been quite eight hundred men in them. No women were to be seen however.

The sailors continued to make friendly signs, and a fine brisk young Tahitian climbed up by the mizzen chains and sprang out of the shrouds, landing on top of the wooden awning over the after end of the quarter-deck.

Wallis made signs to him to come down and held up some trinkets. But the youth only laughed and stared and would not take anything until some of the natives, after making long speeches, threw plantain branches on to the deck. He then accepted a few trinkets and shook hands with Robertson and other officers.

Several other Tahitians now climbed aboard in various parts of the ship, not knowing the proper entrance by the gangway. As one was standing on the quarter-deck near the entrance to the gangway a goat ran up and butted him from behind. The Tahitian turned hastily to see the creature raised on her hind-legs ready to repeat the blow. He leaped overboard, followed by his friends.

They soon recovered from their fright, however, and returned to the ship, where Wallis reconciled them to the goats and the equally unknown sheep and showed them the pigs in their styes and the cocks and hens in their coops. The Tahitians made signs that they had similar creatures. The white men indicated that they should bring them aboard with some fruit, and showing the natives cloth, knives, shears, beads and ribbons, tried to make them realise that they wanted to barter. To emphasise this some of the seamen grunted like hogs, then pointed to the shore, while others crowed like cocks and flapped their arms. The Tahitians grunted and crowed likewise and pointed to the land. But, seeing that the 'children of the glorious princess' already had both hogs and cocks and not understanding the trading mentality of white men, they did not get their meaning. Moreover, the flapping of arms in Tahiti meant a challenge to a wrestling match, an unfortunate coincidence that no doubt set up a bad psychological reaction.

The Europeans now made signs for the men to get into their canoes and bring what was wanted.

Some got into their canoes, but the rest, knowing about iron from the wreck of the *African Galley* – one of Roggeveen's ships wrecked in the Tuamotus in 1722 – were unwilling to leave without some of it, and began to tug at the iron stanchions and the ringballs of the shrouds and stays and seemed astonished that they could not break them. A large spike-nail from the *African Galley* was brought to Tahiti about the year 1725, where it was deposited in a *marai* at Papara; many people were living, even in 1791, who remembered the loss of the Dutch ship; and the Tahitians were also in touch with the natives of the atolls. The white men showed the Tahitians nails, by which they appeared much attracted; but nothing was given to any except the man who had first come aboard.

The Tahitians now began to grow somewhat surly. The *Dolphin* must in their eyes have been a treasure ship such as their world had never seen. Polynesians are unable to understand the apparent greediness of white men. With them, broadly speaking, it is only necessary to ask in order to receive; for it is considered scarcely possible to refuse. The Tahitians never returned thanks nor had they a word to express the idea. The economics of the tribal system and of individualism were in conflict. For the European in such a case, it must be said that he foresees the serious evils that would follow his generosity, as for instance if they had parted with the ringballs. But the Tahitians could scarcely have been expected to understand that the masts and rigging would be down about their ears if they were given all they wanted.

To frighten the natives back into their craft a nine-pound shot was fired over the heads of some in the canoes. Immediately the natives on board the *Dolphin* leaped into the water, while those in the canoes paddled away from the ship and waited about a hundred yards off until the others reached them.

One of the Tahitians had been standing by a midshipman, Henry Ibbot, who was wearing a new, gold-laced, three-cornered hat. Ibbot had been trying to talk to another native by signs. The first seized 'the glaring hat', as Ibbot's shipmates called it, and jumped overboard with it in his hand. When he had swum about twenty yards he held it up and waved it round his head. The white men shouted to him and pointed their muskets at him, but he, not understanding about firearms, got into his canoe. All the natives now began to paddle towards the ship with the intention, it was thought, of trying for more prizes. But perhaps it was merely to return the hat.

Sail was made, and the frigate stood on towards the west. As she sailed much faster than the natives could paddle, they were obliged to abandon the allurements of gold and iron and returned to the shore.

CHAPTER VI

*

THE TEVAS

THE hour-glass-shaped island of Tahiti – roughly half-way between the north of New Zealand and Panama – is about a hundred and twenty-five miles in circumference. It consists of two peninsulas, one about ninety miles in circumference and nearly circular, the other about thirty miles in circumference, oval shaped and connected by a low isthmus about a couple of miles across. Both halves of the island are extremely mountainous, the mountains of the larger or western peninsula being the higher. The larger peninsula is called by the natives Great Tahiti of the Golden Haze. The smaller one is Little Tahiti, or Disturbed Sea.

When the wind from the east – the trade wind – gets far to the south, the clouds collected on the mountains of the smaller peninsula are driven to the west and, striking the high mountains at the south-western end of the island, descend in the form of rain at Papara. So the local clan, the Tevas, were known as The Children of the Mist. 'Teva, the wind and the rain!' was their rallying cry.

With cliffs where it is not palm-fringed, forest-clad, wasp-waisted and mountainous, the island has a peculiar clarity of atmosphere. There is something soft and voluptuous about the light, a fact noticed not only by artists but by the natives, for there is much of the artist in them. A curious shimmering magic seems to hang over the sharply towering mountains with their forests, their lawn-like patches of fern and bamboo, their headlong waterfalls, about the foaming coral reefs and the pellucid lagoons. This applies particularly to the larger peninsula, perhaps because of the greater height of the mountains. Hence the name Great Tahiti of the Golden Haze.

A spirit seems to brood over the startling mountain mass, expressing itself in a race of powerful queens, for it has been said that the island

79

has been inclined always, since men first got there, to favour the feminine. Even about the men with their rounded bodies, for all their good looks and powerful physique, there is a suggestion of femininity: the two sexes tend to approximate more here than in the case of Europeans. Captain Cook considered most of the women to be very masculine.

The first of these queens of whom we know was Hototu. She belonged to the little district of Vaieri or Faa'a on the north-west coast of Tahiti, near Papeete, a hilly place with a lagoon, in which the reflections of palms, crowding down to the shore, lie by day and dug-out canoes are drawn up on sandy beaches, facing the island of Moorea. This beauty spot is shaped like a crested helmet, which raises its blue-shaded pinnacles eight miles away, 'peaked and engrailed like some far distance of Titian's landscapes', across a white line of reef and purple sea.

Hototu was married to Temanu-tunu (Bird That Lets Loose The Army), the first king of Punaauia, by whom she had a son, the Ari'i-rahi (or Paramount Chief) Moanaroa. Punaauia meant 'The trumpet is mine', for the king had been given an enormous conch-shell trumpet by someone who had descended into the hell beneath the earth to get it, whereupon the king exclaimed fatuously – 'The trumpet is mine.'

When a male child of chiefly family was born, the titles and honours of the father were at once inherited by the infant. The original idea of the practice was probably to stabilise the succession, by doing away with the possibility of disputes at the death of the father. But the stated explanation was that the child, as the fruit of both parents, was superior to both, as the fruit is to the tree that bears it. Moanaroa, the infant, thus became the paramount chief, or king, of Tahiti.

Temanu-tunu decided to make a *maro ura*, a red girdle of royalty, the badge of supreme chieftainship, for his son. The girdle, narrow and some fourteen feet long, made of network and thrummed with red feathers, was worn only at the coronations of the Tahitian kings, ceremonies that were attended with human sacrifice. These kings were invested at the age of six or seven with the donning of the royal *maro* and an eye-shade covered with similar feathers, and shaped like those worn by tennis players. They were kept in a sort of sacred ark at one of the principal temples.

Bird-That-Lets-Loose-The-Army set out by canoe for the Tuamotus to collect red feathers, which took some time amid the turbulent, reef-strewn waters which beset the palm-clad atolls.

While he was absent his wife Hototu journeyed down into the district of Papara at the south-west end of Tahiti, where solitary mountains, topped by massive clouds, stand out pyramid-like towards the fringe of palms reflected in the water. 'Papara is the land where the heavy leaves drag down the branches,' says the line of a song – a reference to the frequent rain. Here Hototu met a Fish Body or Shark God, half man and half shark – with whom she was so well pleased that she surrendered herself to his love.

While her husband was still away in the atolls, his dog, Pihoro, returned to Tahiti and, searching for the queen, found her finally at Papara, seated on the ground beside the Shark God. He ran up and fawned upon her, to the jealous disgust of the Shark God, one half of whom said to the other, 'She cares for that dog more than for me. See how he caresses her!'

Angrily he arose and said: 'You will have a son by me who will be called Teva. For him I have built the *marai* at Mata'oa' – a temple in Papara. 'There our son will wear the *maro tea*' – the yellow girdle.

When Temanu-tunu came back from the coral islands and landed at Vairoa on the north-east coast of Tahiti he met the Shark God, whom he begged to return with him to his home. But the Shark God refused, saying – 'Your wife is a woman who is too fond of dogs.'

So Temanu-tunu went alone to Faa'a, where he founded the *marai* of Punaauia, in which his son could assume the red girdle that only the Ahurai chief could then wear.

The Teva family founded by the Shark God afterwards became supreme. The reigning Ahurai chief captured a remarkably beautiful Teva girl. Of her the Tevas soon heard rumours that she had been degraded, and passed down first to the servants and then even to the hogs and the dogs and the fish of the sea. Here surely is indicated

some internal tribal conflict and weakness, possibly accompanied by
the murder of the woman. The insults uttered by her infuriated
father and the story of his revengeful killings were repeated to the
Ahurai chief, who came to Papara to avenge them. On the advice
of their chief the Tevas hid themselves in the shelter of the *marai*
founded by the Shark God, while one of them kept watch from a
famously tall coconut palm. On the arrival of the Ahurai war party
the Tevas arose, defeated them and pursued them, taking possession
of one district after another of the larger peninsula, but they stopped
short of invading the smaller one.

'This is the downfall of Vaieri and the rise of Papara.'

'Let him wear his cloak!' – meaning the rain – were the words of
an old Papuan chieftainess when someone wished to offer her son
protection from the rain as he landed from his canoe.

CHAPTER VII

*

LAND OF THE GOLDEN HAZE

As the *Dolphin* sailed along the south coast of Little Tahiti the white men, shedding their dislike of mountainous scenery, thought it the most delightful country they had ever seen. There was scarcely a hill without a waterfall. The coast seemed to be one continuous plantation from the beaches inwards, with a sort of blue-green metallic lustre of growth; fine level country abounded with coconuts and other fruits.

Beyond the hills – on which were groves of palms and fruit trees – the mountains rose very high. The valleys were thick with tall trees, but the upper part of the mountains was clear of wild wood and as green as any meadow in England, the effect at a distance, although not understood, of the fern and bamboo, with which the mountains of the smaller peninsular are covered in their higher reaches.

The many houses on the plain were neat, well-roofed and like the thatched barns of our farmers, far bigger and better made than any native huts the Europeans had ever before seen.

A foaming line of coral reef, like a wide table of solid rock, ran parallel with the coast, from half a mile to two miles from the shore; on it some natives were walking a long way out, yet only up to their knees in water. Several rivers emptied themselves into the lagoon, and through the reef were openings into deep water, as always happens opposite rivers and streams whose fresh water kills the coral growth as they make their way to the ocean. Within a few miles the officers saw along-shore through their telescopes not less, as they calculated, than six to seven thousand men, women and children.

At three o'clock in the afternoon the *Dolphin* came abreast of a large, V-shaped inlet before the low isthmus of Taravao which

83

divides Tahiti into its two halves. This isthmus was thought by the
Tahitians to be frequented by spirits of the dead and demons, and
so was regarded as an uncanny place.

The huge bay (still not commercialised) into which they now
sailed is called Port Phaeton because it was surveyed by a French
warship of that name in the 1850's. The native name is Te'aua'a.
Here the forests rose to the summits of the mountains. Close to the
water grew the *tamanu*, called by the Tahitians the Healing Tree, a
vast, spreading tree, from whose walnut-like wood they made stools,
dishes, trays, pillows and canoes. It bears a seed, or rather a nut,
which produces a powerfully scented, thick, greenish oil. This, with
other ingredients, they used to perfume their bark cloth and also
used externally for wounds and internally to counteract the ill effects
arising from eating certain sorts of fish.

Along the shore grew the *mape*, the Tahitian chestnut, with ferns
and vines in its branches and board-like buttresses around its base;
also the antedeluvian-looking pandanus palm, standing on a congress
of roots like stilts five or six feet high, its sharp blue-green, thorn-
edged leaves, about six feet long, set in screw fashion. Nowhere else
on the coast was the vegetation of the island so wildly luxuriant and
tropical.

The cutter was sent to sound the beautiful inlet for anchorage.
She did not go inside the reef but sounded close outside, finding as
vast a depth of water as at the other islands. It had not yet been
learned that there is very rarely anchorage outside a reef. If she had
gone inside, good anchorage would have been found.

Tahitians in many canoes began to gather about her, wondering
no doubt what she was doing outside the reef. Wallis suspected that
they intended to attack her and signalled her to return. To intimidate
the natives, he ordered a nine-pounder to be fired over their heads.
The noise of the cannon reverberated among the mountains and
the Tahitians in their canoes were startled by its thunder. For a
century afterwards the comparatively rare thunder and lightning of
Tahiti was thought to herald the arrival of a warship.

That the idea of thunder was intimately bound up with war is
shown by part of a Tahitian chant:

Make way for the king onwards to the Sacred Isle;
Loud peals resound in the sky above, O!
For the red girdle, O!
Numerous are the ura feathers
From the wall of jawbones
In thy red girdle, O my king.
The sky is reached above,
By the great Warrior Sovereign Oro.

(The jawbones referred to are of those killed in battle or massacred after it, which were taken as trophies.)

Thinking no doubt that they were the victims of a supernatural, ill-omened attack, the Tahitians tried to cut the boat off as she began to make towards the ship. But she sailed much faster than they could paddle, and none of the canoes had sails. Some of the natives, however, managed to intercept her and threw stones, hurting some of the seamen. Gore fired a musket loaded with buckshot at the man who threw the first stone, wounding him in the right shoulder. The rest of the men in his canoe jumped overboard, putting the other canoes into disorder.

The cutter was hoisted aboard and, just as the frigate was about to go, a large canoe under a matting sail was seen making after her. Wallis decided to wait for her, as she might have a chief aboard. She sailed very fast and was soon alongside, but no one in her showed any authority over the rest. One man stood up and made a long speech, then threw a plantain branch on to the deck, which the officers understood to be a token of peace. They made a short speech in return and threw the man a branch left by their first visitors. Wallis also gave him toys with which he appeared much pleased.

While the canoe was alongside, the man who had stolen the midshipman's hat came and waved it. Obviously at least one sailing-canoe had followed the ship from the east end of the island, probably within the reefs. The ship made sail, however, and stood off before he could reach her. In both these incidents, which were probably related, can be seen the familiar Polynesian tendency to make things right. They are remarkable people in this respect.

The *Dolphin* stood on to the west along the south coast of the larger peninsula, Great-Tahiti-of-the-Golden-Haze. The shore was lined with men, women and children, and the white men thought it the most thickly populated country they had ever seen. Canoes were drawn up all along the beaches, and the barn-like houses seemed almost without number. There were masses of coconut palms along the shore, with other trees which were not known. There were, of course, many strange trees, such, for example, as the candlenut, the size of a walnut tree; and a large tree bearing a blackish nut about the size of a sheep's heart, which was used for stupefying fish in the holes of the reef.

Behind the beach was fine level country, laid out in plantations. The mountains were even higher than those previously seen, covered half-way up their slopes with what appeared to be good pasture except for a few places seemingly dug up for planting. Above what was actually fern and bamboo the mountainsides were covered with tall trees and the whole was a mass of green, although it was the winter season.

When they were not far from Papara, it was decided to run out to sea and work to windward all night, for fear of being embayed between this high shore and the mountains thought to have been sighted to the south the day before. It was still thick and hazy in that direction and it seemed that these phantom mountains could still be seen appearing through the clouds.

The 'children of the glorious princess' now felt certain that this was part of the Southern Continent. Yet the ship could easily have sailed westward round the island had it been realised that it was an island.

At daybreak she was thirty miles off land, and now returned to the east. A remarkable peak, shaped like a sugar loaf, among the mountains of the interior of the larger peninsula, attracts the attention of nearly all visitors to Tahiti. Bougainville, who arrived there about ten months after the *Dolphin's* visit, compared it to an immense pyramid that the hands of a clever sculptor had adorned with garlands and foliage. This peak is Orohena – First-dorsal-fin – culminating in two gentle rises, in between which lies the lake where live the red-feathered ducks. The plumes of these birds were much sought after for the gods and kings, and men called 'rock-clingers' climbed Orohena's precipitous sides to win them.

Between the north-east point of Tahiti and the northernmost point, which was sighted at noon, is a bay running some twelve miles inland. The houses on its eastern shore were even longer and larger, the inhabitants numerous. The country in the bottom of the bay – forming the north side of the isthmus of Taravao – was strikingly beautiful.

The isthmus was to some extent a sort of no-man's-land between the two halves of the island, although not entirely without houses. It was used, more as a portage for canoes which were often dragged along the track across its neck with the aid of rollers. This was to avoid having to sail round the east end of the island, where there was frequently a dangerous sea off the cliffs.

All the tall trees were green, to the tops of the mountains.

Robertson kept at the mast-head to look out for shoals but saw none. On the west side of the great bay he saw within the reef two islets – Porcupine-fish-stomach and Mud-of-Insects – where, if there were sufficient depth of water behind them, he expected to find good anchorage. But he was mistaken for the narrow, coral-strewn lagoon is on the windward side of the island. Bougainville was to find trouble in losing anchors there; but the shrewd Wallis was not deceived. Robertson would almost certainly have turned it down on investigation.

A shimmering haze of heat hung over the green land. Several sailing-canoes were now running close along-shore, but none came off to the ship. It was supposed that their purpose was to give the alarm to the coast.

At four o'clock the *Dolphin* was abreast of a good river issuing from a valley with fine plantations on either side. Soundings were taken frequently but no bottom was found; Robertson, however, observed the water to change colour about a mile towards the shore, which indicated there was sounding. He reported to Wallis, but the captain did not choose to hoist out a boat to try it.

Cliffs now reappeared, and waves beat on a shore of black stones.

There are blow-holes here in the rocky coast, called Shouting-road, from the whistling sound of the surging sea as it spouts up through the holes in the ancient lava flows, looking like whales blowing. They passed narrow, palm-fringed beaches where ravines ran up into the background, and hills rose from the water's edge with occasional palms outlined against the land's stupendous, cloud-crowned masses. Then the shore again became flat and covered with palms.

The ship approached a low, sandy, tree-clad point about a mile long, from which the coast bore away to the south-west. At about eighteen miles to the west lay high jagged land. This was the island of Moorea. One of Moorea's mountains is curved like a hook and another has a hole through which a god is supposed to have thrown his spear. At the distance from which they now saw it the island is mauve, and the sea from which it rises a deep purple.

Robertson, from the mast-head, saw that beyond the point lay what appeared to be a fine bay with white water, a sure sign of a good anchorage. He reported to Wallis, but it was too late to go in and sound the bay. So it was decided to return to the river they had seen at four o'clock that afternoon.

Due south of the verdant point of Uporu – renamed by Captain Cook Point Venus – is tremendous, pyramid-like Orohena, in the centre of Great-Tahiti-of-the-Golden-Haze. The larger peninsula radiates from three huge central peaks, a riot of valleys, mountain tops, glades and waterfalls, looming – a vast mass of emerald green – out of the blue of the sky, splashed with shadow and white water and red burnt volcanic earth. One of these peaks, nearer Papeete and opposite Moorea, is the Aorai – Earth Meeting Sky, or Sky-world.

The top-sails were triple-reefed, and the ship worked back to windward all night. Wallis and Clarke were very ill, and on the doctor's list were about thirty seamen, some of whom he expected to die if relief were not found on this pleasant and delightful-looking land.

The ship's company spent nearly all the night talking. Most were sure of finding all sorts of provisions, and dismissed the difficulties of procuring them. Others fancied that nothing could be had without blows, and made many idle suppositions regarding the natives' savage disposition. And some thought it impossible to land in the face of so numerous natives, and considered it best to run to Tinian in the Ladrones, where they were certain of provisioning without risk of losing their lives, ship or boats. To attempt to land here, or to anchor anywhere near the shore, where thousands of canoes could surround them, was to incur grave danger to the ship and everyone in her.

But fortunately for the sick, as the master said, it was resolved to try landing here before they bore away for Tinian, 4,246 miles away. Had they been so foolish as to make for that distant island they would have arrived in as much distress as did Lord Anson. (He had given a very good account of Tinian with its herds of wild milk-white cattle, its orchards and its lawns. But 'Foul Weather Jack' Byron had difficulty in catching the cattle and thought it one of the unhealthiest spots in the world.) And it would be disagreeable to discover a beautiful, thickly-inhabited, unknown land, without being able to give a proper account of it, since it was for that purpose that the expedition had been dispatched.

The river, their objective, issued from a deep and beautiful valley, abounding with fruit trees and inhabited a considerable way up its length. (It is the only valley which runs right across mountainous Tahiti, and is called The Room of Refuge. On the other side of the island it opens into the rainy district of Papara.) The *Dolphin*, now off the north coast, was almost exactly on the opposite side of the island to where she had been the night before, when it was decided to alter course so as not to be embayed in the recesses of the supposed Southern Continent. (Regarding this, indeed, the navigators were now becoming a little doubtful.) With nightfall countless lights appeared all along the shore, probably the torch flares of natives fishing on the reefs.

At daybreak two boats were sent out to sound. The instant they left the ship, a swarm of canoes put off from the shore and steered towards them. As they approached the natives appeared to wave the boats off.

In Polynesia what we should consider the military signal to retreat
or keep back, a waving downward with the hand, is an invitation
to come forward, and Tahitians have said that the troubles in which
they were involved with Captain Wallis rose from an unspecified
misunderstanding.

The natives all waved to the boats, and seemed enraged when the
boats stood in for the shore – a natural reaction to their misunder-
stood desire for fraternisation.

The boats found regular soundings, all in fine, black, sandy
ground, and signalled accordingly to the joy of the *Dolphin*. She
made sail, ran in, and anchored in a hundred feet of water opposite
the river, two miles from the shore.

Several canoes were now alongside with coconuts, fruits, fowls
and some fat young pigs. But the natives behaved very insolently.
None of them would trust the 'children of the glorious princess'
with their goods until they got nails or toys. Then several of them
jumped off into their canoes and kept everything. Some carried their
insolence to the extent of striking the seamen, imagining no doubt
that they were dealing with a race of fools, incapable of understanding even the most simple gestures, people who required blows
to assist the process of thought just as their masters of ceremonies at
official gatherings had to lay about them with their wands.

The seamen, not appreciating these niceties, were very unwilling
to put up with it; but the captain had given strict orders that no man
should hurt the natives until their disposition had been tried, so the
British tars, with their traditional good-humoured patience, prepared
to submit to their ill-behaviour.

Wallis ordered Robertson to sound all along the shore and to
look for a place from which the ship could be watered. Several
thousand natives were on the beach, more than a hundred canoes
were alongside the ship, and nearly two hundred between her and
the land, several of them large double-canoes with high sterns and
eight, twelve and sixteen men in each of them.

The instant the barge and cutter left the ship, all the large sailing-
canoes set off after them, their crews hooting and making much
noise, which, with the natives' insolent behaviour in the ship, made

Robertson suspect some hostile design. He therefore told Gore in
the cutter to be on his guard and that he would keep close by him
as the barge sailed better than the cutter.

In a few minutes the sailing-canoes came up and kept so near that
it was impossible to cast the lead to sound. Both boats made all the
sail they could, with the idea of looking for a watering-place, but
again the large canoes came up, and some of their crews attempted
to board the boats. But the seamen avoided them, still making
friendly signs, though at the same time waving to the canoes to
keep off. The natives – thinking, no doubt, that they were being
mocked – behaved even more insolently, or so it seemed.

By the time the boats got close to the shore, more than two
hundred large and small canoes were round them, with nearly fifteen
hundred men in them. The coast was thickly lined with men, women
and children as far as the eye could see.

The boats came to the river-mouth, but there was not enough
water to enter and the surf ran so high all along the shore that no one
could have landed with firearms dry – a necessary consideration with
muskets. The river, Papeno'o – Confluent-waters – at a little distance
inland is about a hundred yards wide and three feet deep. The largest
river in Tahiti, it is rapid and often swollen with inland rains. At this
point an inner line of reef skirts the beach.

The barge and cutter were sailed a little way along the shore in
the hope of being able to sound, but the canoes crowded too thickly
about them. The natives on land waved to the seamen to come on
shore, but they being so numerous and those in the canoes so insolent,
Robertson thought it prudent to return to the ship, as he found it
impossible to do what had been ordered.

As soon as the boats tacked and stood off, the people ashore set
up a loud cry, those in the canoes began to hoot, and several
attempted to board the boats, seeming enraged.

When they were within a mile and a half of the *Dolphin* one of the
large canoes rammed the cutter and carried away her boomkin – a
projecting spar – and tore the mizzen sail, but the seamen and marines
got clear of her by using pikes and bayonets. At the same time another
sailing-canoe attempted to board the barge, but she too got clear.

A few minutes afterwards three of the largest canoes together tried to board the barge. Robertson ordered the marines to point their muskets, but the Tahitians laughed, and struck the prow of one canoe right into the boat's stern, and four of the biggest men jumped on to the prow of their canoe with paddles and clubs in their hands. This was the way the Tahitians fought on the fighting-stages of their war-canoes, in close combat with spears and clubs.

The master ordered a marine to fire his musket right across the canoe, but it only startled them, and when they found that none was hurt they gave a shout and ran directly for the barge's stern again, while the other two canoes came right for her middle. Had they struck the barge their prows would immediately have sunk her. Meanwhile the Tahitians were also trying to board the cutter.

Robertson was furious that the ship took no action, although everything had been seen plainly. Had a nine-pound shot been fired over the natives' heads, it might have frightened them. He now ordered two marines to wound the most resolute pair in the first canoe and the sergeant fired at one man who was killed and another was wounded in the thigh. Both fell overboard and were followed into the water by the rest of their crew while the other two canoes sheered off. The white men pointed their muskets at them, and the natives held their paddles up before their faces and dropped astern.

When the Tahitians swimming in the sea saw the boats go on, they again got into their canoe and hauled their companions aboard. They tried to make one of them stand, and when he could not, to make him sit, but then found he was dead. They laid him in the bottom of the canoe, and while one supported the wounded man, the rest of the crew made sail for the land.

Robertson told Wallis his reason for not sounding, and that it was impossible to land anywhere near the valley without wetting firearms. Wallis asked what had better be done, and the master proposed they should examine the bay seen the previous evening. As it was on the lee side of the low northerly point, they could probably anchor the ship in it and land with dry firearms.

Wallis first approved the proposal but soon rejected it, being otherwise advised by another officer who suggested anchoring closer in to the shore and bringing the ship's broadside guns to bear on the wide river mouth, and to keep constantly firing into the fruit trees, until they got all the drinking water aboard; then they might set out for Tinian.

The following day the weather was cloudy with flying showers of rain. Several canoes came off with hogs, pigs, fowls and plantains, bananas, breadfruit and other fruits unknown, which were bought for nails and other trifles. Most of the natives traded very honestly, but a few attempted to defraud the 'children of the glorious princess' by going off with a nail or toy without paying; but on a musket, or even a telescope, being pointed at them, they returned the nail or toy or exchanged it. All the natives preferred nails and the rate of exchange was one 3-inch nail for a hog of about twenty pounds, a 2¾-inch one for a roasting pig, a 1¾-inch one for a fowl or a bunch of fruit.

The natives now began to understand something about muskets, though they thought their fire was blown through with the mouth. They made signs that two of their companions had been killed and called loudly, 'Bou-bou!' – then smote their chests and foreheads and lay backward motionless with their eyes fixed.

Wallis, who presumably was disappointed in Robertson – the first lieutenant even accused him of cowardice – ordered Gore to take the barge and cutter, find a watering-place and, if possible, to land. If the natives gave any trouble, he was to return, and the ship would fire some round-shot among them.

When the mate got close to the beach, though none of the canoes came near the boats, he found the surf running too high for him to land. The wind here blew right along the shore, raising a huge surf on the side of the ship and on the beach.

Tahitians were lining the shore for two or three miles, and made signs for the white men to land. They refused, but made it clear that they wanted water and showed toys and nails. Some natives came off to the boats through the surf with large sections of bamboo and calabashes full of fresh water. They swam like fish and, as Robertson remarked, dived much faster than anyone could have believed possible without seeing them, for he tried some of them by throwing nails several times into the sea alongside the *Dolphin*, and they dived and caught them.

At noon the boats returned with twenty gallons of water. But after dinner Gore was ordered to take casks and breakers – small vessels holding ten gallons which were filled by the head and had a handle to carry them – and to do all he could to get the natives to bring off water. He had nails and pieces of hoop-iron with which to pay them. When the boats got near the beach, some of the Tahitians came off and took six breakers ashore to fill, but would only return four. The seamen made friendly signs, but they would not return the other two and signalled for the white men to land, and that they would haul their boats up among the trees.

For the seamen, burning with the fires of enforced chastity, the sight of the women on the beach must have been a mixed torment and delight. To get their breakers back, they threatened the Tahitians by pointing muskets at them. The natives made game of it, however, and laughed heartily, not knowing that the muskets could hurt them at that distance. The mate fired a musketoon along the beach, that they might get an idea of their danger by seeing the balls strike the water. But they merely started back a little at the report and took no notice of the balls, which of course it never occurred to them to look for in the angry water, since they were looking only for fire.

On finding that none was hurt, they returned to the waterside beneath the palms, bringing a number of fine young girls, some of a light copper colour, others darker, and some almost white. These attracted the sailors' fancy considerably. They stopped pointing their muskets, and the natives, observing this, made the girls play numerous droll, wanton tricks, and the men made signs of friendship to entice the 'children of the glorious princess' ashore. But they still refused, as they did not know enough about the natives' character.

The seamen had obviously been making indecent gestures to the women as they had done in the Straits of Magellan, when they indicated pointedly that they wanted wives. These were the same men – even longer at sea, and still wanting a little fun. The Tahitians subsequently expressed the view that Europeans were utterly shameless, though it may be that they thought at first that the 'glorious princess's children' had been exhibiting some erotic aspects of the white man's group-dancing, for the Tahitians themselves, as already recorded, gave some of their own repertoire in return, no doubt expecting these exchanges to be followed by a dance on the beach, given by both parties.

Their own single young men made use of lascivious gestures in their dances, which they would not have dared to do at any other time, for however queerly the women acted in public dances, no woman of character would allow improper liberties elsewhere. Any wanton exposures would be condemned in a man as much as a woman. Only in their dances was immodesty permitted, which was the effect of national habit or custom. No person could ever be persuaded to do in private company what, when they danced in public, was allowed without scruple. So declared the first white men to live among them.

In all the districts throughout Tahiti a dance was performed almost every evening. Women, young and old, rich and poor, mixed promiscuously, but no man joined in. They were dressed in their best, their heads decorated with wreaths of sweet-scented flowers. Only the young girls were allowed to wear the snowy-white, waxy-looking, delicately-perfumed *tiare*, the single gardenia, emblem of purity.

Usually in the shade of trees or mountains, they divided into two parties, separated by about thirty yards. One of the best players, taking a small green breadfruit – a large breadfruit is about as big as two fists – ran out about half-way between the two parties and kicked the ball as hard as she could, striking it with the upper part of the foot near the instep. If she sent it through the other party, or past them, her group struck up a song and dance, beating time with their hands and feet. The dance lasted about five minutes.

The other party then kicked the ball. If it was stopped by those who danced first, they danced again. Meanwhile the others stood still. After they had played thus for some hours, they kicked the breadfruit to one side.

Each group then – to draw the spectators, including men, to their own particular dance, for both of them went on simultaneously – produced two or three young girls, normally modest and well-behaved, to take the part of wantons. They stripped off their lower garments and covered themselves with a loose piece of cloth, and at certain passages of the song they threw open the cloth and danced with their fore-parts naked to the spectators, making many lewd gestures. But these girls did not allow the men to take any liberties with them.

To encourage the *Dolphin's* seamen to leave the boats, fruit and provisions were brought and ranged upon the beach, and the sailors were invited to partake of them (in addition, as they thought mistakenly, to partaking of the girls). When they put off to return to the ship without having landed, the women pelted them with the *vi* or Brazilian plum – and bananas, shouting, and showing every mark of derision and contempt. Something culpable had been done, possibly indecent exposures when urinating, or the making of indecent gestures.

The boats got back to the ship with only forty gallons of water, leaving two breakers ashore. This left the ship with insufficient water to carry the company to any known place. Some officers now said it was absolutely necessary to get water at any cost; others said it was impossible, as the natives must now be greatly enraged, especially as Robertson had killed two of them. Robertson replied that what he had done he was ready to do again, if his life or the lives of those entrusted to his care were in danger.

The captain was so ill by this time that he was unable to remain on deck, and he consulted his officers as to what had better be done. The first lieutenant was also ill. Most thought it best to run down to the leeward of the low point, where they thought no man need be afraid of wetting his feet, much less his firearms; and this was agreed on. The plan was to sail under the lee of the sandy point and there to lie to until the boats sounded the bay for anchorage. If any large number of canoes assembled round the boats, the ship was to keep near enough to throw a shot over them if need be. If no anchorage was found, she was to be brought back to her present position and

A view near Hamaniino Harbour in the island of Raiatea. Sketched in 1769.

A *marai* in the Society Islands, with an offering to the gods. Sketched by Sydney Parkinson in 1769.

anchored within a short-mile of the river-mouth, and they would make the best shift they could under cover of her guns. So at day-break the *Dolphin* weighed anchor, and stood away for the bay about six or eight miles to the west.

A shallow river-bed emerged at the end of the tree-clad, brilliantly verdant point which she now again approached, and there, on the end of the point, was a terraced *marai* – a pile of black stones. The mile-long point was the projection of a considerable plain, covered with fruit trees. Several open-walled, barn-like, thatched houses were on the seaward end of the point, which was skirted by a broad, foaming line of reef. Behind the plain a deep valley ran inland between lofty mountains. The river which crossed the plain and emerged at the end of the point flowed slowly from the valley. The river-mouth was calm and enchanting.

D

CHAPTER VIII

*

INTRODUCING PUREA AND AMO

AT THE time of Tahiti's discovery by Captain Wallis, in 1767, the regent of Tahiti was the Teva chief Tevahitua, better known as Amo. Haapaai, the father of Tu (then a child, who later became the famous King Pomaré I) ruled over the northern district. Tutahaa, of Herculean build, was chief of Atahuru on the west coast. The child Tu was his special protégé. These three great chiefs were related. The future Pomarés had atoll blood in them.

Tevahitua lived in his house at Papara, near which once grew the well-known watch-tower coconut palm of immense height, close to the *marai* of Mata'oa. He was married to Purea – the Vahine (the lady) Airoro-Atua i Ahurai – a princess of the Ahurai family of Faa'a. Thus the two old royal families of Tahiti were united. Purea was a descendant of Bird-That-Lets-Loose-The-Army and Queen Hototu. Tevahitua also was descended from the adulterous Hototu, reputedly by the Shark God. Hototu means flatulence.

Purea (the accent on the second syllable and the name means the 'Wished-for') was of true Polynesian strain, in the authentic line of Tahitian queens. She was a lady of enormous stature but even when approaching middle-age she preserved her good looks.

Eighteenth-century England came to know her, more melodiously, as Queen Oberea.

In about 1762 she gave birth to a male child in the *maire* fern house, a small isolated temporary house with scented ferns woven into the walls and roof, where women retired for childbirth. Being – by chance – alone at the time her heart softened towards the babe when it cried out and she spared its life. She had already had several children who had been put to death at birth, for she and her husband were members of the *Arioi* Society. But it was a generally accepted

98

rule that if a child cried out on coming into the world its life was spared, for once it had drawn full breath it was inviolate, being held to have attained its own *iho* or personality.

Tevahitua was uncertain whether the child, who was named Teri'i-rere – Flying-sovereign – was his or not, for Purea was not sparing of her favours to others. (This child was also known as Temari'i and as Terurere, which has led to his being confused as two different people, even in one of the royal genealogies.) Tevahitua was angry that Purea had allowed the child to live, for they both became 'Childbearing *Arioi*'. Moreover, by the laws of inheritance, the infant automatically assumed Tevahitua's rank and titles, and in six or seven years would be king, although Tevahitua would act as regent until the child came of age. The rule of the child becoming the head of the family and receiving the honours and dignity due to the family applied to all classes. Major wars in which chiefs were driven from their districts are known to have been caused by an affront alleged to have been given to a child of a commoner by one of his own class. Tevahitua noted that the child had a habit of blinking, which amused him, and Tevahitua took for himself the name of Amo, 'The Blinker'.

It is not unusual for Tahitians to change their names as a result of any incident or phenomenon which catches their fancy, a habit according with the peculiar, sardonic, self-depreciatory humour of the Polynesians. Thus the most famous of the future kings took the name of Pomaré, which means Night-Cough. Having spent a night sleeping out upon the mountains, he developed a cough which one of his attendants referred to as a night-cough. The assonance of the combination of words took the king's fancy, and he adopted it as the name by which he and his descendants are known.

Amo and Purea quarrelled and separated over the question of the child. Their relations were strained at the best of times, as she was alleged to be in the habit of beating him. She resented his association with a younger woman – an illogical reaction in a member of the *Arioi* Society, but Purea was noted for her troublesome disposition. (Captain Cook remarked on it later, and said that her husband could not abide it.) Purea took up residence on the point of Mahaiatea –

meaning Expansive-migration (one of the Polynesian migrations in the Pacific) – about two miles along the sandy beach to the east of Papara. Here, according to custom, the infant was taken to a comfortable home, called the House-With-Exalted-Walls – enclosed by high stone walls one within another, accessible only by stiles, and guarded by strong men armed with clubs and spears. There the royal mother and infant were to remain for about fourteen months until the child could run about and was ready to be presented to the public. The mother was free, however, to go out during this time.

There was no one now superior in rank to Purea. She was a descendant of the older of the two royal families, married to the regent, and the mother of the future king. Amo's position was somewhat ambiguous. Nominally he was only the regent, but he did not acknowledge the child.

'Wished-for', having separated from 'The Blinker', began to cohabit openly with Tupaia, meaning 'Beaten', as *tapa* (mulberry-bark cloth) is beaten or hammered in its manufacture.

Tupaia, of the modest, sardonic name, was about twenty-five years old. He was a chief of Raiatea, where he had had houses and large estates; but he had been driven from the island by defeat in war by the natives of the neighbouring island of Pora-Pora. The Pora-Porans under their chief Puni were the terror of the adjacent islands and feared as far away as Tahiti, although there are no records of an attack on Tahiti. Their fleet specialised in treacherous night attacks on sleeping communities.

On Tupaia's well-formed body were the scars of a wound where a spear headed with the *aero fai*, the serrated tail-bone of the sting-ray fish, had entered his back and come out just under his left breast. The only way to get such a weapon out without breaking it was to draw it through, as its barbs are like arrow-heads. It was no honour to receive a wound in war except from a spear, for it was thought that a man who suffered himself to be wounded did not know how to defend himself, and even spear-wounds were hidden as much as possible. Polynesian warfare was often highly stylised, and its irrational character in the affairs of men was undoubtedly recognised to some extent. Hence the refusal of all the Polynesians to use their very efficient bows and arrows – as they certainly were in the case of the Tahitians – for anything but sport.

Tupaia, the 'Beaten', was famous for his general knowledge and intelligence, and Purea appointed the refugee to be Chief Priest of Tahiti. His native Raiatea was the centre of the *Arioi* cult, which helps to account for the chief's remarkable learning and prescience, commented on in due course by Captain Cook.

In addition to taking Tupaia openly as her lover and making him Chief Priest, the tall, handsome Purea was filled with the pride of parenthood. She decided that the infant Teri'i-rere must have the largest temple in Tahiti. Temples, intimately linked with inheritance and family prestige, were numerous and Papara was noted for its grand *marai*, ancestral, social and local. According to the Tahitian proverb 'Every point has its *marai*,' and the following Chant gives the proverb point:

'*Marai* were the sanctity and glory of the land; they were the pride of the people of these islands. The ornaments of the land were the *marai*, they were the palaces presented to the gods. Folk did not intrude upon the *marai* of others; they adhered to their own. It was owing to the ancestral *marai* that people could say they had an inheritance.

'A place of dread and of great silence was the *marai;* a person's errand there must be to pray, and none other. The gods could not be deceived. When persons approached a place where stood a *marai*, they gave it a wide berth, they lowered their clothes from their shoulders down to their waists, they carried low their burdens in their hands until beyond sight of it.

'Upon the prominent points were the royal *marai;* in the bays were the *marai* of the nobles; behind them those of the girls, of the common people.

'A holy place was the *marai*, an awe-inspiring place; it was a place that awakened the conscience, a dreaded place.

'Awesome were the *marai* of the royal line; their ancestral and national *marai*. Places of stupendous silence, terrifying and inspiring fear; places of pain to the priests, to the owners, and to all the people. The walls of these *marai* were repelling; when a pig chanced to stray upon a broken wall, its owners never saw it again, it became sacred to the gods. When a canoe passed along the shore, it withdrew afar off as it approached the point where stood the royal *marai;* the people lowered their clothes and paddled lightly until they passed the place.

'Potent were the horns of the *marai;* fugitives who were chased by warriors, conspirators and captives who were chased to be slain, would run to the front of the *marai* for sanctuary. But those destined to be sacrificed found no place of refuge in all the land. When they ran before the *marai,* they were slain there, that was their proper place. . . .

'Dark were the shadows among the great trees of those *marai;* and the most sacred of them all was the *miro* which was the sanctifier. That was the basis of the ordinances; it was the basis of royalty; it awakened the gods; it established the *ura* girdle of the sovereigns.'

Before work was started on the temple, destined to be one of the greatest works of man in Polynesia, Purea imposed a *tabu* on the Teva clan for the benefit of her son. When a national or a royal *marai* was to be built religious restrictions were put upon pigs, fowls and all produce, upon the fishing grounds and upon hand-made chattels. The best of everything was to be ready for the time of building. The restriction lasted for two or three years.

But the *tabu* caused offence among the Ahurai clan, the older of the royal families, as confirming rights and prestige. Purea's mother, Terii Vaitua, decided to come to Papara from her home at Faa'a, with the intention of breaking the *tabu.* When, under the laws of hospitality, a chief or chieftainess of equal or superior rank paid a visit, he or she was entitled to everything that could be given. It was the only way of breaking the *tabu* short of war. Purea was in residence on the point of Mahaiatea, where the new *marai* was to be built.

One day, out of the haze at sea, appeared a double-travelling-canoe shaped like a gondola with high carved stern-posts. A tent, such as was used only by royalty, was pitched on the platform on the forepart. Within the tent sat the old woman.

The canoe was urged rapidly forward by its paddlers so that it seemed as if it was about to fly out of the water and was only held back by the invisible hands of a Shark God, for sharks sometimes participate directly in the affairs of the Teva family.

One of the big rollers rose like a wall of green glass – a spumy flutter of foam flying from the top – about to topple over and crash, boiling, on the reef. A cry burst from the throats of the paddlers.

With another shout the powerful crew, digging their paddles savagely into the sea, thrust the canoe through the reef passage, the water roaring and racing on either side. The canoe shot like a spear into the smooth lagoon and the heaving motion gave place to a gentle gliding.

Incredibly clear, the coral depths beneath seemed never to have been disturbed. Brilliant flame-like fish, silver or green slashed with gold or red, and tiny ones of electric blue, flickered with the beauty of fires among the variegated coloured corals on the white floor of the lagoon.

Straight ahead, on the projecting point of Mahaiatea, grew the sacred *toa* – also called *aito*, the ironwood trees – the emblem of the warrior and of Oro, its wood so hard that it can be wrought only with the greatest difficulty even with tools of iron. The best axe is spoiled on it, as against stone; yet of this wood the Tahitians formed their war-clubs, spears and cloth-beaters, with their own simple implements of stone and bone. Their clubs were from four to six feet long; their spears from fourteen to eighteen feet. Their javelins were from eight to fourteen feet and pointed with the pandanus palm, whose outside circle is very hard. These they hurled under-hand and with extreme precision at a mark set up at a distance of thirty or forty yards. They held the javelin in the right hand and poised it over the forefinger of the left. The ironwood, whose bark furnishes a brown dye, has peculiarly-straight branches and needle-shaped foliage of misty olive-green which hangs from it like tassels. The wind strikes a wailing note in its branches, and the man-of-war bird and the albatross sometimes alight upon them, adding to the awe of the place. Terii Vaitua's canoe entered the passage in an inner line of reef, opposite the point of Mahaiatea, a pass sacred to princes and opened by Rua-hatu, the Tahitian Neptune.

As it entered the passage Purea called out from the shore: 'Who dares venture through our sacred pass? Know they not that the Tevas are under the sacred *tabu* for Teri'i-rere? Not even the cocks may crow or the ocean storm!'

Her mother answered: 'It is Terii Vaitua, Queen of Ahurai.'

'How many royal heads can there be?' cried Purea. 'I know no other than Teri'i-rere. Down with your tent!'

The old woman wept, and producing a shark's tooth scarifier from her clothing, cut her head until the blood flowed.

When a woman took a husband or came of age, she procured a shark's tooth, which was fixed with gum from the trunk of the breadfruit to an instrument which left about a quarter of an inch of the tooth bare. The instrument was designed for the purpose of wounding the head, like a lancet. Some had two or three teeth and struck forcibly, brought forth the blood in copious streams. The strokes were repeated on the head according to the love borne or the violence of the grief. Should a child fall down and hurt itself, the mother would produce a shark's tooth and cut her head, and the blood and tears were mingled. If an insult was offered to an eldest male child, again the shark's tooth was used, for the child, being head of the family, any insult offered to him was felt by the parents more deeply than if offered to themselves.

But, despite the masochistic use of the shark's tooth, the old woman had to return home without having been received by her daughter.

Next a grand-daughter of Terii Vaitua, a niece of Purea's named Tetuanui, made a similar attempt to break the *tabu*.

From Purea came again the cry – 'Down with your tent!'

Tetuanui's canoe brought the twenty-year-old girl ashore, and she sat down on the beach and cut her head until the blood flowed into the white sand.

The High Priest, Manea, Amo's younger brother, came forward from the gathered throng and remonstrated with Purea, saying, 'Hush, Purea! Whence is the saying, the drums of Mahaiatea call Tutunai for a red girdle for Teri'i-rere? Where will they wear the red girdle? In Nuura I Ahurai. One end of the girdle holds Te Pori-o-

Nuu' (The Fatness-of-Hosts – the districts of the north coast of the larger peninsula); 'the other end holds the Tevas; the whole holds the Oropaa.'

He was warning Purea of the folly of arousing the enmity of the Ahurai princesses and of breaking up the unity of the Teva and Ahurai clans, thereby setting free the unfriendly tribes under the chief Tutahaa, a giant of a man, at Atahuru on the west coast and those of the smaller peninsula under the chief Vehiatua. The Oropaa was the sub-division of Papara where Purea stood.

Obstinately Purea answered, 'I recognise no head here but Teri'i-rere.'

The High Priest Manea wiped away the blood shed by Tetuanui and took her to his house, making what reparation he could for an insult which called for blood vengeance. (His action saved some of them when, about forty years later, with the coming of Christianity, Tetuanui took her revenge with the massacre of the family at Papara. The hatred between the women of the family had been well sown.)

The stones of the *marai* were collected in a single day, being passed from hand to hand from all parts of the island. The priests had sent out knotted cords indicating the sizes of the stones required. Care was taken not to remove stones from strange lands, or even from the sea shoals, without permission of the owners; and also not to violate the sanctity of old *marai* sites by taking any stray stones. Death was the legitimate penalty for so doing.

An encampment was made in the woods for the labourers, who withdrew from their families to consecrate themselves; other encampments were made far inland for the old, the infirm, women, children and domestic animals, so that their voices might not reach the appointed place and that they might enjoy freedom. No women or children were allowed upon the scene, but the men went reverently to work, having their food prepared by special masculine hands. No living creature was allowed to approach the site, no fires were kindled along the neighbouring shores, where the people spoke in hushed voices. The runners going away from the labouring, chipping, semi-naked throng, bore messages in the shape of cords tied in knot language by the brown-skinned priests.

Through the moist and tangled forest, with its warm breath of passion and fecund, whispering secrecy, the runners come and go, from or to the deep valley, the Room of Refuge, whose tops run up to the clouds.

The dark-blue tattooing on their loins and buttocks shows like blue-black ink on their clear brown skins, in curved lines, as if to accentuate the action of their bodies in passing through the forest – the tropical forest haunted by a multitude of spirits and demons. They wear a narrow piece of cloth, which, passing round the waist, goes between the thighs, and is tucked in before. Their long hair hangs to their shoulders or is gathered up on each side or in a knot on top of their heads and is dressed with flowers or the long, narrow red tail feathers of the tropical bird. A single scented flower may be worn in the lobe of the ear as an ear-ring.

No able-bodied man was idle, and friends and relations came from other communities. Some provided food and were cooks for the camps. Others, under orders of an artisan, shaped the irregular stones into blocks and slabs with hard stone implements, leaving the round stones in their natural state to fit in between the others. The work took many months.

The men bringing slabs of coral from the inner line of reef left the blocks below the surface of the water, thus making the water bear a part of the weight. The squaring of stone and coral by tools of stone is a work of incredible labour; the polishing is done with the sharp coral sand.

When all the stones were ready, the ground was cleared and sprinkled by the priests with sea water to make it holy, for the sea was the supreme *marai*. A long stone was taken from another grand *marai*, as the Chief-Corner-Stone. A man was killed and placed in the hole dug to receive the stone – his spirit remaining to guard the *marai* – and the erect stone was planted on the corpse, to the accompaniment of prayer. Another stone, called Standing-Towering, was placed at the opposite corner, and these two stones were the horns of the *marai*. Its guardians, drums and treasures were installed in thatched houses. The Tevas' original *marai* was said to have been at Opoa, although this is difficult to reconcile with the story of the Shark God; from here, perhaps, came the Chief-Corner-Stone.

The consecration was performed in vivid moonlight, and the people then silently carried out the stones and placed them in heaps around the place prepared, obeying the directions of the chief artisan. Some pieces of stratified rock, 12 to 18 inches thick, 12 feet long and 9 feet wide, were used, also large slabs of coral which the priests and workmen found were made light in their hands by the gods.

The main part of the temple took the form of an enormous pile of stonework, raised in pyramid form upon an oblong base 270 feet long and 94 feet wide. The foundation was of squared rock stones, some of them 4 feet by 2 feet. The Tahitians knew nothing of mortar or cement and it required all their care to fit the stones regularly to each other, so that the structure might stand. The upper part consisted of ten steps, the first 6 feet high, the rest slightly less. The summit was 180 feet long and 6 feet wide. The vast steps were composed of a top facing of squared white coral stones, some 18 inches high, and round blueish-coloured water-worn pebbles, each about 6 inches in diameter; and the whole was polished.

On the summit of the pyramid stood an image of a whale, shadow of the god Taaroa, made of breadfruit wood charred with the sacred fire to give it the appearance of black stone; there was also an image of stone representing the Handsome-blue-shark of Taaroa. Both images were surrounded by carved wooden tropical birds.

The whole of this gigantic pyramid – whose size and workmanship were almost beyond belief – made part of one side of an area or square, 360 feet by 354 feet, which was walled in and paved with flat stones. About a 100 yards to the west of the building was another paved area or court, in which were several wooden altars about 7 feet high for the offerings, so that the gods in the form of birds might feast on the bodies of the pigs, dogs and the larger fish.

Around the pyramid was the walled square, called the Exalted Enclosure, within which trees grew high and no stranger dared enter. In the back part was a deep pit, called To-Cast-Off-Rubbish, into which were gathered all the cast-off things from the *marai*, still regarded as superlatively sacred. Around this was an embankment of fragrant flowers and herbs to keep the air sweet.

Beneath the pavings surrounding the pyramid were secret vaults, excavated and closely paved by faithful servants, in which they temporarily placed their dead – in time of peace for a year or two, in times of trouble for a few days after the performance of the religious rites for the deceased. The bodies were removed by the same hands to the family vault, a great cavern in a high mountain of Papara, where mats were spread and ornaments and other precious possessions of the chiefs were deposited. Up to recent times the bodies of members of the family have been carried to this place by old retainers, who found that incantations made the work light and easy.

The inauguration of the temple was performed with festivity. The clans of all Tahiti were represented and a feast was prepared on the assembly ground, known as Tiger-shell. All work was done in the morning; and in the afternoon, amid stillness, the people in their best attire followed the Queen. They gathered at the new *marai* and stood in the rear at the place for the congregation.

The first-born young virgins of the royal family represented their respective districts, arrayed in flowing white *tapa* and decked with wreaths and garlands of snowy white *tiare* blossoms. Carrying woven coconut-leaf baskets of the delicately perfumed, waxy blossoms, they led a procession formed by the priests in sacerdotal array, each of whom held a *miro* branch with its bright green, heart-shaped leaves. The Chief Priest's cape was large and bordered with a deep fringe; the chiefs wore their regal raiment. The procession halted on reaching one side of the pyramid and the young virgins then walked around it, casting their flowers upon its enormous steps as high as they could reach, and upon the paving close by.

Tupaia, the Chief Priest, followed, calling upon the gods to fill the place with their presence.

The maidens now returned to the side while the Chief Priest, taking sea water in a gourd, went into the *marai* and sprinkled it everywhere as he called upon the tutelary god to take possession of his new home and make welcome his guests, the crowd of gods.

Extreme propriety was observed at the sacred inauguration feast. The commonalty and the women, except Purea, returned no more to this *marai*, the finest in Tahiti – the finest perhaps made anywhere. Eventually it was destroyed and its stones used by Europeans for making roads.

CHAPTER IX

*

THE *DOLPHIN* IN TROUBLE

IT HAPPENED that as the *Dolphin* approached Matavai (Face of Water) on the north coast, Purea, 'Wished-for', was visiting that settlement of which she was the chieftainess in her own right. She had taken up residence in the guest-house belonging to the Ha'apape district on the plain near the entrance to the valley. This may have been her personal palace, but it was almost certainly the *Arioi* or guest-house. Its name was Atita (Agitation) and it was vast. More than a hundred yards long, with a peaked thatched roof and open walls, it had pillars in the centre of the house which were twenty-five feet high. It was situated half a mile from the beach of the Matavai lagoon near the banks of the sluggish river that emerged from the valley and disembogued at the end of the point which the *Dolphin* was approaching.

Here Purea was living in her accustomed regal state, surrounded by numerous attendants, domestics and relations. No doubt the subject of the approaching ship was eagerly discussed.

The valley has very little descent and the River Vaipopoo – Hollow-waterbed – because of its depth in many parts, meanders leisurely along its course. The valley was lush with vegetation and on both sides the mountains, high and perpendicular, were covered with shrubs and trees. Here parakeets built their nests and a grey thrush verging into brown sang sweetly – that is until it was exterminated by the imported myna bird. The parakeets have also disappeared in the face of immigrant rats, although others have been introduced since.

The natives of the valley were numerous and flourishing. They saw the sun only during the few hours of the day for the gorge runs from north to south and its beams are intercepted by the mountains.

Fine plantations of the *kava* plant – *piper methysticum* – and cloth trees were neatly enclosed in loose-piled stone walls; all the usual fruit and vegetables grew in vast profusion.

Amo, the regent, had arrived at Matavai, having heard that the 'canoe without an outrigger' was making in that direction. There was bustle and excitement among the natives of valley and plain and among visitors to the district, who flocked to the beaches and hill-tops overlooking the Matavai lagoon. 'The Blinker' and his wife, the 'Wished-for', although separated, had again become friendly, and he now acknowledged their child.

When the *Dolphin* was close to the point, the boats went ahead of her with Robertson in the barge. The lagoon on the eastern side of the mile-long point was called Maahonu or Turtle. On that side of the verdant point were hills of shifting sand, undulating like the waves of the sea, believed to have been moved here by Hiro, the giant jester, but actually under the force of the strong trade-wind.

Robertson kept nearest the shore, about two hundred yards from the wide, foaming line of reef which slashed the blue waters. Gore was about four hundred yards outside him in the cutter. Both were constantly sounding. When they got a little way round the point with its enchanted river-mouth, they saw several thousand natives on the shore and many canoes in the bay which they intended to sound.

Robertson was surprised that the ship stood in close after them, since it had been agreed that she was to stay at least a mile from the boats until they made the signal for anchoring.

Robertson called to her to keep off, as he had only eighteen feet of water; but those on board, being nearer the cutter, which had plenty of water, paid no attention. There is a wide opening in the reef on the westward side of the point, and the ship hauled round the reef and stood in, intending to come to anchor. But then she struck and stood fast on a dangerous shoal known as Hiro's Rock. The instant she struck, she came head-on to the wind, and Robertson, thinking she was going about from one tack to another, kept on sounding. (Wallis in his official report blamed the boats for this mishap.) She had paid round with the wind on her beam and her

head to the sea, which made him still think her safe. She was drawing
twenty inches more forward than aft and had swivelled round on a
rock forward, so that her stern had swung in towards the land. When
Robertson got on board the vessel she was striking hard with all her
sails aback – the wind the wrong side of them so that they were
blowing against the masts, or merely shaking.

Wallis and Clarke were on deck giving instructions. Wallis
ordered all sail to be clewed up as fast as possible, had the decks
cleared of lumber and sent the launch out with the stream cable and
anchor, which he ordered to be carried outside the reef so that, when
it had taken ground, the ship might be drawn off towards it by
applying a large force of manpower on the capstan. But outside the
reef, as usual, no bottom could be found, so that it was useless to
drop anchor.

Robertson asked the captain for a free hand to do what he thought
best for the safety of the ship, but Clarke, who had apparently
disapproved of leaving the previous anchorage, interrupted them to
tell the master – in the hearing of all on the quarter-deck – that the
misfortune was entirely owing to Robertson's advice. Now he
would know the danger of contradicting, and when, before long,
they were in the enemy's power, he would know even better!

There existed a peculiar relationship between the master and the
first lieutenant of a naval vessel. Under the Commonwealth, when
Cromwell had brought the Navy to a high state of efficiency, the
master had complete control of working and navigating the ship,
but in the reign of Queen Anne the masters had lost much of their
authority to the lieutenants, on whose orders they were now
dependent. The other warrant officers had at the same time gone
downhill and were even liable, in fact, to be 'caned, bilboed
(shackled) and despitefully treated'. The professional commissioned
naval officer – taking the place of the military element which had
existed in the Navy in its early days – had got the upper hand. The
masters were all Trinity House men – a corporation responsible for
the official regulation of British shipping – and sometimes served
with the merchant marine, hopping backwards and forwards between
the merchant service and the Navy like birds between two perches.

It was, of course, a part of the British naval tradition, and the same sort of thing goes on in time of war to this day.

This situation was now working itself out off remote Tahiti and was causing the usual heart-burning. Robertson replied to Clarke that they would find another time to debate his point but that now was the moment to concentrate on the safety of the ship. She was continuing to pound violently on the shoal, surrounded by hundreds of canoes full of men. They did not, however, attempt to board her but seemed to wait in expectation of her wreck – no doubt anticipating a repetition of the *African Galley's* fate.

Everyone was anxious in the extreme. There is something peculiarly horrible to seamen in a ship pounding on a shoal, it is worse to them than an earthquake on land. And these particular seamen were in an unknown country with natives of uncertain disposition, and there was no apparent possibility of getting back to Europe if they were shipwrecked. They could do nothing more to help themselves, except stave some water-casks in the fore-hold in order to lighten the ship forward, and fire a few big guns to prevent the natives coming nearer.

After an hour the breeze veered round and sprang up from the shore. Robertson ordered the seamen to make all sail and asked the captain if he approved. Wallis said he did. Not so Clarke, who laid hold of the weather forebrace (a rope attached to the yard for trimming sails) to haul it in; but his strength was not equal to it and no one would help him. At that critical moment the man at the lead said the ship was drawing ahead. It was true. She slid off the shoal and was soon once more in deep water outside the reef.

The moment she was clear of Hiro's Rock – ever afterwards known as the Dolphin Bank – the wind freshened. Though it soon moderated, the surf ran so high on the shoal that, if she had remained fast half an hour longer, she must have gone to pieces. She now ran out about a mile to sea, then lay to. The pumps were frequently sounded – drawn until they sucked dry, in fact – but she made little more water than usual.

Robertson went down to the captain's cabin and begged him to let him make another attempt to sound the bay to the west of the point, the bay of Matavai. Wallis agreed and sent up orders to man the boats. Meanwhile Clarke had ordered Gore into the barge to sound off the point and had sent the cutter for another use. He told Robertson that the jolly boat was available for him to go where he wanted; as she drew least water, he would run less risk of losing her. Robertson at first decided to inform the captain, but as Wallis was ill with what he called a bilious colic and much worse for being on deck, he was reluctant to add to his worries. So he asked Clarke to order the jolly boat to be manned and went below to his cabin to write a few lines, doubting if he would ever return to the ship.

He put on a pair of good pistols and took his broad-sword, without the scabbard, in his hand. Clarke – 'my friend Knowall', Robertson called him – met him and told him the boat had been waiting some time. Robertson replied that he was now ready to go in her, small as she was. In the boat were five of the smallest lads in the ship, her proper crew – but no arms for any one of them – and two scarlet-coated marines with muskets; with which stout company he set out to sound the bay.

The *Dolphin* made sail and stood off three or four miles from the shore before she tacked and stood in for the land.

In the meantime the jolly boat entered the Matavai lagoon through the wide opening in the reef near Hiro's Rock, among the numerous canoes. The natives stared hard. Several canoes came round, some so near that Robertson had no room to cast the lead to take soundings. He expected that they would run her down or board her. To frighten them, he ordered the marines to point their muskets, which made them sheer off a little, but soon a cross old fellow called out to his companions and came close to the boat. The master threatened him by having the muskets pointed, whereupon the old man held up his paddle and cleared out.

Robertson found good regular soundings to within two hundred yards of the shore. Everyone in the boat was now very happy, and the poor youngsters declared there was nothing to fear from the natives. Robertson gave each of his company a dram of good old rum, in whose virtues he was a firm believer.

But the moment they turned towards the ship, which was out of gunshot, the Tahitians – annoyed no doubt at the white men not having landed, which they could not understand – surrounded the boat with many canoes and seemed resolved to attack. Robertson expected that Gore in the barge would come down from the point and enter the lagoon to his assistance, and ordered a marine to fire amongst the thickest of the canoes. Most of the Tahitians now moved away, but one threw a stone at the jolly boat without effect; whereupon the master fired a pistol at him. The bullet went through the man's paddle, which he had held up before his face and then showed to some of the other natives, which made them all keep off.

The barge did not go near the jolly boat, to Robertson's surprise. Fortunately for him Wallis was watching through his telescope out of the great cabin window and now ordered the ship to stand in towards the land and had several round-shot fired at the barge to make her go down and enter the lagoon to join the jolly boat. Gore and his people in the barge apparently did not understand this signal and did nothing. But while they were puzzling over the round-shot which were being fired at them, the captain's queer sign was very useful to the little jolly boat's crew, whom the Tahitians were again surrounding. Robertson had another musket fired amongst them, which, with the billowing explosions from the *Dolphin's* guns, so terrified them that they all dispersed.

The captain, writing off the barge as hopeless, ordered the cutter to the master's assistance. By the time she reached him he had crossed and sounded the beautiful bay twice and found it all good anchoring ground. He ordered the midshipmen in the cutter to get into the jolly boat, row to the barge and order her to go to the end of the wide opening in the reef, near the Dolphin Bank, to be a mark by which he could steer the ship into harbour, an ordinary lagoon, enclosed between a coral reef and the land.

Robertson rowed to the ship in the cutter and informed the captain about the bay. Wallis asked why he went down the lagoon without the barge, and he replied that 'Mr Knowall' knew that best. But, if the captain approved, he would take charge of the ship and pilot her into the finest bay he ever saw, for there appeared to be a small river where they could have no difficulty in fetching water.

Wallis liked the idea, though he was still doubtful about the shoal. But Robertson told him that the barge and jolly boat were both now upon its outer end, so there was no danger in going into the bay. Wallis thereupon ordered him to take charge of the ship and pilot her in; which he did, standing at the fore-topmast-head, where he saw the shoal plainly.

In a short time the *Dolphin* was in the lagoon, where she was anchored on good, white, sandy ground in a hundred feet of clear water. Some seamen dived and examined her bottom, but she appeared undamaged except for a small piece knocked off the base of the rudder. But the trestle-trees at the heads of all three lower masts – two strong bars of timber fixed horizontally on opposite sides of the lower mast-head to support the frame of the wide fighting-top and the weight of the topmast – were broken short from the pounding she had received, though this circumstance had not been noticed at the time.

As soon as the ship was anchored Wallis sent Robertson with all boats to sound the eastern part of the lagoon towards the tree-clad point, so that, if he found good anchorage, they might warp the ship up the lagoon – by laying out anchors at the end of cables, and drawing her towards them – and anchor her in safety away from the reef passage. Many canoes were close to the reef and the shore was crowded with natives.

Between noon and sunset they came off in several canoes with hogs and fruit, which were bought for toys and nails. Several other canoes, the natives in them sightseeing, frequently paddled round the frigate; these were 'travelling-canoes' with flat sides, built low for paddling and made of broad planks set above the sides of a hollowed tree burnt out with fire. Near the bow was a platform and a thatched travelling-house, which could be carried on shore to serve as a temporary residence. In some cases only an awning was erected, and here the passengers or persons of most dignity were seated. The sterns were broad and high and ornamented according to the nobility of the owner. Some, fourteen feet high, consisted of carved figures supporting each other on their hands, tier upon tier, surmounted by a sort of fret-work tower or cylinder. (Purea's mother had travelled in one of these canoes on the occasion when she was insulted by her daughter.) According to size, the travelling-canoes were paddled by four to twenty men – they had no sail – and could be used single with an outrigger, or made double.

At four o'clock Robertson returned and reported that there was good anchorage everywhere, and Wallis decided to warp the frigate up the bay early next morning. Three hundred fathoms of hawsers were immediately run out with the boats and she was warped farther into the lagoon by heaving on the capstan.

At sunset the ship's company were divided into four watches, in charge of the gunner and the three mates, one watch to be continually under arms. Each man was armed with pistol and cutlass, the great guns were loaded, some with round-shot and others with grape-shot, all small-arms were loaded, and the men not on watch were ordered to go to the quarters assigned to them at a moment's notice.

As the sun settled down behind Moorea – now a mass of pink peaks and streaming flame – the canoes on the burnished water paddled in to the shore.

CHAPTER X

*

THE ATTACK

THE night was fine, clear and pleasant, but the white men neither saw nor heard any canoes pass the ship, though they saw numerous lights on the reef off the south-west point of the bay towards Moorea, which alarmed them a little, not knowing what might be going on but, as they afterwards found, the Tahitians were merely spearing fish by torchlight. These magnificent, bronzed figures had still to take their stand with poised spear, knee-deep in the foaming water illumined by their flares of dried coconut leaf, while silvery fish leapt in response.

At six o'clock the next morning the seamen began to warp the frigate up the harbour, laying out anchors ahead of her with the boats and heaving on the capstan. About three hundred canoes came off from the shore and lay round the slowly-moving ship. The natives traded very fairly, taking nails and toys for their pigs, fowls and fruit. It was a picturesque sight with the bright, eager eyes in the upturned faces and the lithe, brown bodies among the vivid-coloured fruit in the dark interiors of the canoes.

The squeals of pigs were soon re-echoing about the harbour, provoking a thin crowing of the cocks on the shore and mingling with the chattering and the noise of the straining cables, the creaking of the capstan and the chanting of its gyrating attendants. Perhaps their performance was regarded by the Tahitians as a song and dance, for the capstan was in full view on the quarter-deck; the white men were obviously singing and dancing their 'huge canoe without an outrigger' into the bay. What could be more natural, except that it appeared to be a clumsy thing to move? Did not the *Ariois* perform on platforms in their canoes when entering harbour in their journeying from island to island?

The captain now ordered the gunner and two midshipmen to buy provisions and forbade the trade to anyone else in the *Dolphin*. This was in order to put a stop to the annoyance and indiscipline of private purchases, which had been allowed until then.

Some Tahitians in canoes attempted to weigh the stream anchor which lay out ahead at the end of a cable, but muskets were fired at them and the magic of the 'barking blowers' made them disperse like wraiths from the misty surface of the water.

By eight o'clock yet more canoes crowded round the ship; the last ones were double and very large, with twelve or fifteen powerful men in each. Some of them were singing in hoarse voices, some blowing conches, some playing upon reed flutes which they blew with their nostrils. Wallis was concerned to see that the canoes seemed fitted out for war rather than trade, for they had very little on board except round pebbles. He sent for Furneaux (Clarke being very ill) and told him to keep the fourth watch constantly at arms while the rest of the men were warping the ship.

By now more than five hundred canoes were assembled, and nearly four thousand men sat in them. Most of the trading canoes carried a fine young girl, who stripped herself naked and played numerous droll and wanton tricks which drew the white men on the gunwales to watch them. Yet it is possible that this exposure of their persons was not a salacious act but a studied insult to 'the children of the glorious princess'.

Francis Wilkinson, one of the master's mates and by way of being a poet (he wrote a poem on the back cover of his log-book) made the following observation: 'At ten o'clock the women was directed by the men to stand in the prows of their canoes and expose their bodies naked to our view. As our men is in good health and spirits and begin to feel the good effect of the fresh pork – we thank God for it – it is not to be wondered at that their attention should be drawn to a sight so uncommon to them, especially as their women are so well proportioned, their features rather agreeable than what is styled beautiful. And though they are not so fair as our English ladies, yet I think they are infinitely too much so for their copper-coloured husbands. In this posture they stood for a quarter of an hour, until they judged our men was wholly exposed on the gang-way and booms and forecastle.'

Amo, who sat upon a canopy on one of the large double gondola-like canoes, which lay on the port side of the frigate, at a good distance from the rest of the canoes, now made signs that he wished to come to the ship's side. Wallis intimated his consent and the regent went alongside and gave a seaman a bunch of red and yellow feathers, making signs that he should carry it to Wallis.

The feathers, no doubt, were intended as an offering to a high chief of godly descent. The *Maro Ura*, the red girdle, actually con-sisted of red and yellow feathers thrummed in alternate patches on a belt of net-work some fourteen feet long. A new length was added at each coronation, and from variations in the pattern it was possible to read something of the history of the holders. A long polished needle of human bone was never taken out of it, and it was intended that it should continue for ever. The red girdle was originally peculiar to the Ahurai family, the yellow girdle to the Tevas. The two may have been combined as a result of the marriage of Purea and Amo. The red and yellow feathers should have been lifted at once to the top of the head, then placed above the captain's ear or in his gold-laced tricorne. For in Polynesia to this day a present, even a tobacco pipe or a handful of coins, is always raised immediately to the top of the head, the head being regarded as sacred. According to tradition this feather amulet had been consecrated to the gods and was a powerful means of bringing their aid to bear against the 'offenders' to whom it was presented. Presumably the people had been offended by the sailors' indecencies.

Wallis received the potent bunch of feathers – which, no doubt, he regarded as savages' ornaments – in a friendly way and went below to get some trinkets to give in exchange. But to his astonish-ment, on his return to the quarter-deck, the native had put off his canoe a little way, and upon his throwing up the branch of a coconut palm – the symbol of regal authority in Tahiti – a shout went up from the canoes, which moved towards the *Dolphin*. All trade broke up and a shower of stones poured in from every side.

Tahitians have said that the conflict was the result of a mistake;

but the attack may well have been planned by Amo and Purea in the hope of taking the ship. She had much iron regarding which the 'children of the glorious princess' had been very mean; there were also strange animals and other curiosities; there was the matter of retribution for the white men's indecencies. Or perhaps the Tahitians were angry and imagined that something unfriendly was intended and that their valuable feather offering and ceremonial compliment had been rejected. Had not the white chief merely walked off? The acceptance in the correct manner of a tuft of feathers was a necessary prerequisite of peace in the case of strangers of high rank landing in any island of the Society Group.

In charging a sling the Tahitians held it round their shoulders, keeping the stone (about the size of a hen's egg) fast in it with the left thumb. Then, jumping, they swung the sling three times round their head, holding the left hand grasped on the wrist of the right. The stone was discharged with force sufficient to crack the bark of a tree at two hundred yards, the stone flying with scarcely any trajectory, like a bullet. The slings were made of plaited coconut husk. They also used ordinary throwing stones with great accuracy, pointing at the same time with the forefinger of the left hand as if taking aim. There may be some scientific principle involved here, the left eye usually being the focusing-eye.

In a few seconds the decks were strewn with stones large and small, and several seamen were cut and bruised. They would have suffered much more had a canvas awning not been spread over the deck against the sun and had the hammocks not been placed, as was usual in a man-of-war, in the boarding-nettings. This disposition was intended to provide a screen from small-arms' fire in battle and to get the hammocks out of the way in the daytime.

Wallis decided to use his superiority in arms, especially as many of the ship's company were sick and feeble. He ordered the guard to fire their muskets and two of the quarter-deck guns, three-pounders loaded with small-shot, to be discharged at the same time. At first the Tahitians were thrown into some confusion, then gave another shout and poured stones in like hail, hurting many seamen. The men were now at their quarters and Wallis ordered them to fire the great

guns and to play some of them continually at the part of the beach
where canoes were taking in men and pushing off towards the
frigate.

The guns thundered and recoiled while their crews, amid the
murk and gloom of their own creation, swabbed them out and
reloaded with cartridges containing black powder. They rammed
home the ball or grape-shot with long rammers and fired again. The
smoke, leaping out of the muzzles from the gapped, grinning teeth
of the line of open ports, hung overhead for a time, reflecting the
flash of gunfire amid the masts, furled sails and rigging, while the
ship rocked and trembled to her own blasts.

Robertson said that it would require the pen of Milton to describe
the terror which the round- and grape-shot spread among the
unhappy crowd. When a round-shot struck a canoe it carried all
before it; any survivors jumped overboard and hung by the remaining part of the canoe until some of their friends took them up and
towed off the broken craft. Some of the natives actually dived for
the grape-shot, hoping, it may be, to blow it back in return. Then
they paddled off, the smoke drifted across the lagoon, and the white
men ceased fire, asking themselves how the affair began. Smoke
rolled across the green hills – such sulphurous poison as had never
visited the land since, in distant ages, the bowels of the once terrible
Orohena – now the harmless wooded crater of an extinct volcano –
had ejected their fearful contents.

Next the canoes began to assemble in two different groups, each
about a mile from the ship, one towards the reef, the other near the
shore. By this time it was beginning to be understood how the out-
break had originated: several midshipmen and seamen pointed out to
the officers the canoe which gave the signal to attack. In this canoe
were Amo and several high chiefs, as was later verified. Amo began
to rally his forces near the reef and the chiefs in several other large
double-canoes rallied theirs near the shore. It was decided to disperse
them in order to deter them from making another attempt on the
ship. Two great guns were fired continuously at Amo's canoe and
soon smashed it in two, so that few could have escaped alive.

The thing which most surprised Robertson was the courage of

about thirty men in five or six of the smaller canoes, who kept close by their chief when all the rest fled as fast as they could paddle. These poor fellows – Tevas, no doubt – were so resolute that they not only carried off the dead and wounded but even towed the two shattered ends of the great canoe to the end of the reef near Hiro's Rock. For it was of supreme importance to the Tahitians that the corpses of chiefs should not be captured; otherwise the enemy might work evil on them with appalling results, leading to the extirpation of their families. Hence they often fought more ferociously to rescue the dead than to save the living.

A few shot were fired at the remains of Amo's canoe while she was in tow, and one of the round-shot hit her. Even this did not deter the handful of brave men. When they landed on the reef the guns stopped firing, and the natives carried up the injured and dead on to the reef. Without a doubt they would have defended the corpses to the death.

While this was going on, the chiefs in the large canoes near the beach had assembled more than three hundred canoes, and all began to paddle towards the reeking warship. Perhaps they supposed the white men must now be tired of blowing. It was thought in the *Dolphin* that surely these chiefs could know nothing of the fate of their leader; else they would not have made another attempt. They were allowed to come within three or four hundred yards; then a three-pounder loaded with seventy musket balls was fired into the thickest of them, causing them to sheer off with considerable loss. To add to their terror, two round-shot were fired amongst them when they were about a mile from the frigate. Then they paddled off with all their strength and landed on the shore.

Firing now ceased, and the eight great guns stowed in the hold at Port Famine were got up and mounted in their proper places fore and aft on the gun-deck. The ship was then cleared for action, for another attack was expected later on.

While the skirmish lasted, the shores of the bay and the tops of the hills were crowded with men, women and children. No doubt they hoped to share the nails and toys, besides the pleasure of calling the white men's huge canoe their own, and having all of them at their mercy. How shocked must they have been, thought Robertson, to find their nearest and dearest dead, torn to pieces in a way they never saw before.

Some of the officers thought that they would now look upon the Europeans as demigods, come to punish them for their past transgressions. Others were of the opinion that they would certainly attack the ship again in revenge for the loss of their friends, and that the next onset would probably be at night with firebrands to set the *Dolphin* ablaze; a reasonable conjecture, as the wind was always off shore at night. Two three-pounders, one on each side of the fo'c'sle, were loaded with seventy musket balls each, and firegrapnels for dragging away burning brands were got ready in all the boats. Let the natives attempt what they will, it was thought, they would now get such a reception as would soon put them to flight.

The seamen continued to warp the *Dolphin* up the harbour. By noon she was not far from the river on the point, five hundred yards from the reef. Here she was moored in fifty feet of water, her broadside guns abreast of the river, her bows pointing towards the reef. Not one canoe was seen in the water nor a single person all along the shore. So the boats were sent to sound, and to examine the shore where any natives might appear. The afternoon was spent thus and the weather was pleasant. The master sounded most of the lagoon in the immediate vicinity, which he considered perhaps as fine a bay as any in the world. The water was as smooth as a millpond. Actually Matavai Harbour is safe only for six or seven months of the year, and it is necessary to go farther west in the same lagoon towards Papeete for complete security.

CHAPTER XI

*

SKIRMISH HILL

A DELIGHTFUL land breeze blew all night. It wafted an agreeable scent from the shore, and several officers assumed that spices were growing in the low grounds of the plain, if not on the high mountains.

Robertson and his brother-officers studied the mountainsides at sunrise through a good telescope – spyglass they called it – and saw many trees with flowers of various colours, which they thought must certainly bear some unknown fruit. Not one canoe was to be seen in the calm, cool lagoon.

The casualties ashore must have been heavy, since there was no confining the Tahitians to their houses as long as they were able to move. Nature, however, together with their good constitutions, performed wonderful cures. They generally abominated all bandages and the smell of dressings, flying always to the water when anything of the kind affected them and grating sandalwood over the affected part to take off the offensive smell. If they happened to break a leg it usually killed them, not so much from the fracture itself as from their efforts to crawl to the fresh water, from which nothing restrained them. A broken arm was sometimes completely restored by bamboo splints, which allowed of their going about with it in a sling.

* * *

Softly at night the scent of the Pacific Islands distills itself from flowering forests and palm-clad lowland and goes stealing out across lagoon, reef and ocean, borne by the land breeze on its mission of enchantment and seduction. Sometimes the voyager will sail during the day into a cloud of fragrance compounded of coconut, sandal-wood – the scarce yellow and brown sandalwood, growing in the mountains – and flowers; yet he may pass the island from which the scent has come, too far off for it to be seen. This fragrance is similar to that of the women of the South Seas when anointed with heavily-perfumed coconut oil and their necks and swelling bosoms are hung with heady-scented garlands of flowers mingled with large, scarlet, oblong, scented seeds, the seeds of the pandanus.

The scent of the coconut oil resembles that of roses. The oil, as prepared by the Tahitians, was made by grating the full-grown coconut kernel into a large trough, then after a few days when the oil began to separate, it was poured off gently and mixed with fragrant herbs, flowers, the pollen of the buff-coloured pandanus flower, and sandalwood. The mixture was left to macerate for three weeks to a month, being well stirred every day. When it had acquired a strong perfume, the oil was squeezed out and poured into bamboo containers. Particular families in some islands still seem to pride themselves on their special oil, and in the course of a journey one will detect many variations of scent.

Sometimes a native, lost on a cloudy night in his canoe, will sniff his way back to his island, guided by wafting perfume.

Sometimes the golden girls at night wear garlands of red and green leaves, heavily oiled, on their heads and over their bare breasts, glittering like tinsel in the light; giving that supreme joy when Arcady is here again, a world of strange enchantment, beauty and perfume.

★ ★ ★

The *Dolphin* was unmoored and warped nearer the river, which ran parallel with the sandy beach twenty yards away. She was re-moored about six hundred yards from shore, in fifty feet of clear water. Here, among banks of the branching, brittle coral, fan-shaped or fern-shaped, an entrancingly fragile marine garden, the fantastically coloured tropical fish, large and small, darted in and out.

Robertson surveyed the harbour and at midday reported that there was good landing everywhere on the beach and that the river water was fresh.

Tahitians with small branches in their hands now began to venture off in a few canoes with the tops of plantain trees set up in the bows. The 'children of the glorious princess' treated them coldly and allowed only two or three canoes at one time to come alongside the frigate. When they had disposed of their provisions they were ordered off and others took their place. Before the now chastened creatures got within a hundred yards they stood up, looked hard at the white men and held up the plantain boughs; one of them made a long speech, to which his companions listened with attention. Then they threw their boughs into the water, a sign that the sea was the supreme *marai*, sacred to all; then they paddled nearer, still keeping their eyes fixed intently on the Europeans, if any of whom looked surly, the natives held up the plantain and forced a smile, then laid it down and showed what they had to sell.

If their goods were wanted, signs were made for them to come alongside. The natives then pointed to the plantain-top and made a long speech. Sometimes the speaker would look solemnly up to the heavens, then at the white men, and for some time hold up the tree-top – representing himself – then turn round and point to the shore and his companions. Then more talk, and the plantain-top was thrown on board the ship and trading began.

When the first canoes came alongside, Wallis made the seamen keep under cover and had a small keg of fresh water carried to the natives to show them what was wanted, which they seemed to understand. He ordered a pistol to be shot through the prow of the canoe so that they might understand the nature of pistol-balls. But they immediately leapt overboard. They were soon convinced, however, that he had no intention of hurting them, and got into their canoes again and set off paddling for the shore, taking with them a round-shot and a bag of grape, which Wallis gave them, to show their countrymen.

While the Tahitians were trading quite fairly, a seaman who had been wounded in the head by a stone the previous day, defrauded one of them of two fowls and, when the man wanted to be paid, aimed a blow at him with his fist. When Wallis heard this he had the seaman stripped and fastened to the rigging and punished with a dozen lashes as a warning to others not to swindle the islanders.

It was decided to take possession of the island (as it was now realised to be) with the accepted ceremony of turning up some earth and leaving a flag flying from a staff. The warship's starboard broadside was brought to bear on the projected watering-place, the barge, cutter and launch were manned and armed, and all hands remaining aboard were quartered at the great guns, ready to fire if necessary.

Furneaux was to land with the sergeant and twelve marines, eighteen able-seamen and three midshipmen. Molineux, one of the mates, had command of the boats, with orders to bring all three to anchor in line along shore; four men in each boat were ready to fire the musketoons mounted in them if need be. Molineux was to keep the boats in four feet of water so that the men could jump into them if they had to retreat.

At two o'clock Furneaux and his men landed. They drew up in formation on the beach and went through their arms' drill. On the other side of the river four to five hundred Tahitian men, each carrying a plantain bough, advanced slowly and faced them within pistol shot.

The lieutenant, in his blue uniform, went forward, and, turning a turf, took possession of Tahiti (which had then perhaps 200,000 inhabitants) in the name of King George III, giving the island that name. Then he moved on to the river which was here about twelve yards wide. It was sluggish and limpid and easy to ford. A hot, salty smell came from the lagoon. Beside the river grew the *vi*, or Brazilian plum, with its bronze-green, golden-hued fruit the size of an orange, hanging in clusters of two or three. The *vi*, which is in season most of the year, is a deciduous, beautifully-spreading tree with a tall, straight trunk, sometimes as much as eight feet in girth.

Also growing by the river was the breadfruit tree, about the size of a middling oak, which it much resembles in its branching, with leaves like those of the fig tree and fruit that is like a light-green cannon-ball.

Tasting the water in the shade of these fine trees, Furneaux found it excellent. He mixed some with rum to make grog, and every man drank the King's health. On the opposite bank he saw two old men

The lagoon known as Turtle, from the eastward side of the Point of Uporu. Sketched by Sydney Parkinson in 1769.

A view sketched by Sydney Parkinson in 1769. On the left, the leaves of the edible root *taro*: on the right, a breadfruit tree.

who, confused and terrified, placed themselves in an attitude of supplication. So he made signs that they should cross and one, who had a large white beard, waded through the cool water and advanced on his hands and knees, bringing a small pig and a plantain-bough as a peace offering. Furneaux raised him up and, while he stood trembling, showed him some of the stones thrown at the *Dolphin* and tried to make him understand that, if the natives caused no trouble, no harm would be done to them.

It was afterwards discovered that the old man was a native of lesser rank, a petty chief. Later he came into prominence through the services he rendered the white men. He took the name of Hau, meaning 'Peace'.

Furneaux ordered some seamen to roll two small casks into the river and fill them, and produced hatchets to intimate that he wished to trade for provisions. The native cheered up a little and the lieutenant gave him a hatchet, nails, beads and toys, and ordered some of his men to fix a long spar in the ground and hoist on to it one of the long pennants which usually flew at the *Dolphin's* mast-head.

Several Tahitians now brought over small pigs and fruit and laid them down, each with an emblem of peace. Then they returned to the crowd on the other side of the river and waited until Furneaux ordered his men to put the provisions in the boats and produced toys, nails and two billhooks, which the old man took up. Then Furneaux and he shook hands and they parted good friends.

When the lieutenant and his men had re-embarked with Molineux, the aged man went up to the pennant and danced round it for a considerable time. He then retired into the woods on the other side of the river but soon returned with green boughs which he threw down, once again withdrawing across the stream. These boughs were signs of delegated authority from chiefs.

The boats' crews returned on board the frigate with their two casks of water, which they considered as good as any they had ever drunk, and informed their shipmates that they could water here quite easily. All were happy, expecting before long every kind of provision.

E

The natives now swarmed over the river, each with his plantain-branch, and inspected the place; but all seemed afraid of the pennant. A few began to approach it and Robertson watched them from the quarter-deck through his glass. He saw the two old men advance first with large plantain-tops. They approached as if the pennant had been a demigod, making a stop every eight or ten paces and looking at it very attentively. When they got within two or three yards they fell on their knees and seemingly made a long prayer, then put down their green boughs at the foot of the pole and went back to where the rest were standing. Thereupon hundreds went up to the pennant to lay down their boughs. At one time about a score were on their knees together. When they knelt the air was calm, but presently a fresh breeze sprang up, blowing the pennant out so that the end of it came over their heads. They all started back and ran some distance before they would look round. After this several laid down boughs, but none knelt.

Shortly before sunset the master saw the two old men carrying a large pair of hogs. When they were near the pennant they stood a few minutes, then each laid down a bough, placed the hogs at the foot of the staff and stood looking at the ship and then at their friends. Then they carried the hogs to a canoe full of green boughs and brought them to the *Dolphin*. Each made a long speech and threw some of the boughs into the sea and some on board the frigate, then they made signs for a rope.

The seamen hauled in the two fat hogs, each weighing about fifty pounds, and Wallis ordered the old men to be given presents. They were offered toys and nails but would accept nothing. They still kept talking and pointing to the pennant, meaning, as was later realised, to give the hogs in return for permission to take it.

While this was going on two men threw some stones at the pennant and drove off those who were laying down plantain boughs. (Plantain-shoots were believed to bear away the sins of the people. Even in Tahiti there was human preoccupation with sin.) As soon as the old men landed, however, they lowered the pennant and carried it away.

Soon after dark the noise of drums, conches and flutes was heard, and the glimmer of lights was seen all along the coast. No sound was heard during the night, but large fires were seen burning on the sides of the hills along shore from the river to the south-west end of the island – a signal, it was supposed, to call the people together.

At six in the morning not a native could be seen on shore, but Wallis noticed that the pennant had gone. He ordered Furneaux to take a guard and begin watering, and by eight o'clock three tons of water had been sent on board and another three tons put into casks. While the seamen were filling the casks, several natives approached the opposite bank of the river, among them the old man with the white beard, who waded across, bringing a little fruit and a few fowls. These were sent off to the ship with some of the casks.

Wallis, ill for nearly a fortnight, was now so weak that he could scarcely crawl, but he used the telescope through his cabin window to watch what was happening. At half-past eight a multitude of Tahitians, most of them armed with spears and clubs, came over the top of a red clay hill at the bottom of the bay. In their midst a tall, brisk young man was carrying the pennant flying at the end of a long pole. A number of big canoes now appeared round the western point of the lagoon in the direction of Moorea, keeping close along the shore. The captain looked at the watering-place and saw many natives creeping along at the back of it; probably nothing more than a gesture of respect, but he distrusted it. Thousands were also in the fruit-tree woods, advancing towards the same spot; and canoes were coming very fast round the eastern point, off which the *Dolphin* was moored. Now the captain could see stones piled up like shot all along the shady riverside, and as another skirmish seemed certain before long he sent the jolly boat to tell Furneaux to come off with his men and leave the casks behind him.

The big canoes from the west paddled towards the watering-place, the people in the woods keeping pace with them except for a crowd of women and children who seated themselves on the red clay hill. This eminence, overlooking the ship and beach, had only one tree on it and, although it was about a mile away, it seemed to be almost above the frigate. The canoes from each point, as they drew near her in the blue lagoon, put on shore and took in more men, with large, green, woven coconut-leaf baskets. Though it was not realised at the time, the Tahitians were probably bringing presents of cooked food, which was a Polynesian custom.

Furneaux had seen the supposed danger, and embarked before the jolly boat reached him. He sent the old man towards the natives who were creeping towards him at the back of the watering-place, making signs that they should keep at a distance and that he wanted nothing but water. As soon as they saw his signals – according to their ideas an invitation to come forward – they shouted and advanced faster. Whereupon he retired to the boats and the natives waded across the river and took possession of the casks, delighted and rejoicing, no doubt believing them to be presents.

When Furneaux and his men were embarked in the boats, Wallis ordered a few random shots to be fired into the fruit-tree woods to disperse the natives. But until a few round- and grape-shot were fired among the crowd nothing happened. The natives then began to run towards the solitary tree on top of the hill, where the women and children were sitting. The white men called it Skirmish Hill; the native name is Tahara'a, 'the Setting'. The Tahitians compared the appearance of the rock that projects from the outer side of the tunnel-like cave at the extreme end of the bluff to the stern of the *Dolphin*, which served to fix the appearance of the ship in their minds for generations.

About a hundred canoes lay abreast of Skirmish Hill and the natives in them sent some of their party ashore. Some returned and held a council in the canoes. Then they began to paddle very slowly towards the warship. It was supposed they were waiting for many canoes that were paddling up from the south-west, before they attacked the ship.

The captain determined to make the action decisive. He ordered his men to fire first upon the canoes which were in groups. The seamen bound handkerchiefs tightly over their ears, as was the custom, that the thunder of the guns might not deafen them for life. The cannon thundered and roared. The nearest canoes to the west made towards the shore as fast as possible, and those to the east, getting round the tree-clad point, were soon beyond the reach of the guns.

Most of the natives ran their canoes ashore and scuttled into the woods. Fire was directed into the woods, where the guns had tremendous power, being so near in shore. The Tahitians soon saw that they had no protection from the round and double-headed shot, as several trees and many branches were brought down about their heads and were shown to 'the children of the glorious princess' afterwards.

The head being sacred, this must have distressed them particularly. They had, for example, an aversion to comparing the size of any food to a person's head, regarding this as a species of blasphemy and insult. A hand laid on the head would be a high offence. (One of the *Bounty* mutineers, who later resided on the island, outraged their customs by carrying provisions on his head and was regarded with horror as a cannibal. Indeed, all the mutineers were regarded at first as cannibals because they were so fond of meat.) The cuttings of hair were buried at the *marai*. If anything touched a child's head before certain rites were performed, it had to be deposited in a consecrated place railed in for that purpose at the child's house. And if the branch of a tree brushed the child's head, as sometimes happened in carrying the child about, the tree had to be cut down; if in its fall it injured another tree so as to penetrate the bark, that tree also had to be felled as unclean and unfit for use.

The remaining canoes which were coming up from the south-west put ashore at seeing the warship blowing, except for six which paddled up until they got among those beached at Skirmish Hill. The Europeans fired a gun loaded with round- and grape-shot at them, sending their occupants also to the top of the hill. Eighty large canoes now lay on the beaches off Skirmish Hill and it was assumed that their owners were planning a night attack.

Wallis ordered the carpenters and any others who could wield an axe to destroy all these canoes. They landed from the boats with a guard and cut the canoes in the middle, the ship continuing to fire round- and grape-shot until they returned. In three hours they put the canoes out of use. Many were sixty feet long and three feet wide, lashed together to form a double-canoe; most were new. In the woods were found two of fifty feet by one and a half, handsomely carved.

Several Tahitians now came down through the wood to intercede for their canoes. The guard fired at them and put them to flight, and they retired to the top of the hill, where were seated several thousands of their people, among them Amo – who, unknown to the white men, had survived the fight with the ship – and Purea. Wallis ordered the breeches of the two stern-chasers to be let down, and four shot fired towards them so that they might not suppose themselves safe. The first shot fell short by a quarter of a mile; the second ploughed up the earth within fifteen yards of the solitary tree. Here all the people, including Amo and Purea, retreated to the back of the hill in terror, apparently from the firing of that shot. Indeed, none of the ship's company except the captain expected it to carry this far.

Nothing was found by the axemen in the canoes beyond stones and slings, a little fruit and a few pigs and fowls.

When the boats returned from damaging the canoes, the guns ceased firing and many men and women began to assemble on the beach to the north of the watering-place on the sandy point, bringing green boughs, pigs, fowls, fruit and white bark cloth. They planted the boughs near the beach in sign of welcome, placed the other things beside them and called to the white men to take them away. It was supposed that they wished to make peace so as to save their canoes. As the *Dolphin* was about six hundred yards off, 'the children of the glorious princess' did not know exactly what to make of the gift. They recognised cloth and hogs, but seeing other animals, whose forelegs appeared over the back of the neck, rise up several times and run a little way erect, they imagined that they were some strange, unknown animal and were eager to have a closer look at them.

After dinner Furneaux took the barge and cutter, manned and armed, and the launch, loaded with empty water-casks, which he anchored off the watering-place. He landed by the peace-offering and walked a few steps towards the canoes hauled up on the

beach as if he meant to axe them as he had those to the south, off
Skirmish Hill.

The natives were frightened and made signs of friendship, pointing to eight large hogs, four pigs, a dozen fowls, fruit, six large
bales of paper cloth – from sixty to eighty yards in each bale – and
two fat dogs with their forefeet tied on their backs. (When the
Tahitians were tired of a war, two young dogs were among the
presents exchanged by the opposing parties.) The lieutenant ordered
his men to put the fruit and livestock in the boats, except the dogs.
(Dogs, being intended for food, the Tahitians fed them exclusively
on vegetables. Captain Cook was to say – 'It was the opinion of
everyone who tasted it that they never eat sweeter meat, therefore
we resolved for the future never to despise dog's flesh.') These two
dogs were unbound and ran a long way before they stopped to look
back at their liberators.

Furneaux signed to the natives to take the cloth, as he thought it
of little use to him and a severe loss to them; but they were afraid
and made signs for him to remove it. He laid down hatchets, billhooks, nails and toys, and beckoned them to take these and their
cloth. None would come near, being sure that peace was not concluded. Furneaux then went to the watering-place with his men and
sent off six tons of water, finding all the casks undamaged. Only
some leather buckets and funnels had been taken.

He returned with his men to the ship, but the Tahitians waved
green boughs round their heads. Someone guessed the reason, and
Wallis sent two boats for the cloth. The instant 'the children of the
glorious princess' touched it, joy appeared on every native's face.
The seamen signed to them to take the presents, which they did and
brought more pigs and fruit for which they were paid with nails
and toys.

★   ★   ★

Among the crowd were some particularly handsome girls, on whom
the young seamen feasted their eyes. Some of the natives observed
this and drew several of the young women out of the crowd – some
of them of a light copper colour, others darker, and some almost

white. The old men caused them to stand in a row and made signs to the seamen to take those they liked best, and as many as they wanted. And supposing that the 'children of the glorious princess' might be unaware how to use the girls, they made signs as to how they should treat them. The boats' crews seemed to need no enlightenment and begged their officer to allow a few of the young women on board, making signs to the girls that they were not so ignorant as supposed. The old gentlemen appeared delighted at seeing the white men so merry, but the girls were a little frightened.

The officer, having no orders to bring off any natives, refused to receive the girls but made signs that he would see them later. He ordered his men into the boats and returned to the ship. The boats' crews swore that they never saw finer-looking women in their lives and declared to a man that they would rather live on two-thirds of their allowance of food than lose so good an opportunity to get a girl apiece. The news made the men mad keen to land. Even those who had been on the sick list for weeks vowed they would be happy if they were allowed ashore, saying that the young girls would make excellent nurses and speed recovery much more effectively than the doctor.

Wallis ordered every man to have as much fruit and as many coconuts as he wanted, and that hogs and pigs should be killed to make broth for all hands. Several of the men had bought fowls, and all fared so well that the sick began to crawl up on deck, and all hands passed the night in making merry, supposing the hostilities were over.

The land breeze that night brought off the same sweet scent from the shore.

The following morning Hau, the old man with the white beard whom they had seen dancing round the pennant set up by Furneaux, came to the far bank of the shady river, where he made a long speech; he then waded across to the watering-party. Furneaux showed him stones piled up like cannon-balls, brought there since his first landing, and some slings and bags filled with stones taken out of the canoes. He tried to make Hau understand that the natives had been the aggressors and that the white men had only acted in self-defence.

The old man understood and obviously dissented, but he made a speech to some of the Tahitians, pointing excitedly to the stones, slings and bags. At times his looks, gestures and voice were really furious, but he calmed down by degrees and Furneaux, who regretted that he could not understand a word of the speech, tried to convince him by signs that the white men wished to be friendly. He shook hands and embraced Hau and gave him several presents. Finally, he made him understand that he wished to trade for provisions, that the natives should not come in large numbers and that they should keep on the other side of the river while the white men kept on theirs. Hau went away well pleased.

Before midday trading was well established ashore. The Tahitians brought bunches of plantains and bananas, breadfruit and the *vi*, which 'the children of the glorious princess' called apples, but which they said should rather be termed peaches, seeing that they had a large stone and were formed more like them, but much larger and better. The 'stone' is actually a core covered with flexible spikes, and the flavour of the fruit has been compared to the quince, pineapple and mango as well as to the peach.

The white men thought these 'apples' to be the finest fruit in the world, the best to eat off the tree and making the best pies, tarts and puddings. The plantains and bananas, so they said, were much larger and finer than those of Jamaica – then perhaps the most important of British tropical colonies – and the breadfruit not a bad substitute for bread when properly cooked.

So many pigs were aboard the warship that Wallis ordered fresh pork broth to be made every day, with plenty of breadfruit and chopped-up bananas and plantains – a good substitute for potatoes when green – boiled in it. It was a wonderful diet for restoring strength and spirits to the 'poor distressed seamen', as they called themselves, who had had to exist so long on salt provisions.

CHAPTER XII

GETTING ACQUAINTED

THE seamen were right; hostilities were at an end. After many tribulations the hard-pressed, exhausted men had found their paradise – Calypso's Island, the Hesperides, the Fortunate Isle, the Isle of the Blessed, the Happy Island, the Amorous Island – where nearly all their dreams came true. There it was, conveniently in the offing, warm and alluring, with its firewood and fresh water, its meat and fruit, and beautiful and accessible girls, while the ship lay at anchor in a good harbour. Rarely can collective dreams have been so completely realised.

The carpenters made some necessary repairs in *Dolphin* and she was repainted in her original bright colours. Seamen moved about aloft like spiders, repairing the rigging; the sailmakers, squatting on the decks, repaired the sails, all of which were loosed and dried the following day.

★ ★ ★

From three to six p.m., when the tide was ebbing (the tide rises and falls only eighteen inches at the point), natives were fishing on the great south-west reef which runs down eight miles to Papeete, forming a lagoon all the way. At low water the Tahitians went on to the reef and gathered conches, mussels and other shell-fish, which they ate raw with cooked breadfruit before coming on shore. When angling in the lagoon – which ranged in colour from pale turquoise to a pellucid green – they stood in the water up to their shoulders, using a long bamboo fishing-rod with hooks of mother-of-pearl, which also served as bait. Here they caught many kinds of fish, such as sea-chub, white mullet, parrot, gropers and others. The red mullet was usually caught in seines and used as bait for the albacore and bonito, fished for far from shore. Some of the canoes were fitted with primitive cranes to lift the larger fish. They were not afraid of sharks and other dangerous creatures of the sea. In fact, it is said that a Tahitian shark has never attacked anyone. If one came in among them while they were surf-bathing and they could manœuvre it into the breakers, which the sharks normally avoid, they would force it ashore with nothing but their hands. They also caught small sharks from their canoes, with a running noose, getting the shark's head above the water and beating it with a club, as the Samoans do to this day.

The Tahitians were strong, well-made, active and good-looking. The average height of the men was from five feet seven to five feet ten inches though some, especially the chiefs, were taller. A short chief was almost unthinkable. The women ranged from five feet to five feet six. The men's complexions were olive or tawny, but those who went much upon the water tended to be redder than those living on shore. Their hair, which was neat and anointed with coconut oil, was usually black, but in some cases brown or red; while with young boys and girls it was often bleached. It was usually tied up, either in a bunch in the middle of the head, or in two bunches, one on each side. But some wore it loose, and it then curled tightly.

Most of the women were handsome, and some of them extremely so and light in colour, their cheeks suffused with red. Their hair was cut short on the neck.

Both sexes went naked until the age of six or seven. At thirteen or fourteen – earlier in the case of females – began the operation of tattooing. The instruments for tattooing a chief or head of a family were sent to the *marai* and destroyed as soon as the work was done. The females marked their hands and feet with a number of small figures and their hips with arched lines, guided wholly by fancy as to their number and thickness; the men tattooed their arms, legs and thighs as well as their buttocks. A person without these honourable marks would be reproached and shunned.

In the tattooing of men and women there was a small spot on the inside of each arm, just above the elbow, which showed that such a person might eat or touch his father's and mother's food, without rendering it *tabu;* it was a sign that all the *amoas* had been performed and was generally put on when the head was made free, which was the last *amoa* except that of friendship and marriage. The tattoo artist was called in at the pleasure of the parties and no constraint was used. The young people would not allow him to leave off as long as they could endure the strokes of the instrument, though they made cries and lamentations as if he were killing them. The girls were attended by female relatives, who held them while they struggled, encouraging them to cry out in order to alleviate their pain. When it became excessive and they could endure no more, no compulsion was used.

No one ever lifted his hand to strike a child; on the contrary, young girls would often strike those who in pity urged them to suspend the operation. They were not regarded as grown up until it was finished, which sometimes took a year, or even more, from the beginning of the process.

Both men and women were gracefully clothed and in rather a similar manner, the cloth (called *tapa*) being made of the fibre of an inner bark (usually the paper-mulberry) spread out and beaten after being soaked in the bed of a stream. The men wore a narrow piece of this cloth which was passed round the waist and between the thighs, and was tucked in before. It was called the *maro*. An oblong piece, not a yard wide, called *taputa*, with a hole in the middle for the head, hung down to the knees, the sides being open so as to leave the arms uncovered. A square piece of doubled cloth, sufficient to pass one and a half times round the waist of the men and above the breasts of the women, under the *taputa*, was called *pareu*. On the man it came down to his knees, on the woman to the calf and often to the ankles, and it was sometimes tucked in at the corner or confined by a girdle of cloth, plaited hair or fine matting. Sometimes the women wore another cloth, white and fine, thrown over as a cloak. The other garments were of what colours they most fancied. In place of the *maro* the women wore a smaller *pareu* as an under-petticoat. If persons of rank appeared with more than the ordinary quantity of cloth around them, it was designed for a present; and they usually honoured the recipient by winding it round him with their own hands.

The women uncovered their shoulders and breasts in the presence of a chief, or on passing sacred ground. They wore green eye-shades decorated with flowers, particularly jasmine. These were often changed as they cast them away on passing the *marai;* but they were replaced in a minute by weaving coconut leaves, and for this they preferred the bright yellow leaves to the green. Both sexes wore garlands of flowers and feathers.

The cloth-plant, or the paper-mulberry, of which two kinds were in use, was carefully cultivated and protected from the pigs by fencing. When the plants, which shoot up like osiers, were ten to twelve feet high and three inches in circumference, they were cut down and stripped of their bark, of which the finest white cloth was made. The rind, being taken off, was carried to the water, the outer cuticle scraped off carefully and well washed, till the sap and slime were separated. It was then wrapped in plantain leaves and left for three days until it became clammy and fit for working into cloth. Next it was spread in a regular thickness on the beam where it was to be beaten into widths of about eight inches. Now plantain leaves were laid on the ground, and on these the cloth was spread to bleach in the early morning dew for several days, being removed as the sun grew high. When perfectly bleached, it was dried and rolled up in bundles for use. If the natives wished it to be clouded, they broke the outer bark with a stone and wrapped the shoots in leaves for three or four days before they barked them.

They also mixed the inner bark of the tender branches of the breadfruit tree with those of the paper-mulberry, and prepared it in the same manner. When a chief or man of substance required some cloth, he sent his mulberry plants in bundles to his tenants to be prepared. If he needed a piece of exceptionally large dimensions, he gave them ample notice for occasionally there might be required a piece as much as 240 feet long and 24 feet wide to be given away on some great ceremonial occasion.

The cloth could be stained black or in many shades of crimson, yellow, grey and brown. The black dye was obtained from the sap of the mountain-plantain, or under the roots of such coconut palms as grew in wet and swampy ground, where the cloth was alternately soaked and dried several times in succession until it became a deep black and was then washed in salt water to be fixed. The brown was tanned with the bark of several trees, especially ironwood, which gave a fine bright colour, heightened by the sun. The yellow was extracted from turmeric; the grey was the *tapa's* natural colour when unbleached; after being half worn it might be dyed brown, and lined with white, by pasting two cloths together. The very lovely and delicate red was produced from the *mati* berry.

When the brown cloth was worn out they barked the branches of the breadfruit and mixed the old brown cloth with the new bark. This they dipped in a light yellow dye prepared from the root of a tree called *nono*, which gave it an attractive appearance. They infused perfumes into the yellow dye and lined the cloth also with white. Another kind of cloth used for upper garments was also made of the mulberry bark, half beaten. It consisted of several layers of irregular thickness, and the *Ariois* were particularly expert at making it, although it was reckoned women's work, and required much skill and nicety in the joining to prevent the part pasted on from stiffening the cloth. They painted it with the beautiful crimson *mati*, mixed with the leaves of the *to*, a low tree with wide-spreading branches, of which they made scoops for baling the canoes. They imprinted the cloth with sprigs and leaves by wetting them with this juice, and impressing them on to the fabric.

The berries of the *mati* are brown when ripe and the size of a sloe. Two or three drops of *mati* berry juice sprinkled on the leaf of the *to*, worked up with water, sufficed for one leaf. Colour was laid on with a small brush of stringy fibres. The women liked the crimson dye to remain on their fingers both as an adornment and as a tribute to their industry.

There were other trees from which cloth was made by the same process. Sometimes they pasted together pieces of different colours cut into curious shapes, in which display of taste the *Ariois* excelled.

The men provided the materials; the women made the cloth. The beam on which the bark was spread was about twelve feet long, made of a hard wood, squared to six or eight inches and finely smoothed on the upper side. The beetles were made of ironwood, about fourteen inches long and two and a half square, with grooved sides of four different sizes, according as the cloth was to be made of a finer or coarser thread.

In the heart of the mountains to the west of Papara lies a large fresh-water lake; the natives said it could not be sounded with any line and that it contained eels as thick as a man's body. Those who dwelt on its shores had no breadfruit, using in its place the mountain-plantain. Here they made vast quantities of a greyish cloth, beaten from the bark of a mountain-sloe. A number of *Ariois* frequented the place for that purpose, preferring the cloth to any other as being the strongest and best for wear. They crossed the lake on rafts made of the purple trunk of the mountain-plantain.

Ornaments consisted of feathers, usually stuck in the hair; flowers, worn behind the ears or as ear-rings or in the hair and also used as garlands; and pieces of shell and pearls. The pearls were worn mostly by the women, hanging down about two inches from the ear in a plait of hair.

* * *

The natives made no attempt to trade with the *Dolphin*, but some ventured to remove what they could of the damaged double-canoes. First one man would steal down, launch a single canoe and paddle her close along shore, keeping his eye upon the warship for fear of being fired at. When he got away without the white men seeming to take notice of him, ten others would crawl down to the beach beneath Skirmish Hill on their hands and knees and launch one of the double-canoes. The instant she was afloat two powerful men jumped into her and paddled off to the south-west as fast as they could while the rest ran into the fruit-tree woods. And so they carried off all the canoes not fairly cut in two, except two which were brought on board the frigate and split up for fuel. At first it was proposed to use up all the damaged canoes, but it was then felt that this would be too hard and would distress the poor natives; so they were allowed to remove the rest without interference.

At sunrise the following morning, while the launch crew were filling casks and getting them into the boats, eight marines and eight seamen stood on the riverside to protect them. About two hundred Tahitians came to the far bank of the river bringing fowls and fruit and made signs that they wished to trade. The gunner, in charge of the party, signed to one of them to bring the provisions over, but it was long before any of them summoned up enough courage to do so.

The white men saw ear-rings in all the women's ears but at that distance could not tell what they were made of, and none of the women would risk crossing. The natives kept staring, rather frightened, until the guard grounded their arms. But, when several men waded into the river, Harrison waved the others back and allowed only Hau to bring over a fowl and some fruit, giving him a two and a quarter-inch nail for the fowl and a one and three-quarter-inch nail for the fruit. The old man went back for more provisions.

According to one of the midshipmen, the natives sent a beautiful fan as a present, the sticks made of mother-of-pearl and the rest of feathers of a shining blooming colour. The Tahitians never allowed a fly to touch their food if they could help it, and should they find one dead in their puddings, would throw them to the pigs. So they all carried fly-switches, usually made of feathers and fixed to a wooden handle ten to twelve inches long, sometimes carved, sometimes plain. The wing bones of the largest fowls were also used for handles. Whenever you entered a house or approached a place where provisions were being prepared, it was the first thing offered you. When the provisions were cooked and hot before you, the boys who assisted the women with the cooking continued to fan away the flies, nothing being more offensive than that a fly should get into the mouth. Their aversion to touching them with their hands was such that should a dead fly be found on any part of their body, they would go instantly to the river and wash themselves. The flies at times were numerous and of two sorts, the common black fly and a grey fly which could sting sharply. There were also butterflies, butterfly-moths, mosquitoes, lizards, scorpions, centipedes, beetles, crickets, grasshoppers, small ants, sand-flies and other insects, none of them dangerous or really troublesome.

Tropical birds build their nests in holes of the cliffs, and as their long feathers were wanted by the Tahitians for their war-helmets and mourning dresses and as ornaments, they procured them in the following manner. From the top of the high cliffs, beaten by the waves beneath, a man was lowered down by a rope, seated across a stick. He searched all the holes from bottom to top, swinging himself from point to point with the aid of a staff he held in his hand and by the stones which projected or the shrubs which grew there. When he found a bird on her nest, he plucked out her tail feathers and let her fly. When he could find no more birds or was tired of the labour, he gave the signal to be drawn up. Though they swung a hundred or more feet down and perhaps eight times as many from the bottom, few accidents ever happened though the sport was often continued for many hours together.

The people set a particular value on the shiny black feathers of the man-of-war birds and they watched for their arrival, being birds of passage, in the rainy season. As soon as they observed the bird approaching, they launched a float of light wood, baited with a small fish, and stood by with a long pole within reach of the float. The moment the bird pounced on the fish they struck at him with the pole and seldom failed to bring him down. If they missed their aim, the bird could not again be tempted to approach. The cock bird was the more valuable and sometimes fetched a large hog in exchange.

As only Hau was allowed to trade, he was unable to bring over even a tenth part of the available provisions. So when the boats came off to the *Dolphin* with all hands for dinner at noon, the gunner brought only a few fowls and a little fruit. All the Tahitians went away, it was supposed to dinner.

Tahitians had three meals a day when at home and were hearty feeders; nothing pleased them more than to see a stranger eat with relish. Everyone was at pains to procure abundance for the stranger even though he should himself go short. The main part of their diet was vegetable, and the lower classes seldom enjoyed animal food. But whatever the sea produced they ate, affirming that nothing unclean could come from water. Yet there was a fish of the conger eel kind which was poisonous and could produce great swellings in the body, hands and feet, and even deprive the limbs of sense and motion. They had, however, found an antidote which in a few days expelled the poison. This eel is about twenty inches long, the fins edged with green, the skin of a brownish hue. It was caught about the reefs, and some varieties were harmless though the Tahitians could not always distinguish the good from the bad. There is also a small red crab, no bigger than a horse-bean, but deadly.

In eating they sat cross-legged on the ground or on leaves. First they made an offering to their god, then washed their hands and began stuffing their mouths full of breadfruit and dipping their fish or flesh in a coconut shell of salt water, which was their salt-cellar. They were ever ready to divide their provisions with those who had none and any place served for a dining-room. They often squatted on the grass, or under a shady tree, and always ate a little apart for fear of inconveniencing each other with their fly-switches. Green leaves from the nearest tree gave them a tablecloth, and before them was also a coconut shell of fresh water. Like the ancient patriarchs, the chiefs assisted in preparing and cooking food for their visitors.

★   ★   ★

The news that some of the women had been seen wearing ear-rings encouraged the men in the ship with the hope of finding something valuable when they could explore the island. But Wallis gave strict orders to Harrison not to let any of his men cross the river nor to allow more than two or three natives to come over to his side. And as he thought that the men would probably trade privately with the Tahitians, thus becoming involved in continual disputes, he ordered all trading to be transacted through the gunner and told him to see that the natives were neither swindled nor ill-treated. And he was enjoined at all costs to secure the services of the old man, Hau. The other warrant officers suspected the gunner of having persuaded the captain to give this order – Wallis and Clarke were both so ill that they were usually confined to their beds – with the idea of monopolising the trade. It was decided not to let any canoe trade alongside the ship.

Many Tahitians assembled at the watering-place the following day, but none was allowed to cross the river except Hau and his son, a boy of about fourteen. Harrison had the pair working in his interest by making them presents. The midshipmen realised that Hau's performance offended the other natives, particularly some of the first rank, and that he was of lower rank and paid them much respect. They had servants with them and large quantities of stock, but would send none of it over by him. At noon the trading party returned with twenty small pigs, a lot of fruit and a dozen fowls.

The next day a sail was carried ashore to make a shelter for the guard, and a tent in which the coopers could set up water casks. The gunner now allowed several natives to cross the river to sell their goods.

As it was supposed that by now the Tahitians would be peaceable, Dr Hutchinson told the captain that the sick should go ashore every day. Wallis agreed, and told him and Furneaux to find a suitable place. They reported all places equally healthy, and recommended the watering-place as being under the protection of the ship's guns and the guard and a locality where the sick could easily be prevented from straggling and be brought off to the ship for their meals. Wallis ordered a sail to be taken ashore as shelter from the sun and rain, and forbade any wandering away into the woods.

On the 1st July the weather was pleasant, with refreshing showers. The men in the *Dolphin* continued repairing her sails and rigging and finished the painting. At sunrise the traders and waterers were sent ashore accompanied by a score of liberty-men, most of them sick, but all able to walk about a little. They accompanied the waterers in the boats, and the gunner was in command of a party of sixteen armed men, four midshipmen and the sergeant of marines. Upon a little island in the middle of the shallow, shady river a tent was pitched for the sick. All those fit enough were given a cutlass to defend themselves in case of need, and two midshipmen and four marines stood guard over their tent to prevent the invalids from straggling. They were not to go off the end of the islet nearest to the gunner, who was conducting the trading.

The doctor, having seen them settled, took his gun and started off on a walk. Presently a wild duck flew over his head. He shot it and it fell dead among some Tahitians standing on the far bank of the river. These started to run away in a panic, then thought better of it; and the doctor then signed to them to bring the duck across. One of them risked it and, pale and trembling, laid the bird at his feet. Several more ducks came wheeling overhead with the curiosity peculiar to their species. The doctor brought down another three with one shot and it was thought that the ease with which the Tahitians were kept at a distance was largely due to this incident.

Some young girls crossed the water and traded with Harrison for their ear-rings, pearls of a fine lustre, but spoiled in the boring. It was supposed that the natives must have metal to bore them, but they were probably pierced with a shark's tooth.

The next day the liberty men were sent back to the islet, where they found some hundreds of Tahitians ready to trade and carrying no weapons, not even a stick. But again the gunner allowed no one to cross the river but the old man and his son. The Tahitians, who had with them fine fat hogs and fowls, were disgusted, and most of them returned home with their stock. The ship got only four young pigs, two hogs and some fruit.

After dinner Clarke, who was better, went with a party of seamen to haul the seine in the lagoon. The Tahitians had enormous nets with very small meshes, with which they caught quantities of fish about the size of sardines; but while they were using nets and lines very successfully, the white men could not catch a single fish with either. They obtained some of the natives' hooks and fibre lines, but still had no luck.

* * *

During the rains the Tahitians caught quantities of small fry at the mouths of the rivers. They formed a large net or bag of the coconut husk sewed together with a wide mouth to receive the stream; and this was held open and secured by stones to the bottom. With coconut leaves stripped and tied together on a line, they swept all before them into the bag-net and caught bushels at a draught. Sometimes the women would take bag-net and basket, forming a line across the river, and would hold them to the bottom by their feet, keeping the mouth open with their hands. When they had filled their basket, they went home and cooked the fry. They seldom returned empty-handed, and the queen herself and her mother were as often engaged in this work as any others. The Tahitians constructed fishing-tackle displaying the greatest ingenuity, exceeded only by their art in using it. The fisherman built his own canoe, made his lines, hooks and bait, and all the necessary apparatus. The hooks were ground, with coral, from pearl-shells, bones, the boars' tusks and sometimes hard wood, made in different shapes and sizes. Some were formed like artificial flies, serving for bait and hook together; and though not bearded, seldom lost the fish once it was hooked. Although the form appeared to the Europeans rude and clumsy, the natives would succeed where they, with their best hooks, could not.

The seines were of all sizes, from thirty feet to three hundred, and from six to seventy-two feet deep. Seines and lines were made of the bark of a shrub called *roa*, which seldom grew larger than hemp and when dressed looked like it. There were several other sorts of inferior quality. The fishermen twisted the filaments on their thighs with their hands, then wound the thread up into balls, some of two, some of three threads. But lines of more than two threads were rarely used, even for dolphins. Those of three threads were more liable to kink and foul when of any length; and, as dolphins were always played, were more apt to snap. The hooks made of pearl-shells were of different sizes and shapes: some were made to represent flying-fish, others for putting on real fish or whatever bait the fish would take.

For dolphin the Tahitians fished in sailing canoes four or five miles from the land. They never put out a line until they found a fish; and then they made sure of him by baiting with flying-fish prepared for the purpose. When the dolphin was hooked they played him till he was spent, then brought him gradually alongside and laid hold of him by the tail, never depending upon hook and line. When they got to the fishing ground they plied to windward. About fifty or sixty canoes from Matavai were employed in this fishery during the season, which lasted about six months, as these fish follow the sun.

While the sun is to the north they are scarce, but when it passes the line, very plentiful. They spawn about March, when the fishery ceased. Thereafter the canoes were otherwise employed, either in trading to the islands or in fitting for the albacore and bonito fishery.

While the dolphin fishery lasted, quantities of larger flying-fish were caught. White sticks, six to eight feet long, were prepared and weighted with a stone to keep them erect in the water. To each of these the natives fixed a short line and a hook of bone baited with coconut kernel. These they cast into the sea as they were standing off at a distance from each other; and, on taking them up on their return, usually found a fish on every hook. If, therefore, they had no luck with the dolphins, at least they did not return empty-handed. Sometimes they also brought in sharks and other fish.

For albacore and bonito they used a double-canoe, on which was fixed a sort of crane. The skipjack was caught with a long bamboo and line, but from its size was more easily lifted in. Most of the other fish were taken with seines, which would sometimes also net a turtle, or by hook and line from small canoes; if they hooked a large fish, they steered the canoe after him till he was spent, then lifted him in. The canoe being light bore little strain, and the fish was soon exhausted. Flying-fish were caught in seines about seventy or ninety feet long and nine feet deep. With these the natives went out in small canoes and shot them round the fish, splashing the water and rapping the sides of the seine with their paddles till the fish darted into the net. If the weather was calm and a number of canoes fell in with a shoal of fish, they joined their nets and surrounded them; then all leapt into the water and dived, rising with a fish in each hand and adding them to those already meshed. Those who fished for dolphin-bait remained out most of the night, and the darker the better. When thus employed they sometimes met sword-fish, which would strike through the canoes and repeat the stroke in two or three places before the sword stuck fast enough to hold him. They leapt overboard immediately with rope and running noose to secure him, then made hastily for the shore, to prevent the canoe from sinking.

Quantities of fine rock fish were caught in pots made from a running shrub or vine (also used in thatching to fix the palm-leaf to the rafters, for railing to the houses, and for lashings that were more durable than cord). The Tahitians were also expert at diving after rock fish and hedgehog fish, which they seldom caught in any other way. The latter takes refuge, when pursued, under the coral rock. Thither the diver pursued him and brought him up with a finger in each eye. The men could remain under water an astonishing while, chasing the fish from hole to hole and sometimes surfacing with one in each hand. The weather had to be calm for good sport, as the least ripple on the water obscured the bottom.

On dark nights the Tahitians used torches to draw the fish around the canoes and had landing-nets ready to scoop them up. When the fish came into shoal water to spawn, the natives stripped coconut leaves from the stem and, knotting them on a line, swept the reefs and shoal places till they forced the fish to the beach where, with lade-nets or small seines, they took large quantities.

They also used two- or three-pronged forks of ironwood which were flung a considerable distance at the prey. Others, with many prongs, were hurled into a shoal from the canoes and sometimes struck two or three fish at once.

★ ★ ★

Wallis was still extremely ill and the doctor feared that he might die; but the seamen were recovering fast. That night it was dark, dismal and squally, with much lightning, to fit the crisis in the captain's illness. But at sunrise the weather cleared and the traders, wooders and liberty-men were sent ashore. The men remaining aboard heeled the ship over by shifting the guns and ballast, scrubbed her sides between wind and water, and paid the line with warm tar. Her copper bottom looked as clean as on the day she sailed from England and, much to their satisfaction, as sound.

Many Tahitians arrived at the watering-place, but brought very little stock. They included some of the principal people, with their servants carrying low stools cut out of a solid block of wood for the convenience of their masters and mistresses. Still the gunner allowed none to cross but Hau and his son, and when any of the others set their feet in the water he ordered the guard to point their muskets at them, which made them return trembling to their own side and often go off into the woods, not to return.

The gunner was at great pains to make Hau and his boy get him some pearls from the women, but most of them, seeing themselves treated like slaves, took the pearls out of their ears. The implications were fully realised by the midshipmen. The Tahitians attached much value to their pearls, particularly as they were an ornament which would stand immersion in water. At noon the shore party went aboard with one hog and six small pigs.

On the 4th July the sea provisions were overhauled, a thorough clean-up was made of the ship, the yards and top-masts, which had been struck, were got up and the yards and standing-rigging tarred. Salt provisions were served, there not being sufficient fresh pork on board.

All the liberty-men who were sufficiently fit to do so were ordered to cut grass, to make hay for the sheep.

The poetical Wilkinson said in his journal: 'This day, a party of our men went on shore to make hay by way of refreshment, there being good grass here for that purpose. The natives assisted them in their work with great cheerfulness, and it was no unpleasant sight to see our men pass and repass the river where we watered, every one carried by his native.

'Though everything seemed to be so agreeable on both sides, we were always on our guard. The women were far from being coy. For when a man found a girl to his mind, which he might easily do amongst so many, there was not much ceremony on either side, and, I believe, whoever comes here after, will find evident proofs that they are not the first discoverers. The men are so far from having objection to an intercourse of this kind, they brought down their woman and recommended them to us with the greatest eagerness, which makes me imagine they want a breed of Englishmen amongst them. They become wives at ten or eleven years of age, and have children in their arms at an age when our European young ladies are nursing like babies at that age.'

Extreme youthfulness in mating applied only to the lower-classes and partly accounted for their smaller stature as compared with the chiefly families. A man might cohabit with two sisters, and a woman with two brothers, at the same time if all were agreeable; and it was considered a friendly act for a man to have sexual relations with the wife of his *taio* ('adopted friend') if she were willing. The adopted friend was regarded as a brother. For that reason the Tahitians were eager to allow their *taios* among the white men, with whom theoretically they had exchanged names, to have sexual intercourse with their own wives or sisters-in-law, yet not indulge in liberties with the sisters or the daughters since these were considered as his own sisters or daughters. Nor would any temptation make them violate this bond of purity. It has been said that a *taio*ship formed between different sexes imposed the most solemn barrier against all personal liberties; but there is considerable doubt about this. So it was that the natives recommended their wives to the haymaking liberty-men. But they were soon to suffer a disturbance of this idyllic situation.

In the scale of rank, birth enjoyed singular distinction. A chief was always a chief; and though expelled from his command, losing his district, or having his honours transferred to his child, he remained noble and respected. On the other hand, no acquisition could raise a common man to a higher station than that held by the near relations, younger brothers or *taios*, of the chiefs. If there were more chiefs than one, the district was divided into different parishes, and each chief had deputies under him. Their estates were three times the size of a gentleman's. Yet the meanest natives lived in no slavish dependence. They rendered honour and respect to their chief, through force of custom rather than from fear of punishment. They were admitted as their companions on all occasions, and treated with perfect freedom; indeed, in outward appearance they could hardly be distinguished. The king was not averse from conversing with the least of his subjects or from visiting them; he never treated them with *hauteur*. His retinue was often changed and no man served him longer than he pleased. They had no wages nor were they engaged for any stated time, though some remained in the same family all their lives. These ancient domestics were as much respected as were relations, giving directions to the cadets and managing, as stewards, the affairs of the household without control.

The Tahitians laid not the least restraint upon their children from the day they were born. Being the heads of their families, they were indulged in everything. They had their own amusements, called *heiva tama ridi*, of which, unfortunately, practically nothing appears to be known; but they were certainly of sexual significance. As the children grew up and advanced to manhood, these were generally abandoned; but none was controlled by any authority, and anyone might continue them if he pleased. All the earliest observers seem agreed that the Tahitians were the happiest race of people in the world; and no pains should be too great to discover all that can now be unearthed regarding such matters.

One of the marines, 'a dear Irish boy' according to Robertson, received a severe beating from his companions for not beginning his love-making more decently, in some house or at the back of some bushes or a tree. 'Paddy's excuse was his fear of losing the honour of not having the first.' It would certainly qualify as a classic Irish 'bull' – equal to, 'It is impossible that I could have been in two places at once, unless I were a bird' – but it is more than that, for he influenced history more than might easily be imagined.

Herman Melville, writing about a century ago, remarked on the curious way in which Polynesians are in the habit of making bosom friends at the shortest possible notice, a custom, he said, which had its origin in a fine, and in some instances, heroic sentiment. Filled with love and admiration for the first whites who came among them, the Polynesians could not testify the warmth of their affection more strongly than by making instant and abrupt offers of friendship. Hence, he said, one may read in old voyages of chiefs coming off from the shore in their canoes and performing strange antics to express this desire. In the same way their inferiors now accosted the seamen.

CHAPTER XIII

*

HANDSOME-SHARK

FROM the deck of the *Dolphin* that afternoon, some of 'the children of the glorious princess' tried their luck at fishing for sharks – always a favourite occupation with seamen when the opportunity offers, the weather is sultry, they have time on their hands and are unable to go ashore.

It is quite a pleasant way to pass an afternoon in harbour, even if nothing is caught. The steel hook, on a length of chain, is baited with a lump of pork; the water gurgles softly against the side of the ship, whose wearisome pitching – if she be a sailing ship which pitches – is over; and to a lazy, drowsy sense of well-being is added an interest centred on a dangerous foe.

A large female shark was hooked. She had perhaps been attracted into the lagoon by the human carnage reddening its waters, a week and a half before. After she had taken the hook the seamen had to give her several musket-shots and run one of the gunner's pikes several times into her belly before she died. She was found to measure twelve feet six inches. The officers ordered them to tow the carcase ashore to the watering-place to show the natives, then to come off immediately after landing it so that they themselves might see, before night came on, how the Tahitians would behave.

Robertson watched the proceedings through the telescope. The instant the boat put off from the shore the natives assembled in a large body some thirty yards from the shark, then advanced slowly until within ten yards of her and waited while some of them went off to fetch green boughs. Having done so, two of them stepped up to the carcase very slowly and laid boughs at its head, then started back some paces, stood some minutes and made a speech, gazing steadfastly at the shark.

The two men again stepped up slowly, and several of the rest came with green boughs and laid them down. The ceremony took nearly an hour. Then one put his foot upon her tail and, not seeing it move, took hold with his hands and gave a strong pull. Another began to look narrowly at her head and thrust his fingers into the shot holes. Then all stood still and gazed at the frigate.

Robertson supposed they were wondering how it was possible to kill so huge a monster. Yet when young whales got entangled in the reefs or were hurled over them by a heavy surf, the Tahitians sometimes killed them by surrounding them with their canoes and thrusting at them with their war spears; but often they had their canoes dashed to pieces.

The officers sent a boat ashore and the seamen made signs for the natives to carry off the carcase. In a quarter of an hour they cut it up in large pieces and removed it, appearing very cheerful. It was supposed that they cooked and ate it that same night. The seamen reported that there were about twenty young sharks in the belly of the old one.

Perhaps the ceremony was performed because this, the great blue shark (which the Tahitians did not consider rapacious) was thought to be the shadow of Handsome-shark, the beloved of the god Taaroa, who now swims in the Living-water of Taaroa, the Milky Way. There is a hint in Tahitian mythology that the shark is merely a seaweed-eater. Taaroa took up the original shark and protected it because two youths tried to kill it on the suspicion that it intended to eat children (there is kindness involved in all this) and it now eats clouds in the lake of the Vairoa of Tane – the God of the Winds – the dark space in the Milky Way. The killing of the shadow shark by the Europeans was probably of dubious propriety.

Next morning the traders, waterers and liberty-men were sent ashore and Harrison allowed the natives to trade; but as soon as he had paid them, they had to return to their own side of the river. They were very merry. Some young girls brought fowls and were paid with two and a quarter-inch nails; and the midshipmen gave them ear-rings and the gunner tied beads about their necks and wrists, which made trade go well. The girls were delighted and some of them ventured across to the islet to the liberty-men, who received them very cheerfully and gave them small presents. These gained the girls' hearts and they gave the liberty-men a signal. The honest-hearted tars, as Robertson called them, would willingly have obeyed but were at once ordered back to the ship, to which the gunner returned with eight hogs, four pigs, eighteen fowls and much fruit. Fresh pork was served and broth was made of the fat hogs.

Wallis thought that trade had improved because Hau, after an absence of three days, had returned to the market-tent that day and given Harrison to understand that he had been up-country to persuade the people there to bring their produce, of which the places nearby were nearly denuded. Several Tahitians not seen previously had arrived with hogs larger than any yet brought to market.

The old man paddled off to the *Dolphin* in his canoe bringing a roast pig as a present for Wallis, who, much pleased, gave him an iron pot, a looking-glass, a drinking-glass and several other things which no other Tahitian possessed. When Hau had the pot, he and his friends ate boiled meat every day. The natives were very astonished when they first saw the gunner, who used to eat ashore when he kept the market, cook his pork by boiling.

Tahitian puddings were made by wrapping the ingredients up in leaves and baking them in the oven. Of mountain-plantains a pudding was made which tasted like gooseberry-fool, while the root resembled yam. The Tahitians had fifteen different sorts of plantains including the maiden, the horse-plantain and the mountain. Of plantains they also made a pudding mixed with *taro* – a large root of the arum lily tribe – and coconut. The coconut was grated on coral and mixed with its own milk, then wrung dry in a stringy grass that expressed the white juice and left the substance of the nut behind. Into the juice the natives grated *taro* and mixed the ripe plantain, tying the whole up in plantain leaves toughened over the fire. These bag-puddings remained in the oven all night and, when taken out, might be eaten hot or cold and would keep for many weeks. Another good pudding was made of breadfruit and coconut milk mixed in the same manner and often cooked on heated stones.

Another was made of the same materials, with the tender leaves of
taro broken into it. The Samoans make a pudding of the cream-like
expressed coconut juice and young *taro* leaves, baked in breadfruit
leaves, which is astringent and delicious. Another was made with the
gratings of a cassava-like root and expressed coconut juice. When
well made it resembled a suet dumpling, although the root itself, if
eaten in any quantity, could cause giddiness. So a flour resembling
starch was made of the root, which, mixed with water, also formed
a paste for joining and thickening pieces of bark cloth.

★ ★ ★

On the 7th July Wallis was much better. On leaving his bed after
nearly a fortnight, he found the ship's company so fresh and healthy
that he could scarcely believe they were the same men. During all
his illness, he said, he was not troubled with any business nor had
the mortification to hear a single complaint or appeal. He decided
to take an airing round the harbour in his barge. Robertson went
with him to sound the south-west of the bay, which he had not
previously had an opportunity to do.

Natives in several small canoes were fishing outside the reefs but,
on seeing the boat sailing down the lagoon, they paddled ashore,
except for those in one canoe, who came near and exchanged a few
fish for some trinkets. The Tahitians were so fond of fish that they
normally parted with them with reluctance. But the idea of trading
was now firmly implanted in their minds, and there is reason to
think that a *tabu* had been put on their own consumption of pork.

The boat's sail and mast were struck when two miles from the
Dolphin, and the white men lay for some time looking at the people
fishing on the reef, with several big canoes close by. Knowing that
the canoes sailed much faster than their boats, it was thought unwise
to go near the reef to see what fish the natives were catching, for
fear that the poor creatures might be foolish enough to attack them
and put them under the disagreeable necessity of killing some in
self-defence. It was therefore decided to row back to the ship but to
keep close in shore, to get a good view of the coast.

Several fine streams were seen and good landing for boats and canoes in every little palm-fringed bay and cove. Near the beach, upon a reef, lay a large double-canoe about fifty feet long, which could have carried nearly eight tons. The two hulls were raised about two feet with several large logs under them to dress their bottoms, as a ship would have been raised in Europe to put on a new keel. The place was in the Pari district, where was the next harbour to the west of Matavai. The district of Te-pori-o-nuu – The-fatness-of-hosts – extended from Faa'a, west of Papeete, to Skirmish Hill. At Papeete there is an excellent harbour; and Pari – Fortification – was a sub-division.

As the boat rowed along the Pari shore a temple came into view. According to the *Bounty* mutineer James Morrison, writing about twenty years later, a new *marai* was built near here. Its name was Taputapuatea, which he mis-spelt and consequently translated 'Sacrifice The White Hog'. The name of the *marai* in the *Dolphin's* time was probably Tara-hoi. It was a building made of round stones. The outermost part, close to the sea, was nearly fifty yards long, six feet high and about eight feet broad on top. Another wall, four feet high and nearly as broad, stood on top of this. Within it and sur-mounting all was another wall three feet high and very broad; in other words it was a stepped, truncated pyramid. The building was about sixteen yards wide. The back (the side facing the land) had seven steps, each two feet high. Close by were some images rudely carved out of large trees, and there appeared to be several burying-places.

Protecting the shore was a reef which prevented the white men rowing close to it; and it was thought dangerous to land and walk round to look, as the natives were assembling on the beach in great numbers, though none went near the building. Robertson said that he often wanted to have a full view of the place but never had the opportunity. However, apart from his account of the back, he gave what is probably the best description ever written of the *marai* – which has long since been destroyed. A sketch of it was made two years later for the young naturalist, Captain Cook's companion, afterwards famous as Sir Joseph Banks and President of the Royal Society (see page 225).

Pigs and fowls were running along the shore and the trees were laden with fruit. Robertson wondered how the pigs and fowls came to be brought to the island, unless the high mountains to the south were a part of New Zealand, which he thought likely. Actually the mountains were an illusion, while the general extent and the east and south coasts of New Zealand, more than two thousand miles away, were not then known by Europeans. The north and west coasts had been discovered by the Dutchman Tasman, and a couple of years later New Zealand was mapped by Captain Cook.

If the high mountains were a part of New Zealand, thought Robertson, both breeds might be supposed to have come first from India to Sumatra, Java and New Holland (Australia), in time to New Zealand, and thence here. There were then no swine in New Zealand, although the Maoris knew them by name. They were introduced by Cook. Robertson thought it reasonable to suppose that the people of this island had originated from the same quarter of the world, in which he was probably right. 'There is three distink colours of people here, which is a thing most difficult to account for of anything which we have yet seen, the Red people are ten times more numerous nor the Mustics, which is a Medium between the Whitest sort and the red or Indian colour, and the Mustics are near ten times as numerous as the Whitest sort.'

Robertson's handwriting here has also been interpreted to read 'Mustee', and *mustee* (or *mustafine*) is the Caribbean term for the offspring of a white father and an octoroon mother. In fact, there were four racial types, for there was a negroid strain remarked upon particularly by Bougainville and probably derived from Melanesian canoe-slaves and concubines picked up in New Guinea and the Western Pacific by the Polynesians during the migrations.

Off Skirmish Hill 'the children of the glorious princess' lay on their oars and traded for fowls, fish and bunches of plantains and bananas, paying with beads and buttons. Many men, women and children came to the beach, and Wallis sent several strings of beads to the young children, pleasing the old people immensely. Here there were two places walled-in like gardens, containing nurseries of young trees.

The captain and Robertson got back to the *Dolphin* at noon. The traders had brought off only four pigs, a few fowls and some fruit. A midshipman told Robertson that a new form of trading had taken up most of their attention that day; but this, said the master, might more correctly be called the 'old trade'. The relations with the women had been commercialised for the first time on the basis of frank prostitution, brought into line with the trading. 'Civilisation' was on its way in.

★ ★ ★

That day Wallis read to the ship's company the Articles of War (having reference to mutiny) and ordered James Proctor, the corporal of marines, to be flogged. The corporal had not only left his station ashore and insulted the gunner, but, when he came aboard and was ordered into confinement, knocked down the master-at-arms, the petty officer responsible for discipline on the gun-deck.

After dinner the captain sent the trading party ashore for more pigs. They returned with only a few bunches of plantains and bananas, but the 'old trade' had proceeded merrily.

After dark numerous lights were seen upon the long south-west reef, others along-shore by the water, for fishing. Beautiful and full of mystery is the spectacle of the torch-flares in the soft dark Pacific nights as seen across the lagoon. This, and graceful, bare-breasted girls discerned through the palm trees as they carried their blazing torches swiftly in single file along the edge of a lagoon, might well have suggested to the more educated of the beholders a picture from classical mythology.

At sunrise the traders, waterers and liberty-men were again sent ashore. For fear lest the gunner's party would do no better, Gore was dispatched with a party of twenty armed men to trade along-shore from house to house, beginning at the foot of Skirmish Hill and coming up to the watering-place. All hands returned at noon. But the 'old traders' brought only three small pigs, some fowls and a little fruit, while the mate's party brought four small hogs, two pigs and some red and white yams. These grew wild in the mountains, from one to six feet long and of different thicknesses. They

F

were good eating, but being procured at a distance and with more trouble, were little sought after in the breadfruit season. The liberty-men meanwhile had continued their pursuit of the girls. Clarke was again very sick at this time but most of the seamen were fairly well. All those able to go ashore recovered fast. Warrant and petty officers were served with two fowls amongst three men and as much fruit as they wanted.

Wallis now landed for the first time to walk a little way along the shore and was much refreshed. That evening Robertson saw a large fire near the *marai* at Pari, but did not know what the natives were doing nor did he know the purpose of the *marai*. No lights appeared on either reef.

The next day the gunner and his people went to the watering-place at sunrise, but Gore was not sent ashore with his party as he declared that the natives' stock from Skirmish Hill to the riverside was exhausted. That morning Wallis, Furneaux and the doctor were ashore with an armed guard, taking the air. Robertson was busy in the ship making out a plan of the bay. A midshipman, who had charge of the watch on deck, came down to the cabin and told him that he had observed a great number of large vessels approaching from outside the south-west reef, and more than three times as many men on the reef as he had ever seen there before. On a previous occasion several thousand people had been seen there, fishing.

Robertson went on to the quarter-deck to scan the vessels through Wallis's telescope and saw them coming round the reef, all under sail. At first they appeared like large schooners or sloops, but on their rounding the reef he had a better view of them and likened them to the double-canoe under repair. About twelve of them were nearly double her burden – sixteen tons – and the rest smaller. They flew long streamers like pennants, red, white, blue and yellow.

As soon as they entered the reef passage, several small canoes came out to welcome them and returned with them towards the shore. By this time the shore abreast of them was crowded with people, and the natives on the reef went ashore after them. The large vessels seemed to be full of men, and this circumstance, with the quantity of small canoes gathering round the larger ones, made Robertson suspect them to be planning an attack on the ship. However, they all went round a point of land about a mile and a half from the place where lay the canoe under repair.

On seeing all of them disappear together, the master supposed the newcomers to be strangers from another country or the crews of trading vessels returned from a distant voyage, and that their friends and acquaintances were welcoming them home. The larger vessels were loaded with something, but with what he could not make out.

They were, in fact, the fighting-stages, for although the canoes may possibly have been those of the *Arioi*, it is far more likely that they were the giant Tahitian war-canoes, which could carry up to three hundred men each, flew coloured streamers, had such a superstructure, were double and up to ninety feet long. There was a Tahitian naval dockyard, so to speak, at the place where these canoes put in, which was visited later by Captain Cook. Tahiti could muster several hundred of such craft, and Cook on his second voyage to the Pacific saw a tremendous review of them, one hundred and fifty-nine great double war-canoes, although they were only the canoes of the small Faa'a district. He saw canoes carrying one hundred and seventy-two men each, one hundred and forty-four paddling, eight steering and twenty warriors on the fighting-stage, also some canoes ninety feet long.

The war-canoes had high bows, on which were carved rude images of men; their sterns ran tapering up to as much as twenty-four feet, and were ornamented with similar figures. The bottoms were sharp, the sides rounding in towards the top in the mid-ship frame like the ace of spades; they were built of short pieces of wood about six feet long, except for the keel, which seldom exceeded three pieces of twenty to thirty feet, and sometimes was formed only of two pieces. The short pieces were lashed together securely with sinnet (coconut-husk twine) the seams caulked with fibre and paid with bread-fruit gum. But a heavy sea could open the seams and make them leaky, and the Tahitians had no method of clearing the water other than by baling, wherefore five or six hands were thus constantly employed at sea. In port the canoes were hauled up on dry ground to prevent their sinking. The breadfruit plank was preferred for durability, for, though not a close-grained wood, the salt-water worms would not touch it. On the top of the masts there was a kind of basketwork of the shape of a funnel used in Europe for pouring liquids.

When Wallis returned on board, Robertson reported what he had seen and proposed to inspect the river or harbour the vessels had entered. Wallis at first agreed that he or Furneaux should go, but later thought it too much of a risk to allow the boats out of sight of the ship.

Afterwards, at various times, more large canoes came through the reef passage and entered the same river or harbour.

CHAPTER XIV

*

CHIEF PRIEST TUPAIA

Amo, the regent, afraid lest 'the children of the glorious princess' should revenge themselves upon him for his attack on the ship, had retired to his home at Papara. He added the stolen pennant to the *maro ura*, the girdle of royalty, for it was seen in due course in that situation by Captain Cook and later by James Morrison and other *Bounty* mutineers. Assuredly it could have been put to no more sacred use. The white men, knowing nothing of its strange fate, still thought that Amo had fallen a victim of the skirmish. Purea was still living in the gigantic *Arioi* house named Agitation, near the entrance to the deep valley; but of this 'the children of the glorious princess' were unaware.

To the Tahitians the *Dolphin* appeared almost as a floating island; her masts like the trees of the forest; her rigging like the lianas of the undergrowth; with streams running from the decks in water gushing from the pumps. An island capable, she seemed, of belching forth death-dealing bolts with attendant thunder and inhabited by jovial, even lecherous, yet hasty-tempered and always unpredictable white men, whom for all their obtuseness in some ways, they were finding it advisable to treat with respect and precaution. Yet they were also, the Tahitians thought, creatures for whom it was possible to feel affection; not altogether, in fact, a bad reputation and certainly one which could appeal to women.

It had not been realised by the Europeans, in this curious coming together of cultures, that the new arrivals in the lagoon had been war-canoes. So on the following day the trading party and the liberty-men went ashore after dinner without concern. The liberty-men and the Tahitians were now so friendly that they walked arm-in-arm. At sunset the captain went to take the air in his barge, but returned feeling rather poorly. Again at sunrise next morning the traders, waterers and liberty-men were ashore, and Gore took a party of men to the woods at the nearest end of Skirmish Hill to cut firewood.

Many Tahitians were assembled here and showed signs of uneasiness when the white men began to fell the first tree. One old man made a long speech and seemed troubled as if he was thinking of the axed canoes and fearing that it was intended to destroy the entire plantation. On finding that he was the owner, the mate made him understand that he wanted only about a dozen trees, gave him a seven-inch spike-nail for the one felled and drove another nail into the next old tree, directing him to take it out, and the woodmen to cut down the tree. The only spike-nail Tahitians had seen previously was that from the *African Galley*. Soon the ancient had pointed out more trees than Gore needed, and delighted in showing his nails to his friends, highly pleased with his bargain.

The forge was set up, and the armourer and his mate were put to making small iron gouges, which it was thought the natives might like better than nails; but they preferred nails to anything else. They formed a nail into an excellent fish-hook and used the larger ones for boring holes in the planks of canoes.

Robertson went ashore for the first time, carrying a pistol and his broadsword, and walked about a mile up the shady bank of the river, where grew only breadfruit and *vi* trees, towards the valley, accompanied by two midshipmen armed with cutlasses and a seaman armed with a musket. They passed several well-built houses but saw very little livestock about them and scarcely anything in the way of furniture. The master supposed that fear had made the natives remove everything of value away into the country; but in point of fact what with their pleasant climate and easy-going mode of life, the Tahitians had but little need of furniture.

★   ★   ★

The common dwellings were about eighteen feet in the ridge-tree, oblong and rounded at the ends. The furniture consisted of a few wooden trays and stools for making their puddings and posts on which to hang their baskets of provisions; the floor was spread with matting and cloth, on which they slept. In fine weather many slept in the open air. Their pillow was shaped like a low wooden stool, neatly wrought out of one block. Their usual seat was the ground, their posture cross-legged; but they had seats with which they were always ready to compliment a stranger.

If a man ate in a house with a woman (in the absence of a women's eating-house) he took one end, she the other, and they slept in the middle. If a woman had a child, its provisions could not come in at the same door as the mother's; there was an opening like a window, through which they were received. It would have been considered abominable in the highest degree for her to eat whilst suckling her child. The unmarried women slept beside their parents, at one end of the house; the unmarried men at the other. The servants usually slept in the women's eating-house, or near it. Their bedclothes were the garments they wore, if they had no other, which was frequently the case with the common people and servants, who, in that warm climate, troubled themselves little about clothes or the care of them.

Though generally there were no partitions in their houses, Tahitians had in many instances more refined ideas of decency than Europeans. James Morrison declared that he never saw any appetite, hunger and thirst excepted, gratified in public.

During the night, if strangers lodged with them, they burnt candle-nuts stuck on skewers, that their guests might find their way in and out of the house without inconvenience from those who slept on the floor, sometimes to the number of fifty or sixty persons. It was not unusual for them to get up and have food ready in the night; and some sat and chatted and told stories, with which they were always delighted.

They were very fond of dogs, especially those with a bushy tail, whose hair they used in the breast-plates worn in battle. The women not only fondled the puppies but would even suckle them at their breasts.

*　*　*

As the Europeans were returning to the boats they were accosted by three exceedingly handsome young girls. One smiled in Robertson's face and made a sign, holding up her right hand with the first finger upright, then taking hold of her right wrist with her left hand while still holding the finger straight. Then she crooked all her fingers and kept playing with them.

The master stopped to inquire what she wanted and, supposing the midshipmen better acquainted with such matters than he, who had never seen any of the girls before except at a distance, asked one of them to explain the sign. Both assumed a grave look and said: 'We don't understand her signs.'

Supposing she had something to sell, the master made signs that she should show her goods, but that seemed to displease her. Then another girl laughingly repeated the sign, which set the midshipmen laughing as heartily as the maiden.

The master insisting upon an explanation from the young men, 'The girls,' they said, 'only want a long nail each, but we have never seen them make a sign for one longer than their fingers. They must think that you carry longer nails than other white men because you are dressed differently.'

Robertson wanted them to explain the second part of the sign – the girl crooking her fingers and playing with them – that he might understand it all; but the well-mannered midshipmen begged to be excused.

He gave the girls a nail each, and they parted good friends. Then he walked down to the market-tent to see how trading was going and told the gunner what had happened with the girls. Harrison explained the whole matter in a few blunt words, remarking that 'Your young friends are not quite as ignorant as they pretend to be.'

The gunner continued, 'The price of the "old trade" is now fixed at a three-and-a-half-inch nail each time, and the liberty-men deal so largely in this way that I am much afraid of losing my trade in pigs, fowls and fruit. The natives deal very cunningly. If they bring three or four things to sell, they always try to sell the worst first; and if they get what they want for any trifling thing they can easily spare, they take back their more valued produce.

'I have often seen them conceal their best things until I purchased others of less value, which makes me afraid that they will buy up all

our nails and toys by means of the "old trade", and, of course, bring
no other goods to market. So I advise you to try to put a stop to it
when you go aboard by preventing the liberty-men from coming
ashore.'

'That is out of my power,' said the master. 'Most of them are on
the sick list.'

Harrison retorted that even the most sick traded a little and could
scarcely be as ill as they represented themselves aboard the ship.

Robertson promised to put the case to the commanding officer
and the doctor, and the gunner added, 'Your young friends deal a
little too, and might likewise be prevented.' But the midshipmen
boldly defended themselves by declaring that Harrison dealt more
largely than any one of them and thus was himself the greatest
spoiler of the trade.

Robertson, alive to the situation, advised them all to deal
moderately for fear of losing the broth and other good fresh food.

When aboard the ship he informed Furneaux (who was in charge),
the doctor and their 'good, merry friend' the purser, of how things
were going ashore. They consulted other officers as to what had
best be done. Some thought it would be best to detain the liberty-
men for some days; others, that it would ruin all trade to keep them
on board. The doctor, who was credited with taking all possible
care of his patients, declared that keeping them confined aboard the
ship would ruin their health and constitution, for, said he, 'anything
that depresses the minds and spirits of men must certainly hurt them'.

So they questioned some of the men on the sick list and threatened
to stop their liberty for spoiling the gunner's trade. Their dismal
expressions confirmed the truth of what the doctor had said. It was
therefore agreed to prevent the men, so far as possible, from taking
nails and toys ashore. The doctor affirmed upon his honour that no
man on board was affected with any sort of disorder that he could
communicate to the natives of this beautiful island.

* * *

The seamen had now lost all fear and associated with the Tahitians
with complete assurance. Gore's main difficulty when getting timber

– which the natives carried to the boats, being paid with one-and-three-quarter-inch nails – was to keep his men from straggling into the woods, where the painted silence of the cool paths, shaded by palms, breadfruit and *vi* trees, was very conducive to love-making. Therefore he and the gunner agreed to let the men have a stroll through the woods in turn, which made all parties happy.

The groves of these trees were intersected in all directions by paths going from one house to another, so that the whole locality was in one shade, most grateful in a climate where the sun was so powerful and the shade was the most beautiful imaginable. The houses were mostly without walls (some had walls made of poles fairly close-set, like a bird-cage), so that the air, cooled by the shade, had free access in whatever direction it blew. Little gardens of plantain or banana and the cloth tree were around the houses, which were about fifty yards from each other.

Round each house enough ground was clear to prevent the moisture that dropped from the branches from rotting the thatch. Two houses were often built close together, one being the women's eating-house. The floor was covered some inches deep with soft hay, upon which were laid the mats.

* * *

Two days after Robertson's discussion with the officers, the mate was seeking firewood to the north of the river, where were several old trees, each bought with the now customary spike-nail. If the owner removed the nail and kept it, the woodmen cut down the tree; but if he returned it or pointed to another tree, the first one was allowed to stand and the other was felled.

A midshipman now stuck in a spike, and an old man, apparently the owner of the tree, who had a house close by, withdrew it; but another man, powerful, good-looking and presumably a chief, took the nail and kept it. Words followed between them, then the old man gave up the argument and went into his house.

A few minutes after this incident had occurred Purea arrived, accompanied by a retinue who showed her great deference. Some of the bystanders telling her of the dispute, she sent for the old man, who appeared before her trembling. She said a few words to him, then spoke angrily to the one who had the nail. At once he returned it to the old man and walked off very frightened.

Soon afterwards the Queen withdrew into the woods with her attendants, and then arrived Tupaia, Chief Priest of Tahiti and lover of Purea. At noon the traders and the woodmen and liberty-men came off to the frigate for dinner, bringing Hau's son and Tupaia with them. Tupaia, who was obviously a chief, was about thirty, well-made and with good features of the 'Mustic' colour. The officers found him sensible and well-behaved. They showed him the ship, and he noticed everything and seemed much surprised at the vessel's construction. Wallis and Clarke, who by this time were able to sit up, joined the officers and the chief at dinner in the gun-room.

The officers, apart from the captain and his guests, shared a common table and every day invited one of the petty officers.

After the cloth was spread they sat down, Tupaia carefully examining the chair before seating himself. He subjected the plates, knives and forks to the same scrutiny, but, when the dinner was put on the table, laid down his plate and touched nothing until he was invited to do so.

The dinner was good: chicken broth, two roast fowls, a roast pig, yams, plantains, bananas, soft bread, biscuit, 'apple' pudding and 'apple' pie. He observed the way the officers used their spoons, knives and forks and helped himself as they did; but at first, when he stuck a morsel upon his fork and tried to feed himself, found difficulty in guiding the fork. By force of habit his hand came to his mouth and the victuals at the end of the fork went away to his ear.

There was some good claret together with Madeira, port, rum and brandy grog, and excellent London porter. Tupaia smelt and tasted the wine and grog, but liked neither. (Two years later he got most gloriously drunk on the royal birthday, to show his loyalty to King George III.) He responded to toasts in water and was much pleased when all the officers touched glasses with him. But it made him a little uneasy to see them wipe their mouths with their pocket handkerchiefs before drinking, for he had nothing in the nature of a handkerchief and was unwilling to use his *tapa* clothes.

Robertson therefore gave him the corner of the tablecloth for wiping his mouth, which so shocked the fastidious Mr Clarke that he would eat and drink no more, but kept growling at the chief and the master during the rest of the time they sat at table. He took up the cloth several times and tried to make the Tahitian understand how impolite it was to use it, which distressed Tupaia, who could not understand his meaning and thought he had done something very wrong.

This made Robertson uneasy, so to please the chief he hob-nobbed with him the more and wiped his own mouth with a corner of the cloth which reassured the Chief Priest. He made signs to Clarke, who was still fretting, that he would bring him a fine young girl. This suggestion put an end to the growling and Clarke replied graciously, 'Well done, Jonathan. If you perform your promise, you shall be rewarded.' (This, incidentally, was the first Christian name bestowed on a Tahitian, and to the officers 'Jonathan' he remained.)

After dinner they showed 'Jonathan' a looking-glass, which at first surprised him. But he soon began to pluck his beard, perhaps because the officers were clean-shaven. They then gave him a pair of tweezers, and he began to pull his beard and the hairs out of his nose. The Tahitians extracted every hair from the nose and body to prevent its harbouring any dust or foulness, and their beards were usually neatly trimmed with shells. But their hair was worn short or long, according to taste. The women, except for those who affected to be prophetesses, wore their hair short and decked with flowers, and they paid the nicest regard to their persons. They plucked their eyebrows and clipped their eyelashes if they were too long, forming the eyebrows into regular arches. Nor were the men less attentive to their appearance or less meticulous with their toilet. A black coconut-shell filled with water served for a looking-glass, fish-scales or shells formed their tweezers, shark's teeth their scissors and bamboo their combs. Fragrant oil served instead of pomatum, and powder and civet could hardly have adorned greater beaux.

Tupaia was particularly pleased and astonished when the doctor showed him the miniature of a handsome and well-dressed young lady. The officers made him understand that it represented the women of England, and, if he went with them, he should always have one to sleep with. That put him into raptures. He hugged the miniature to his chest and kissed it repeatedly (obviously he had seen white men kissing Tahitian girls) and made several other significant gestures to show how happy he would be with so fine a woman.

After dinner the usual shore parties were landed and at sunset Wallis and Clarke also went ashore to take the air. When they landed 'Jonathan' at the end of the point, he was received by a multitude of natives, who seemed delighted at his accounts of his reception in the ship. Scarcely any went to the usual landing-place; nearly all waited to receive Tupaia, and Wallis gave him and some of his friends several presents.

The next day Tupaia came off to the ship with two very handsome young girls. The officers took him and the girls over the *Dolphin* and showed them everything of interest. It was assumed that the girls were Tupaia's sisters; but, when they came down to the gun-room to dine, he gave the officers to understand that he was fulfilling the promise he had given them the day before, and to make up matters with Clarke offered him the choice of either.

Several natives of superior rank, who had treated the woodmen very generously, had come off in their boat. To find what would most please them, Wallis laid down before them a guinea, a crown piece, a Johannes (that handsome gold coin of the Portuguese King John V), a Spanish dollar, a few shillings, some new halfpence and two large nails, making signs that they should take what they liked best. They first seized the nails very eagerly and then a few halfpence, but the gold and silver lay neglected.

On the 12th July Robertson landed for the second time and walked from the river to the foot of Skirmish Hill, where he saw several well-built houses with large pillars in each corner, and one, two or three in the middle, supporting a neat, well-thatched roof. Several had small partitions but he saw no furniture except drinking coconut shells and calabashes, a few wooden trays and many kinds of mats.

Close by the houses were set up several images rudely carved out of tree-trunks. One represented five human figures on top of each other. The lowest was a man; on his head stood an equally large woman; on her head was another man, smaller than the one below; and on his head another woman of about his own size. On top of them all was a great powerful fellow with all his parts proportionate. The other images had two, three or four figures, but the uppermost was always the largest and a man. Robertson said that the natives, while scarcely skilled carvers, imitated some aspects of Nature so exactly that no man could mistake the sex they intended to represent.

The master kept looking at the figures until some natives started to gather round. He began to handle the figures, looking gravely to see how the natives would react. But they merely smiled and said nothing. He then led one of them up to an image but could not persuade him to touch it. Robertson pushed at it with his broad-sword, but still they kept smiling to each other. Then he chipped a small piece off one of the wooden men with his sword, whereupon the natives turned round and walked off, but seemed not at all angry. Their behaviour made him suppose that they did not set up these images to worship them but rather to commemorate deceased members of their families.

The figures were, in fact, the *Ti'i-potua-ra'au* – Back-to-back-wood-fetchers – carved from large logs in the national *marai*, dedicated to spirits and erected with pomp in the presence of the king and queen whenever a general restriction of food on land and sea had to be proclaimed. Sickness, misfortune and even death were said to befall those who disregarded these restrictions, and few ever ventured to do so. When the restrictions were raised the *ti'i* were taken down and put away for future use, and the spirits abandoned them until invoked again.

There were also other images. As a child became the head of his family, the boundaries of his land were newly marked with crude figures. If the new-born infant was only of the rank of a gentleman, little flags were set up in different parts of the boundary. To these emblems, whether figures or flags, all persons of inferior rank had to uncover as they passed, whether by day or night; should this sign of respect be omitted the child's mother flew to the shark's tooth and cut herself, and the offender had to make his peace-offering with the plantain-stalk. If he also refused to do this, the father and mother would tear the clothes from his back and drub him well into the bargain. This might lead to the arming of friends and relations on both sides, sometimes with fatal consequences; but people seldom or never fought because of any personal quarrel. Questions at issue were referred to a bystander, and the party whom he declared to be in the wrong would submit and make the other a peace-offering, which was never refused.

There were also enormous images marking the boundaries of the royal lands, to which all persons uncovered, lowering any burden from their shoulders. Here there were no special penalties, as anyone neglecting the proper procedure was deemed to be insane.

As Robertson returned to the watering-place he met some men with sugar-cane in their hands, and bought a piece for a small nail. He found it not nearly so sweet as the cane of the West Indies.

The gunner had obtained a fine roast pig from Hau, who brought it from his house wrapped in green plantain leaves. Robertson ate some of it with Harrison, the old man and some midshipmen. It was as well cooked and clean as any pig he ever saw; Leadenhall Market in London – then the meat market – could have produced none better.

Pigs prepared for eating were either drowned or, more usually, strangled. If it was a large one the natives put two or three turns of strong cord about its neck and with a stick, twisted till the breath was stopped, stuffing the nostrils and fundament with grass so that the animal died quickly, and also perhaps because with many primitives the soul of an animal was thought to escape through these parts. Having wetted the carcase all over and wrapped it in dry leaves or grass, they singed off the hair, scraping it with sticks, coconut shells and rough stones till the skin was perfectly clean. Then, opening the belly with a split bamboo, they took out the entrails and congealed blood, mixed them with some of the internal fat and heaped them into coconut shells; these they covered with hot stones to make a kind of black pudding, an appetiser while the pig was baking in a pit. The pit was some six inches deep and two or three yards in circumference, the bottom well paved with large pebble-stones; it was there permanently in the established cook-house – a small, shed-like building. In it was kindled a fire made of dry wood, leaves and coconut husks, which generated a terrific heat. When the stones were hot enough, the natives took out the embers and raked up the ashes on every side, covering the stones with a layer of green coconut leaves. The pig, surrounded with breadfruit, yams and *taro*, was covered thickly with plantain leaves, hot embers and grass, and the earth dug out was heaped upon it till it was ready. If the animal was large they split it, and a pig of moderate size took at least two hours to bake. The leaves were placed so carefully that not a particle of earth reached the food, and the meat was tender and juicy.

The Tahitians liked their food well cooked, except for fish, which they usually preferred raw. Small fish might, however, be baked in breadfruit leaves, large ones in plaited coconut leaves. Bonito, a red-fleshed fish, was generally eaten raw with sea water. Cookery was a matter of baking or broiling on the open fire. The Tahitians, having no knives, used shells and pieces of bamboo, with which they carved very dexterously, always cutting away from themselves.

Bamboo grew in abundance on the hills, the clumps sometimes rising to a height of sixty feet. The natives used segments of the fully-grown bamboo as receptacles for their oil, water and other liquids. Bamboo also made good fencing, and split fine it served for carving-knives. It was used also for fishing-rods, for hooking down breadfruit, for quivers, arrows, flutes and many other things.

To protect their food from the rats which swarmed everywhere the natives hung it up in baskets from the beams of their houses or on the boughs of trees.

★ ★ ★

On the 13th July after dinner the usual parties went ashore, and 'Jonathan' came aboard with a present of two excellent roast pigs and some fruit. The officers asked about the two girls, and he made signs that they were crying ashore and could not get away from their friends; but if, he added, the two gentlemen with whom they were most friendly would go ashore and sleep with them there, the girls would be very happy. But as the captain had ordered that no boat should be away from the ship after sunset, the swains in question were unwilling to risk a whole night ashore for fear of accidents. In the light of Polynesian etiquette there was probably little risk involved. Had the two officers felt able to accept the invitation, it would no doubt sooner or later have afforded them an unforgettable experience, a warm, dark night illumined only by the glow-worms in the bushes, steep mountains blocking out vast areas of the starlit sky, and the chirping of the crickets providing an *obbligato* to the sighs of love.

But at sunset, when Tupaia's canoe came for him he had, much to his disappointment, to return ashore alone.

* * *

Heavy rain fell all that night, and at sunrise the natives were at work cutting through the beach to let the river run into the lagoon abreast of the *Dolphin*. They were concerned to prevent flooding, for the beach was at a higher level than the low grounds behind it.

Tahiti is intersected by narrow valleys and these collect innumerable streams from the hills, some of them falling in dramatically beautiful cascades, filling the rivers that meander through the valleys to the salt-water lagoons. The streams, swelling into torrents during the heavy rains, loosen rocks and trees and carry them down into the valleys, where they sometimes cause much damage.

Perhaps that is why the Tahitians were animists, attributing everything to the procreative power, convinced that what at first was made by the gods then dissolved and dropped away, other things being created in their places. The whole system of nature, they held, kept constantly changing, some things dying and some being born every day, the rivers running to the sea, the trees rotting, the rocks falling from the mountains. All of this had gone on from the beginning of the world, yet nothing disappeared without something else taking its place.

Heavy rain fell all day, so no boats went ashore at first; but Tupaia and Hau came off in a canoe, each bringing a roasting pig. The old man paid 'Jonathan' much respect and was clearly ready to do whatever he wished. Furneaux and Robertson rigged Tupaia out with a complete set of clothes (he was about five feet nine) and derived much entertainment from showing him how to put the garments on, especially the breeches, which puzzled him most of all. But when he found how to wear them he liked them better than anything else except the shoes, which pleased him beyond measure and he walked up and down the quarter-deck in highest spirits.

After dinner he went ashore in a ship's boat, wearing his English dress and exceedingly happy. When the barge landed him, he called to some natives to carry him for fear of wetting his shoes. It was shoal-water where the boats landed, and the officers were always carried ashore. On getting to the river he made two of his servants carry him across. Previously he had always waded through without ceremony. On the far bank he delighted in showing himself to his people, who crowded round him.

That was the last the *Dolphin's* company was to see of their friend 'Jonathan'. Purea probably ordered him back into the island lest her lover should leave Tahiti with the white men. Indeed, a couple of years later, at the nadir of his fortunes – Purea had then another young lover, the second of three who are definitely known – Tupaia accompanied Captain Cook on his first voyage in the Pacific. After visiting New Zealand – where he was able to converse with the Maoris to the extent of being able to instruct them in the origins of their religion and was listened to most attentively – and the east coast of Australia, where he took part in the famous landing at Botany Bay, he died at Batavia in the Dutch East Indies, where many of Cook's men perished from the extreme unhealthiness of the place.

Cook's ship was known to the Maoris as 'Tupaia's ship', and the white men were considered to be goblins, presumably in his service. Undoubtedly Tupaia's death was a severe loss to the world. But for it we might have had valuable information regarding the *Arioi*

Society, for Sir Joseph Banks expected to derive much profit and entertainment from his conversation and proposed to support him, saying that it would cost no more than it did his neighbours to keep lions and tigers. Tupaia, moreover, was not without influence on the exploration of the Pacific. With the assistance of Pickersgill he drew for Cook a map of the Pacific (now in the British Museum) on which he recorded many of the island groups, some of which he had visited by canoe.

From the viewpoint of Europeans Tupaia is probably the most important of the Polynesians, although he has received little recognition. In this respect he shares the fate of a significant English character of the Pacific, the *Bounty* mutineer, James Morrison.

CHAPTER XV

★

TAHITIAN QUEEN

PUREA had probably no intention, in any case, of letting 'Jonathan' steal all the limelight. He had perhaps gone rather too far in assuming English dress, in which in due course he welcomed Captain Cook. She was touchy on that point: for she told Captain Cook and Joseph Banks that she had beaten and sent away her next lover – a handsome young fellow – because he had stolen English clothes. Yet she had declared her intention to spend the night with Banks in his tent; and English artists and versifiers of the day made merry over the rumours which reached Britain of the amours of the young scientist and the Tahitian Queen. There was a story (supported it seemed by the official account of the voyage) that after a night of love the amorous Queen had removed Banks's clothes:

> 'Rise Oberea, rise my Queen,' you said,
> 'Some thief has stol'n my breeches from my head.'

This was rather unfair, as everything was stolen but his breeches.

Be that as it may, Harrison came on board the *Dolphin* in the afternoon of the 11th July, accompanied by a person, described by Wallis as a tall woman about forty-five, of most majestic bearing. The gunner said that she had only recently come into this part of the island and that, seeing much respect paid her, he gave her some presents and was invited to her house, which he said incorrectly was about two miles up the valley. She gave him gifts in return and expressed a wish to go on board the ship. He thought it right that her wish should be gratified.

Wallis found Purea an easy guest. In his living-cabin he threw over her a large blue mantle reaching from her shoulders to her feet and gave her a looking-glass, beads and other trifles which she accepted gracefully and with obvious pleasure, behaving all the time she was aboard the frigate with the easy freedom of conscious superiority and the habit of command. She realised that he had been ill and pointed to the shore. Understanding that she meant he should go there to complete his recovery, he signified that he would do so the following morning.

When she was ready to return ashore he ordered the gunner to accompany her, and Harrison attended her to her residence, which he described as 'a prodigious large house', full of guards and servants.

The captain went on shore next morning (for the first time, by his own account, but this is not strictly correct) and 'my princess' (as she was called in the published story of his voyage although not in his manuscript journal) soon came to him at the watering-place, followed by her attendants. Seeing that his illness had left him very weak, she ordered the servants to carry him and the other invalids across the river and all the way to her house. The captain's guard – marines in high sugar-loaf caps and scarlet tunics – followed with bayonets fixed, the sergeant of marines carrying his halberd, and the officers wearing blue frock-coats and gold-laced tricorne hats. Purea held a coconut leaf, the symbol of regal authority in Tahiti. The natives were dense about them as they passed beneath the fruit trees, but at a wave of the hand or a word from the Queen they withdrew and left a free passage for the distinguished throng.

On the way Wallis noticed several walled-in places enclosing little sheds; outside the walls were figures of men, women, pigs and dogs crudely carved on posts driven into the ground. He was told that wherever the ship's parties had been, they had seen similar places. From time to time people had been seen to enter these areas with slow step and dejected face, from which it was supposed that the enclosures were repositories of the dead.

The posts or upright carved planks were signs that various families might worship at that particular *marai*, and the dejected-looking men were the priests of the *marai*, assuming a properly suitable expression in their approach to the gods. Wallis said later that he found not the least trace of religious worship among the natives, although they were probably among the most religious of all Polynesians. In

Tahiti, as the worship of Oro increased, the people used to cry –
'Bowed down, forsooth! Crushed will be Tahiti before the *marai!*'
The temples were cleaned at stated intervals by the chiefs and priests,
weeding from west to east (could it be because the Polynesians
came from the west?) amid solemnity and restrictions. These inland
marai, however, were probably those of the commoners. None were
buried in the *marai* except those offered in sacrifice, those slain in
battle and the children of chiefs which had been strangled at birth.

As the party neared the *Arioi* house, Agitation – thought to be
Purea's palace – many men and women came out to meet her.
Indicating that they were relations, she presented them to the captain
and, taking hold of his hand, made them kiss it. Apparently the
officers had been kissing her hand. Kissing is unnatural to Polynesians,
their intimate salutation being to rub noses or rather to sniff cheeks,
drawing in each other's breath and sometimes almost suffocating
each other in their fervour. Their breath was perfectly free from
taint, and they were scrupulously clean, so that one might be
among a vast crowd without suffering the least inconvenience on
that account, which was more than could be said then for most
Europeans. Their constant bathing prevented any disagreeable smell
from perspiration, and their mouths and teeth, being washed at
every meal, preserved their teeth white and their breath sweet.
The Tahitians wondered that Europeans could express affection by
wetting one another's faces with their lips.

The enormous, open-sided and open-ended house, as specified by
Wallis – everyone estimated it differently – was 327 feet long and
42 feet broad, having a peaked roof, thatched with palm leaves,
raised on thirty-nine wooden posts on each side, with fourteen pillars
down the middle each thirty feet high. Beneath the thatch were
reeds of which the fences were made; they lay under the thatch and
supported it. These reeds grew thick on the mountains and were
sometimes burned to clear the ground. They were probably what
Robertson had mistaken for good pasture and places dug up for
planting on first sighting Great-Tahiti-of-the-Golden-Haze. The
thatch itself was made of the pandanus palm, the leaves overlapping
each other and attached to the reeds with the stem of a coconut leaf,

a sharpened pig's rib serving as the thatcher's needle. Beneath the eaves was a low wooden fence to keep out animals, and round about grew coconut palms, plantains and breadfruit trees. In the background were the mountain-tops which marked the entrance to the valley.

As soon as the party entered the house the Queen made them sit down on mats spread on the floor. There was dried grass beneath the mats. The Tahitians as yet had no fleas, for which pest they were indebted later to the importation of cats.

Calling four young girls, Purea assisted them to remove Wallis's buckled shoes, pull down his white stockings and take off his coat, then directed them to chafe his skin gently with their hands. The same was done for Clarke and the purser, but not for those who were well. This pleasant and beneficial massage of the whole body, which involves some muscular tweaking, given by the young women, is a custom widespread among all Polynesians. It is designed to relax muscles, perhaps fatigued after a long journey, and usually lulls the patient to sleep. Tahitian women also gave it to their men after they had been drinking *kava*. The *kava* could bring amorous dreams, and a sudden awakening could dispel pleasant illusions. So no noise must be made and not even the cocks were allowed to crow. The women waited, massaging the man's limbs until he awakened, when their ideal scenes of bliss were realised.

Afterwards the couple might bathe in some stream or pool, then attend the district evening dance, and later repeat the round of connubial pleasure. Charles Stoddard, an American writer of the end of the last century, said: 'The crowning luxury of savage life is the multitudinous bondsman who anticipates your every wish, and makes you blush at your own poverty of invention by his suggestions unimagined joys. Mats – broad, sweet, and clean – lay under foot, of and served our purpose better than Persian carpets. . . . Wherever we lay, pillows were mysteriously slipped under our heads, and the willingest hands in the world began an involuntary performance of the *lomi-lomi*. Let me not think upon the *lomi-lomi*, for there is none of it within reach; but I may say of it that, before the skilful and magnetic hands of the manipulator are folded, every nerve in the body is seized with an intense little spasm of recognition, and dies happy. A dreamless sleep succeeds, and this is followed by an awakening into new life, full of proud possibilities.'

Polynesians can even massage away a headache. Their massage is remarkably effective in dealing with sprains and wrenched muscles, in which highly skilled branch it is practised by experts. These are usually men of high rank, who in applying it anoint the body with coconut oil treated with healing herbs. The rapidity of their cures is often surprising, sometimes a matter of only a few hours. A variant of the treatment – the *tui-tui* – is a gentle, rhythmic drumming on the bare flesh with the lower side of both fists, applied by the young girls who are liable to continue their *lomi-lomi* so long that one will awaken to find them fallen forward asleep across one's legs.

The doctor, who was feeling the heat and also, perhaps, that his professional province was being invaded by sirens, now took off his wig to cool himself. A sudden exclamation drew attention to his action, and in a moment every eye was fixed on the prodigy and every operation suspended. For some time the whole assembly remained motionless in silent astonishment, which, as Wallis said, could not have been expressed more strongly if it had been discovered that his friend's limbs were screwed on to the trunk. Presently the young women resumed their treatment and after about half an hour dressed their patients, not unnaturally a little clumsily. Already the patients felt much better.

It should perhaps be explained that the preparation of Tahitian *kava*, a shrub of the pepper tribe (the root looks much like an ash root) was quite different to that in most of the other Pacific islands, where the root was sun dried and used merely in a ceremonial drink. In Tahiti the green root was used after being chewed by the women, who were careful to exclude saliva as much as possible, and some of the chewed stem and broken green leaves added to green coconut milk. A quarter of a pint was quite enough to drink at a time. This explanation is necessary, otherwise its qualities as an intoxicant and aphrodisiac will certainly be denied. I myself have drunk quantities of ceremonial *kava*, and am satisfied that the evidence on this subject is overwhelming and conclusive.

Purea now caused some bales of bark cloth to be brought out and with these she clothed Wallis, his officers and men in Tahitian fashion. Wallis sought at first to decline the favour for himself, but, being unwilling not to seem gratified with what was intended to please him, ultimately submitted, which must have pleased the marines.

Next she ordered a very large sow in farrow to be taken to the boat, and accompanied her guests to the landing-place, telling her people to carry the captain. As he preferred to walk, she took him by the arm, wearing his Tahitian dress, and whenever they came to a patch of water or mud, lifted him over it as if he had been a child.

The following morning Wallis sent the gunner to her with six hatchets, six billhooks and other things. Harrison found her in her house, giving an entertainment to about a thousand people. The dishes were brought to her by the servants who prepared them. Purea distributed the food in coconut shells with her own hands to the guests, seated in rows around the house. She then sat down on a pile of mats and two women, one on each side of her, fed her, placing the food in her mouth.

When she saw the gunner she ordered food for him. He was uncertain what it was, but supposed it to be fowl shredded small, with 'apples' cut among it, and seasoned with salt water. However, it 'tasted very well'. (The Tahitians used sea water as sauce, stored in long, wide sections of bamboo.) On festive occasions in Polynesia foods are distributed which are never seen at ordinary times.

After the establishment of these friendly relations provisions became much more plentiful. But although pigs and fowls were brought every day, the gunner still had to pay more for them than at first, the trade having been spoiled by the nails which the seamen and marines had stolen and given to the girls. 'Yet everything was as cheap as dirt,' noted the captain in his manuscript journal. He ordered that every man should be searched before he went on shore and that no woman should be allowed to cross the river.

It is difficult to determine how much Wallis knew of what was going on with the girls, for he seems to have anticipated Nelson with his useful blind eye. He probably had no alternative, situated as he was by the shore of an almost inconceivably remote and previously undiscovered island in an almost unknown ocean, and faced, unless he handled his men with tact, with the possibility of mutiny. He was not a man to look for trouble, and allowance must be made for his sickness.

When unable to get at the nails brought for trade, the men stole iron and drew nails from different parts of the *Dolphin*, particularly those fastening the cleats (used for belaying the ropes which manipulated the sails) to the ship's side.

This practice, like most currency inflations, wrought a double mischief: damage to the ship, and a considerable rise at market. When the gunner offered small nails for medium-sized pigs, the natives refused and, producing large spikes, intimated that they expected nails of the same size. Eventually Wallis instituted a searching inquiry into this state of affairs. A large reward was offered for information against the culprits, but none was obtained. He said that he was mortified at this, but still more so by a fraud practised by some of his men.

When no nails were to be procured, men would steal lead and cut it up into the shape of nails. Many Tahitians thus swindled brought these leaden spikes to the gunner, requesting him to exchange them for iron ones. Obviously Harrison could not comply with the request, and from that time the market was very badly supplied. The natives refused to sell provisions at the usual price and made signs for large nails. It was found that all the belaying-cleats had been ripped off and scarcely a hammock-nail was left. Wallis now ordered all hands on deck and told them that until the thieves were discovered, not a man should go on shore. This produced no effect except that Corporal Proctor again behaved mutinously, for which he was instantly flogged.

In the edited record of his voyage Wallis said that he often wondered why the *Dolphin* was in danger of being pulled to pieces, for the sake of the iron and nails which held her together. He puzzled himself to account for it, for the whole ship's company had as much fresh food as they could eat daily. He said that his health was very bad at Tahiti and he was largely confined to his bed, so his account of the place and transactions there was necessarily much less full and accurate than he might otherwise have made it. There are serious discrepancies in the dates of various occurrences as given by Wallis and Robertson. By Wallis's admission, a lot was kept from him.

He had busied himself playing with nails and coins with natives when the two 'Mustic' girls were brought aboard; and this was the episode which he reported to the Admiralty; not that naval officers of the period seemed frightened of what they reported to the Admiralty. Their recorded thoughts are often astonishing; for example, Cook's comments on the happy condition of the Australian blacks as compared to Europeans. They were dealing with men of the world, and theirs was a less hypocritical era than those which followed. Nails and coins: curiously symbolical, perhaps. He had heard the promise made to Clarke. Did he know nothing of the sequel? Or might the blind eye have come into operation? In any case, some sexual licence was natural and necessary for the avoidance of sadism, very apparent in parts of Cook's long voyage a couple of years later.

While his men were on shore, said Wallis, several young women crossed the river, not averse to granting personal favours but knowing their value too well not to stipulate for a consideration. The fathers and brothers, who conducted them to the far bank of the river, would show a stick of the size of the nail which was the girl's price. They seemed fully conscious of the value of beauty, and the size of the nail invariably bore a proper relation to the lady's charms. If the white men agreed, she was sent over to them, for they did not allow the Tahitian men to cross the river. This traffic went on for some time before the officers discovered it, for, while some of the seamen and marines straggled a little way to receive the girl, others kept a look-out. Wallis said that, when he was enlightened, he no longer wondered that the *Dolphin* was in danger of being pulled to pieces.

Later the Tahitians accused Europeans of using things of which the white men knew them to be fond to tempt them to commit acts of which in their innocence they were ashamed. If, for example, they could secure iron at the expense of their virtue or if they could steal it, they would do so. They said that Englishmen were ashamed of nothing, and had led them to public acts of indecency never before practised among themselves. From their experience with the men of the *Dolphin* they undoubtedly derived the belief that open, public and unabashed fornication was the white man's custom; was, in fact, his mode of greeting members of the opposite sex at sight. The experiences of subsequent navigators, particularly of Bougainville and Cook, whose voyages are amusing to read in this respect, show that they, for their part, believed the converse, namely that such was the custom of the Tahitians. Hence from Bougainville's voyage, about ten months later, the learned world of France found confirmation of Rousseau's theories regarding free love among men living in a natural state uncorrupted by society. The *Arioi* Society, of course, was based on a theory much more complicated: the psychology of war.

The Polynesian's idea of life in Europe is often rather staggering to the white man who can get at it. The Polynesian girl, for instance, is apt to think that all European girls sell their favours. She regards amused protests as mere conventional lying designed to uphold racial prestige, and assures one earnestly that it is very shameful and that these things should be done only for love, as with her.

The price demanded for the girls, Wallis considered, was not great, but it was one which his men were not always in a position to pay.

Hau made himself very useful, keeping the guard alert and soon bringing back stragglers, at least so Wallis was told. The Tahitians sometimes pilfered, but, by holding the threat of a gun over their heads, he made them bring back what was stolen. One day a native crossed the river unseen and stole a hatchet. Harrison, missing it, made the old man understand and got his party ready as if to go into the woods after the thief. Hau signed that he would save him the trouble, and quickly returned with the hatchet. The gunner insisted that the thief should be handed over. Very reluctantly Hau complied. When the man was brought along, Harrison recognised him as an old offender and sent him as a prisoner off to the *Dolphin*. Wallis wished only to frighten him and, after entreaty and intercession, set him free again. The Tahitians were astonished and overjoyed, receiving him with acclamations and carrying him off into the woods. The next day the man brought the gunner a quantity of breadfruit and a large roast pig as a peace offering.

The day after Wallis had sent his presents to Purea there was heavy rain, and the Tahitians were scarcely stirring out of their houses. While Harrison was on shore, an old woman came to the far bank of the river and cried for a long time. Having attracted his attention, she sent a young man across the river with a large plantain branch. He made a long speech and laid the bough at the gunner's feet; then went back and brought over the old woman and made another man carry across two large pigs. The old woman looked round upon Harrison and the guard, fixing her eyes sometimes upon one and sometimes on another, then began to cry again. The tears poured down her cheeks, which shocked the gunner who did not know the meaning of her sorrow. The young man who had brought her made a second speech, but her distress was still a mystery. At length she made Harrison understand that her husband and three of her sons had been killed by the *Bowis*, as the Tahitians called the big guns, representing no doubt the explosion and barking of the cannon.

Two years later Joseph Banks wrote: 'How the *Dolphin's* men, who were here much about this time, came to find so great plenty of breadfruit upon the trees, is a mystery to me, unless perhaps the season of this fruit alters. As for their having met with a much larger supply of hogs, fowls, etc., than we have done, I can most readily account for that, as we have found by constant experience that these people may be frightened into anything. They have often described to us the terror which the *Dolphin's* guns caused them, and when we ask how many people were killed, they number names upon their fingers, some ten, some twenty, some thirty, and then say *worrow worrow*, the same word as is used for a flock of birds or a shoal of fish. The *Dolphin's* journals often serve to confirm this opinion. "When," they relate, "towards the latter end of our time provisions were scarce, a party of men were sent towards Pari to get hogs, etc., an office which they had not the smallest difficulty in performing, for the people as we went along the shore, drove out their hogs to meet us, and would not allow us to pay anything for them." '

The old woman was so affected that she sank down unable to speak, and the young men – apparently her remaining sons or some very near relations – supported her and took much care of her. Harrison tried to soothe and comfort her. When she recovered she ordered one of the young men to give him the pigs and shook hands with him, but would accept nothing in return although he offered her ten times as much as would have bought the pigs.

Here be it remarked that by custom the relations of a man killed in war sought out his slayer and made him presents. A special set of dancers was hired to perform at his house. In the dance, the daughter or nearest female relative of the dead man took a leading part, verging out from the floor towards the killer and touching him with a wand. He was then adopted by the relations of the deceased, whom he entertained for several days, and was regarded by them in future with affection. Here, again, we find the Polynesian tendency to make things right. The intention behind the custom was no doubt to eliminate the possibility of blood feuds; but 'the children of the glorious princess', of course, knew nothing of it. The old woman was clothed in red cloth, and Hau (according to the gunner) explained that this denoted mourning. But this is improbable for red was a favourite colour of the chiefs.

The next day trade went tolerably well. The gunner brought off four hogs, four pigs, ten fowls, plenty of fruit and some yams, and managed to buy some mother-of-pearl fish-hooks and a few pearls. The weather was fine and pleasant. That afternoon no boats were sent ashore other than the barge, in which the captain and Clarke went to take the air at the end of the point. Here there was a long house, open and airy, with several smaller houses around it, all abandoned by their inhabitants since the ship arrived in Matavai lagoon.

Wallis and Clarke usually walked up and down inside the long house, enjoying the breeze, but unable to bear the heat of the sun until it had nearly set. While they stayed there in the shade, with a guard to attend them, the officers and midshipmen who accompanied them sometimes walked into the woods, where there were several small houses, but never went any considerable distance.

The instant the boat landed, numbers of Tahitians came flocking round, particularly young girls, who seldom failed to carry off a nail from every man of the party. The liking of the girls for nails may be said to be due to their communal spirit. In some islands of the South Seas, in the twentieth century, girls were more apt to prostitute themselves for dynamite than for any other consideration since with dynamite fish can be killed in the shallow lagoons for the benefit of the whole community, and some tribal approval earned.

Wilkinson had seen what Robertson called 'a very handsome little woman' who lived near this long shady house, and had made her several small presents at different times without, however, finding her as kind as the other girls. Today he gave her some large gifts, or so they appeared to her, and she gave him the usual signal – that which had puzzled Robertson – by crooking all her fingers and playing with them. He obeyed by walking after her into the woods.

When they got out of sight of the others, she pointed to a little house and made him understand that there he was to be rewarded for all his presents. But just as he was going in, he saw a strong, well-made man coming towards the hut. The woman looked frightened and called out words which led Wilkinson to suppose that it was her husband. She re-entered the hut and returned to the doorway with a fowl and some fruit; and, when her husband came, she was selling the fowl and Wilkinson was offering double the normal price. But she would not agree, until her husband came.

She talked to him and he began to smile, and tendered the fowl and fruit for what had been offered to his wife. Wilkinson gladly accepted them, and seeing the man appeared to be a carpenter, gave him several nails into the bargain.

The barge returned to the *Dolphin* at sunset, bringing two pigs, eight fowls and several bunches of bananas. Wilkinson was sore at his disappointment, but Robertson told him he had double reason to be happy: that the strong fellow did not catch him and give him a good drubbing, which Wilkinson admitted him well able to do, if he had got hold of him without his sword.

Wallis's guard of marines had relieved one another regularly, and got value, as they expressed it, for their nail, and returned to duty in the shady house. Some of the fellows were so extravagant that they spent two nails. Wilkinson remarked that, 'It was owing to the great variety of goods which came to market.'

At sunrise Wallis sent Furneaux with sixty men and six midshipmen in all the boats down the bay towards Papeete, to look at the country and see what they could get. Furneaux landed with thirty armed men between the point of land behind which the fleet of canoes was seen to enter and the *marai* at Pari, but did not examine either. He ordered all the boats to keep rowing up the lagoon abreast of his party, that he might embark if necessary and also to take in the pigs and other stock as he bought them. He noticed no difference between the country down there and the coast about the river-side; there were a few places walled-in with stones and earth which he supposed were burying grounds; but he paid no further attention to them.

So far were the *marai* from being ordinary burying grounds that only those were buried there who would add to the sacredness of the place. If a little boy chanced to break away from home and go to his father at the *marai* during some great solemnity, the father would say resignedly to the high priest: 'Take this child and slay him for the gods! Behold, the order of the *marai* is disturbed by him, the thread of the prayers to the gods is entangled. He is my son, I begat him, but I must not regret losing him, because he has erred in coming here to the assembly of the gods.' Then the high priest would have the child seized and slain as a sacrifice to the gods and buried near the *marai* to add to its sacredness – as he would his own child.

Furneaux and his party marched several miles back to the ship through attractive country, free from bog, fen or marsh. Scarcely a tree did not bear fruit, and there were pigs, fowls and vegetables in abundance. There was no undergrowth and he saw no mosquitoes. The inhabitants, scattered but numerous, were, however, unwilling

The attack on the *Dolphin*: Amo seated on the canopy. From an engraving in *Hawkesworth's Voyages*.

The fleet of war-canoes which assembled at Pari and was inspected by Captain Cook. Engraved from a painting by W. Hodges.

to part with any of the provisions most wanted but gave Furneaux a few coconuts and plantains and at length sold him nine pigs and a few fowls. Their reluctance – probably only overcome by fear of the white men – was no doubt due to the fact that that part of the island came under the sway of the chief of herculean stature named Tutahaa. This man was hostile to Purea and Amo and within a couple of years (in alliance with Vehiatua of the smaller peninsula) overthrew them, thus paving the way for the rise of the Pomarés and the fall of the Tevas and, incidentally, of Tupaia.

According to a member of Purea's family her downfall was to be attributed to 'outrageous disregard of the courtesies which took the place of international law between great chiefs'. It was further remarked that – 'If a family must be ruined by a woman, perhaps it may as well be ruined thoroughly and brilliantly by a woman who makes it famous.' 'Jonathan' had got wind of this plot and urged Purea to have Tutahaa put to death. She refused, preferring, like most Polynesians, to await the need for action; and Tupaia, seeing the explosion about to take place, fled to the mountains for safety, and Purea and Amo barely escaped to the mountains with their lives; but all this, of course, lay in the future.

* * *

On his way back to the ship Furneaux saw many large canoes drawn up on the beach, and some in course of construction. All the tools being used were made of stone, shells or bone, suggesting that these particular natives had not been engaged in the trading. The Tahitians made their stone tools from a blackish lava obtained in the hills; it had a fine grain and was neither hard nor apt to splinter, so could fairly easily be brought to an edge. But at almost every stroke the adzes required whetting, which wasted an immense amount of time.

For the large canoes many sorts of wood were used. The small canoes were of the hollowed trunk of the breadfruit tree, which is light and spongy and frequently about six feet in girth and twenty to the branches. The purpose of the high sterns – sometimes twenty-four feet high – and heads, and the extreme length of the big canoes,

G

was to facilitate their landing and launching in the surf, in which they were far better than European boats, landing dry where our boats could scarcely land at all.

The war-canoes were built by general levy. The chief issued his orders to his deputies, they to the gentlemen, who called upon their tenants for the meat, cloth, oil and other supplies required by the carpenters sent to do the work. These first examined the hills, then pitched on the proper timbers. The owner of the land where a selected tree was found sent men to cut it down and hew it in the rough, under the carpenters' direction, that it might be easily removed. When the timbers were collected, they were laid under the shed where the canoe was to be built. A feast was then made to engage the favourable assistance of the god. This was most acceptable to the workmen, who celebrated before the tree was cut, again at the outset of the building, and on making fast every course. The war-canoes were six feet deep. When the first strake or bottom was completed, there was a great entertainment, and so it went on until the whole was finished.

The porcine offerings for the war-canoes were brought to the *marai* of the chief in whose district they were built. There the priests strangled the animals and cleaned them, smearing them over with their own blood and placing them on the altar with young plantain trees, to the accompaniment of lengthy prayers. The entrails and guts were cleaned and eaten at the *marai*. Sometimes the pigs were cooked before being offered on the altar, and there left to putrefy or to be eaten by birds which frequented these places. These were, especially, the heron and the woodpecker, birds respected as sacred and never killed. For it was believed that the deity descended in them when he visited the *marai* to inspire the priest and give an answer to their prayers.

Being animists, the Tahitians regarded the trees as living personalities and were at pains to avoid giving them offence. If a tree on being felled discharged much frothy sap and its severed roots did the same, they were supposed to be weeping for each other and the log was abandoned. Normally the tree was cut into the length required for the plank. One end of the section was heated till it began to crack, and it was then split down with wedges of harder wood and the sides were smoothed with small adzes. Six or eight men were sometimes at work upon the same plank, every man having by him a coconut shell filled with water and a flat stone, with which he continually sharpened his adze. The planks were about an inch thick and could be from fifteen to twenty feet long.

To fasten them together, holes were bored with a piece of human bone fixed into a stick. Plaited coconut fibre was passed through the holes and the planks were drawn tight together. The Tahitians prepared their pitch for paying the seams, by wrapping the gum of the breadfruit tree round candle-nuts stuck on skewers of coconut-leaf ribs. When these were lighted, they let the pitch drop into a tray of water and, squeezing out the aqueous particles, spread it on the plank edge and laid coconut husk beaten fine upon it. They then smeared it with the pitch and fitted on the next plank, pressing it powerfully with ropes and levers and securing it in its place with lashings. The seams were caulked with dry rushes, and the whole of the outside of the vessel was paid with gummy juice from the trunk of the breadfruit. If, in burning the breadfruit sap, the carpenters saw that the fire, instead of being all red, burned partly red and partly with a pale flame, they thought it a sign that the canoe would not be inaugurated before war broke out, or that the canoe shed would catch fire.

Considering the magnitude of the work and the beauty of the execution, it was astonishing how, without the use of iron, without rule or compass, with only a stone adze, the leg or arm bone of a man sharpened as chisel, gouge and gimlet, with coral and sand, the Tahitians could carve so neatly and finish so smoothly that the most ingenious European workman could not excel them. To form their planks with such instruments out of the hardest and most solid of woods, and to build vessels capable of carrying three hundred people required a remarkable combination of technique, labour and perseverance.

None of the travelling canoes came near the warship except on the first and second day after her arrival in Matavai lagoon. But three or four times a week a procession of eight or ten of them passed at a distance with streamers flying and smaller canoes attending them, while hundreds of islanders ran abreast of them along the shore. They usually paddled to a point of the reef about four miles to the west of the frigate, where they stayed for an hour and then returned. Those who manned the big canoes were fully dressed while those in the other canoes wore nothing but loin-cloths: those who paddled and steered wore white; those who sat upon the awning and under it, white and red; two men mounted on the double prows of each of the large vessels were dressed in red only. They constantly opened and folded up pieces of white, red and spotted cloth. The white men sometimes went out in their boats to watch them.

What they were witnessing was probably a mixture of two ceremonies. In suing for peace, a man called a 'Messenger-flying-for-Peace' was sent forth in a 'sacred canoe'; the 'sacred canoes', like the war-canoes, being built by general levy.

In one hand the man carried a Bird-of-Truce – a bunch of red feathers and a small red flag fixed across a staff in the form of the letter T. In the other hand was a sheet of *tapa*, one side white and the other red, called a Pledge-of-Peace. If the enemy were not ready for peace they tore the Bird-of-Truce in two and threw it into the sea, signifying a determination to fight to the bitter end. Otherwise, they too presented a Pledge-of-Peace, and both sheets of *tapa* were fastened together amid invocations that curses might fall upon those who dared to rend the alliance. This was then confirmed with a Wreath-of-Peace, made of *maire* ferns – the fern used at childbirth – interwoven by both parties, and the exchange of a couple of young dogs. The essentially irrational character of war can clearly be seen running through all the ceremonial, former enemies become allies, dogs and the link with childbirth.

The second part of the ceremony appears to have been that used for the resanctification of a desecrated land, when it had been trampled down by the enemy, its gods and temples profaned, and concluding with a performance called Sending-off-the-canoe-bearing-away-sins, a sort of marine scapegoat.

The canoe was fitted with mat sails, pennants and a long steering handle attached to the stern; it was manned with images made of plaited coconut leaves and dressed in loin-cloths, capes and turbans, with cloth masks for faces, and holding paddles on each side alternately. Abundant food was placed round the images, with presents for the gods of the ocean. The priests drew the canoe out to the edge of the reef facing the open sea, then the high priest, addressing the effigies, would have said in this district, according to the formula:

'Paddle this canoe past Short-border, Border-receding, Border-advancing, and onwards to Trackless-ocean. The sins of the people will be cleansed in Trackless-ocean; the pollution of the land will be cleansed in Trackless-ocean.

'When the gods hover over the ocean and inquire, "From whence is the canoe?" say, "It is from Tahiti." "From what place in Tahiti?" "From Ha'apape; the mountain above is Orohena; the assembly ground is Vale-of-visions; the river is Hollow-waterbed; the point outside is Uporu; the *marai* are Blooming-hibiscus and House-of-beds; its queen is Purea. It is a canoe bearing away sins – cast it into Vortex-ocean." '

Ha'apape included the Matavai district.

Then, setting the canoe before the wind, the high priest would have said as it sailed away:

'Behold the arriving of the gods! There comes Tane; there comes Low-cry-that-awakens; there comes the Lord; there comes Source-of-Armies; there comes Taaroa, father of the gods; there comes Oro, slayer of men, and his daughter Axe-with-eyes, with her waiting maids.

'And behold the arrival of the gods! Arrived to accept, arrived to give power, arrived to save.

'May your people here live, may your shadows (priests) live.'

The smaller, outrigger canoes, hollowed out of a single tree and carrying from two to six men, were used mainly for fishing, and these were the sort that were continually upon the reef.

Others of different sizes constructed of planks sewn together, held from ten to forty men. Single canoes had one mast, double ones had two. The mast was fixed with shrouds and stays. The sails were made of matting, long and narrow, and had a kind of sprit laced up and down the after-leech, reaching one-third higher than the mast-head, forming a bow from the height of the mast upwards and keeping the weather-leech of the sail tight from the mast-head to the sprit-end, to which was usually fastened a long pennant made of feathers.

As the Tahitians had no method of reducing their sail at the head, being only able to cast it off at the foot and roll up a part, they were driven to extremities when overtaken by bad weather and were frequently dismasted, overset, or blown off the coast and heard of no more. When a squall came on, they luffed the head of the canoe to it; if she was likely to fall off, they jumped overboard and held her head to windward till the gust of wind was passed. When overset, their first care was to lash everything fast and tow the canoe round with the mast-head to windward. Having a line fastened to the sprit-end, they got all hands on the float of the outrigger, which was as long as the canoe. Then, hauling the head of the sail out of the water, they swung off with their whole weight and, the wind getting under the sail, righted the canoe. Two or three in the water continued to hold her head to the wind, and when the canoe was clear proceeded on their voyage. This accident frequently happened on returning from fishing; and, so little danger did they apprehend from being thus overset four or five miles from land, that they never thought of assisting each other. Nor did those who were in the water call for help, though they might lose so much ground as to have to run down to Moorea or Raiatea.

With these craft, the *Dolphin's* people noted, the natives sailed far out of sight of land to bring home plantains, bananas and yams.

CHAPTER XVI

*

THE QUEEN'S MOTHER

THE morning after Furneaux's expedition no boats were sent ashore to trade, but Wallis went to take the air in the long shady house on the point, where numbers of natives assembled and 'the old trade' went on as before. Every man of the captain's guard of amorous marines laid out his nail, and some men spent two nails.

The beautiful woman brought Wilkinson a large pig and her husband brought a large bundle of fruit and wanted to give both. Wilkinson insisted on giving them triple value, and made signs that they should go on board the *Dolphin*. The husband was unwilling – if he was the husband; but, from some words the woman spoke, he may have been a near male relation and so may have regarded Wilkinson as his *taio*. On the other hand he may well have been the non-complaisant type of husband.

The woman pointed to the ship and called out words understood to mean – 'Tomorrow! Tomorrow!' Literally they meant – 'The beginning of the day!'

At sunrise next morning Harrison and his party were sent ashore to trade. Twenty men had liberty to ramble up and down in sight of his guard, but were ordered not to go into the woods under penalty of a severe flogging. For in twos and threes liberty-men had been benefiting by the privilege given them by making a habit of wandering a mile or so into the woods and foregathering with forty or fifty Tahitians. Some would go inland as far as one of any of the young girls chose to take him, perhaps passing a hundred Tahitians, not one of whom attempted to molest him. This friendly behaviour on the part of the natives made some of the officers suppose that they intended treachery.

Shortly after nine o'clock the beautiful woman, accompanied by

199

the man thought to be her husband, and with her father, her mother, and a young girl thought to be her sister, came off in a canoe. The officers showed them over the ship, where the husband examined everything very closely, particularly the chairs, chests and tables. He measured the length and breadth of every joint of the chairs and the gun-room table, and marked his measurements on a piece of line he brought with him, making different knots for the length and breadth. His scrutiny presumably was the origin of the large chests on which Tahitians took to sleeping when fleas became troublesome.

While he and Robertson were thus engaged, Wilkinson and his charmer were trying to get clear of the old man and his wife, while a midshipman took care of the sister and showed her some curious things which pleased her. But the instant the carpenter saw his wife and Wilkinson go into the latter's cabin, he went after them, ostensibly to see what curiosities they had there; a disappointment that cost Wilkinson a suit of clothes for the husband – it would be interesting to know what Purea had to say to that – and a shirt for the wife besides the trouble of showing the inquisitive man everything in his cabin.

The young woman, however, had evidently decided to be co-operative. She slipped out of the cabin and cast loose their canoe, which the wind soon began to carry across the lagoon, and called loudly for her husband. There was nothing for him to do but throw off his clothes and swim after the vessel.

Wilkinson was alarmed, thinking of the huge shark – the shadow of Taaroa's handsome blue shark, caught about a fortnight before – and asked Robertson to send a boat after the canoe, and nobly took hold of the carpenter to prevent him from jumping overboard. And so it came about that Wilkinson got hold of the husband instead of the husband getting hold of Wilkinson. But the 'artful little creature', in Robertson's words, put herself into such a passion that the man twisted himself out of Wilkinson's hands and jumped out of the gun-room port. The moment he was in the water she slipped into Wilkinson's cabin, laid hold of his coat, pulled him in, and 'enjoyed the reward of her art and cunning'.

In about ten minutes the carpenter returned with his canoe and made it fast to the gun-room port and jumped into the gun-room where his wife met him with a few large nails acquired in his absence. He was much pleased, not knowing how the nails were procured and probably thinking them a compensation for having to swim after the canoe, as in a sense they were. The family were then given a few presents each and sent ashore.

Meanwhile the liberty-men had cut quantities of grass along the riverside and brought it to the liberty-tent, where it was made into hay to feed the sheep on the homeward voyage and lasted them as far as Tinian. The following morning, the 18th July, Robertson went ashore for the third time, taking a midshipman and a quarter-master with him, all armed. They proposed to go to the top of one of the hills to get a better view of the country. But they were disappointed. As soon as they were half-way up the hill they observed a signal for all boats to come on board, so had to return without seeing anything of particular interest except two young girls making bark cloth in a little stream: they had a smooth, broad stone on which they laid the bark, then beat it with two pieces of iron-wood. By the time the party got down to the landing-place all the men were in the boats.

The gunner said to Robertson: 'I have waited for you for some time. I am afraid I shall be reprimanded by Mr Clarke, who ordered the signal to be made, and soon afterwards sent the jolly boat to order all hands on board. He said if anyone had strolled away in the woods, I was to let them wait for another opportunity, even if it was you, as he knew no business that you had for going out of the way, any more than he himself does when he goes ashore.'

'If you have done amiss in waiting for me,' Robertson replied, 'I will bear the blame.' They got aboard the ship an hour before the usual time. Robertson inquired the reason for the boats being recalled so soon. The midshipmen of the watch on deck could not tell him; but the gunner was told to report to Clarke immediately. The master sent in word to the captain that he had come aboard, and went down to his cabin. He heard no more until dinner.

Clarke then said, 'I was surprised how you detained the boats from coming off after the signal was made.'

'I was a good way back in the country when I observed it,' replied Robertson, 'and made all the haste to get down that was possible.'

Said Clarke with a sneer, 'I suppose you were disappointed in finding out gold and silver mines?'

'It is very possible that there are mines,' answered the master, 'and I know no reason for there not being such things in this country, as well as in South America under the same parallel. And, by all accounts, the country here has the same appearance as Chile and the Brazils.'

(As a matter of fact, there were no minerals in Tahiti.)

'You might have stayed and looked for gold and silver mines and not kept the boats!' said the first lieutenant.

'I acknowledge the boats ought to have come off on seeing the signal,' replied Robertson, 'but as there was no kind of necessity for them on board, but to disappoint me from finding gold and silver mines, that end was best answered by letting me come on board. For had I been left with the young gentleman and the quartermaster who was along with me, we would have gone as far in search of such trifling things as the light of day would have permitted us to go and return.'

More words passed, and the master said that if the only intention of their voyage was to obtain good eating, they had no need to go further than the market-place. But he supposed it was their duty to discover the produce of the country, for the sake of trade.

Clarke's answer was, 'Damn trade!'

Robertson begged that for the present he would drop the subject, and Clarke retired growling to his cabin.

Wallis was again very ill, and now Furneaux too began to complain. He was popular, and humane to all the ship's company, most of whom were much disheartened at seeing the captain and second lieutenant so ill, and the first beginning to recover. For he, according to Robertson, was heartily hated by all on board. He seemed to take a delight in crossing every officer, except the gunner, who was his favourite.

Furneaux's sickness worried Wallis, as Clarke had obviously

not fully recovered and he himself was extremely weak. To add to his anxieties, he had to punish Corporal Proctor again, with twelve lashes and confinement in irons, for drunkenness and insolence.

Purea had been absent for a day or two, but the Tahitians had made the 'children of the glorious princess' understand that next day she would be with them. She came down to the beach the following morning, and soon many natives, not seen before by Harrison, brought every kind of provisions to the market.

Wallis read the Articles of War to the ship's company, and awarded Proctor another dozen lashes for the same crime as before. He was then released.

Trade was now more brisk than ever. The gunner got fourteen hogs. He sent off word that he would dine ashore with his party, if this was agreeable to the captain. Wallis gave his consent, and most of the liberty-men dined there too; they were given their choice, and only four wished to return to the ship.

While the rest were eating, Midshipman Pickersgill (who was to make at least three voyages to Tahiti) and the sergeant of marines strode a long way into the woods and fell in with a multitude of natives assembled at Agitation, where an entertainment was being prepared for the assembly. Purea was present, dressed in red, which was thought to be mourning.

The two Europeans were afraid, and would have withdrawn without going very near, but several Tahitians came to them and invited them to the feast. They feared to refuse, knowing that they were a long way from the guard and scarcely knew their way back; so they accepted the invitation and sat down with about five hundred natives in the enormous, open-walled house until dinner was ready. The food was prepared at a distance, where there were several huts or cooking-sheds.

When the meal was ready, all the people formed a ring inside the great house and sat down on the floor round the Queen; she was seated on a fine mat with two extremely handsome girls standing by her.

The food was laid down before her by the servants and she then ordered the two girls to distribute it in dishes, which were given to the servants to pass round, beginning with the people of the first rank sitting next to Purea.

The guests maintained a grave demeanour and muttered a few words with their face towards the sun, then threw a small portion out of each dish as an offering to the gods. It is a custom to which even white men living in Samoa conform to this day when drinking *kava* with natives, pouring a little of the liquid from the coconut-shell cup on to the coral floor.

They began to eat very heartily. When the notables had been helped, three dishes of meat, prepared differently, were brought in and set before Purea, who invited Pickersgill and the sergeant to eat with her. They excused themselves and pointed to some fruit just pulled off the trees, preferring this to sharing what seemed to have been cooked for her own eating.

On finding that the two white men were diffident about eating with her, the Queen ordered the two girls to feed her, which they did by turns, washing their hands in bowls of fresh water changed between each mouthful. She ate from the fingers of the girl's right hand, with a good appetite, and when she had finished the two girls seated themselves at a little distance and ate in their turn, attended by a considerable number of other young women. Maids of honour in the Pacific usually have a sort of attendant beauty chorus. Lastly the servants sat and ate at a considerable distance from the guests.

The Tahitians washed before and after the meal, which took a little over an hour. They observed strict silence throughout and conducted the whole with much ease and everyone appeared cheerful and merry. Afterwards Purea stood up and made a speech, then ordered two of her attendants to conduct the Europeans back to the landing-place.

Soon afterwards she came off to the *Dolphin* accompanied by six chiefs in canoes. Wallis was very poorly, so she could not be taken into his cabin. But she brought a present of livestock which provided for all hands for two days, and the captain ordered that she should be given a gift in return.

Her principal attendants ate and drank with the officers in the gun-room, but the Queen would do neither. Women did not eat or drink anything touched by men, although they employed as servants boys and young men who assisted with the cooking and were exempt from the rules of this *tabu*. It was not unusual to find young men of the first families performing these menial duties. Men could eat food touched by women; but if a husband so much as touched his wife's cooking utensils, she had to throw them away and get a fresh set.

Purea was entertained by being shown the officers' curiosities. The chiefs ate heartily, and each drank two glasses of Madeira and a tumbler of water, but would take neither rum nor brandy grog. She and the chiefs were then shown over the ship. In the galley they were interested and amused to watch the roasting of a pig and two fowls, one of the chiefs taking hold of the spit and revolving it three times, and all examined the cook's shining coppers. Then they walked aft to the quarter-deck, where they were shown the geese and turkeys in the coops. One of these geese was to figure in the history of Tahiti, after the *Dolphin's* departure. The officers then pointed to the rigging, which astonished them more than anything else, probably owing to their inability to reduce a sail at the head. Robertson considered them smart, sensible people, especially the Queen who tried to learn the use of most of the things shown her. She was plainly dressed in a red gown with a red and white sash and a white and yellow petticoat. Her undergarment, which Robertson called her shirt, was white. She wore no head-dress; but the sergeant of marines remarked that when he first saw her she had three very large pearls in each ear, which were soon removed.

Wilkinson wrote in his journal: 'I cannot omit mentioning a large house which I saw here, of 376 foot long, 36 foot broad, and 20 foot high. It is ingeniously contrived and I believe has been the habitation of one of their kings. At present it is inhabited by a woman whose power seems to be equal to that of a queen. She came, with some of her attendants, on board, with the sergeant of marines, for whom she has a particular liking, and, by their assistance, we are not likely to eat salt meat while we are here. The above-mentioned house is about half a mile from the beach, standing near the riverside that provides us with water.'

That apparently is the only true record of the position of the guest-house, Agitation.

But Midshipman Ibbot, the one whose hat had been stolen, did not think quite so well of the Queen. In his journal Ibbot said: 'There are two different sorts of people among ym, one having long Black Hair and of a dark copper Colour, in gen'ral Stout, well made & handsome featur'd, & by what I saw of ym, are the poorer sort such as Fisher Men & (which appears to be their chief employment) Canoe Builders; tho' in short I take ym to be in gen'ral lazy and indolent. The most part of them go naked except a Bag where they put their Privities. The other sort have short curly Black Hair, are not so yellow as a Mulatto, all of ym go wh ye Cloath above mentd and are in gen'ral, I dare to say, as tall and stout as the Patagonians.

'Of the women I saw some that were quite white and had a red colour in their Faces: they are in gen'ral very small, but quite handsomely Featur'd. The Men of both sorts all wear their Beards, and one thing very remarkable which I never heard of any people before, that is, Both Men and Women having their backsides Black'd, which is done by pricking it in, and some of the Old Men I have seen wh their Arms, Legs & Bodys Black'd in sev'ral parts.

'Their love of Iron (Nails) is so great that the women (or rather Girls, for they were very young & small) prostitute themselves to any of our People for a Nail, hardly looking upon Knives, Beads, or any toy. Yet I must say yt the Girls wh were of the white sort would admit of any Freedom but the last, which they would not, every one having by what I saw a Man or Husband.

'Pettycoat interest here, as well as in other parts, is the most prevailing, the principal person here about who appear'd to have any authority over the rest being a Woman, whom we stiled the Queen; she was the stoutest woman I ever saw there, & had a very commanding aspect, but not handsome, being upon ye decline. She lived at a House which we call'd the large House . . . and in the whole, allowing for the Materials, is something very clever: there was no partition in it, but all open. They sat upon Mats (as I take it every family by itself) either cross-legged or on small low Stools.

'Their chief food is Pork, Fowls, Fish, Bread-Fruit & a various composition of different Fruits Mixed together. When they eat there is Plantain leaves spread on the ground wheron their victuals is laid, and two Cocoa Nutt shells of Water by every person, in one of which they wash their victuals before they put it in their Mouth, & dip their Fingers in the other before they touch their victuals again. Here the Queen serves it out to her Attendants, herself is fed by two fine young Girls.'

Purea's demeanour was cheerful and merry. Shortly before sunset the captain, wishing to take the air ashore, ordered his barge and the Queen accompanied him with two of her head men, while the other chiefs went in their canoes. Several hundred natives assembled on the shore to receive her. When she landed she made a long speech to them, and not a whisper was heard while she spoke. On ending, she pointed to Wallis and the other officers, signifying that they were the principal people in the ship. She took her leave with a short speech and marched off with a large number of her people.

She and her attendants appeared to be well pleased with their reception aboard, for more stock was obtained that afternoon than on any of the three previous days: forty-eight hogs and pigs, four dozen fowls and a large quantity of fruit.

At sunrise the liberty-men and traders were sent ashore, and the traders were again very successful. The current range of prices was a nine- or seven-inch spike-nail for a hog of fifty or sixty pounds, two four and a half-inch nails for one of thirty to forty pounds, two three and a half-inch for one of ten to twenty pounds, a three and a half- or four and a half-inch for a good roasting pig, a three-inch for a fat fowl. One and three-quarter-inch nails bought fruit and curiosities such as shells and mother-of-pearl fish-hooks.

But, despite this satisfactory state of affairs, the gunner told Robertson that the 'old trade' had increased about a hundred per cent, which made the master wonder how the seamen got the nails. He sent for the carpenter and told him to examine his stock of nails. The carpenter replied that he had, and took care to keep the people from thieving them. Harrison brought off from the shore twenty-seven hogs and pigs, six fowls and some fruit.

The following day after dinner (the date conflicts with that given by Wallis, who antedated the first part of the occurrences, but not the sequel) the traders and waterers had been sent from the ship into the boats alongside, to go ashore. But as the master was ordering the liberty-men into their boat, the carpenter came and told him that every cleat in the ship was drawn. The boatswain at the same time informed him that most of the hammock-nails were drawn, and two-thirds of the men were forced to lie on the deck for want of nails to hang their hammocks to the beams.

Robertson referred in his misplaced journal (mentioned in the Epilogue) to, 'a new sort of trade that they have carried on, or rather the old trade, which in a few days had very near laid the whole of our men flat on the decks. Before this was found out, there was scarce a hammock nail in the whole ship; the men drawed the whole and lay down contentedly on the deck, for the sake of the old trade. Every hammock nail purchased a whole day's diversion'.

The master stopped the liberty-men from entering the boat, called all hands on board and told them that no one should go ashore as a liberty-man until they informed him who drew the nails and cleats, and what use they made of them. None knew anything about drawing the nails and cleats, but all said they knew to what use the nails went.

'It is very surprising,' replied Robertson, 'that you know the use they were put to, but know none of the men!'

Some of the midshipmen then told him that all the liberty-men carried on a trade with the young girls, who had raised their price, for some days past, from a three-inch or three and a half-inch nail to a four and a half-inch; some indeed were so exorbitant as to demand a seven- or nine-inch spike. It was plain proof of the way the large nails went.

Robertson reported to Wallis, who ordered him to stop all liberty until he discovered who had drawn the cleats. The master told the ship's company that none should have liberty to set foot on shore until he was informed. He then ordered off the boats for trading. At

sunset the trading party returned with eight hogs, six fowls and
plenty of fruit.

That evening Robertson heard a loud and continuous murmuring
among the seamen. He slipped forward to see what he could find
out, unseen because of the dark. The galley was full of men cooking
their suppers, and some blaming the others. He found that most of
them were involved. Several said they would rather receive a dozen
lashes than have their liberty stopped. At last they conducted a sort
of trial among themselves, and six were condemned for spoiling the
'old trade', by giving large spike-nails when others had only a
hammock-nail, now become unacceptable to the grasping young
women. But two smart men cleared themselves by asserting that
they had obtained double value for the spikes. This claim to sexual
prowess led to a free fight which forced the master to reveal himself
and restore quiet.

He sent the boats ashore at sunrise, but no liberty-men. At noon
the trading party returned with ten hogs, six fowls and fruit.
Robertson told the traders that they were to go ashore after dinner,
but none should go on liberty unless some who drew the nails were
discovered. At length three concurring witnesses proved that a poor
fellow, one Pinckney, who was flogged some time before for
thieving, had drawn one of the cleats. This man was treated for
venereal disease after the ship left Cape Town on the homeward
voyage, being said to have contracted it there: a point of some
significance in the future history of Tahiti, for men under treatment
had their pay stopped and so might have concealed the disease.

Bougainville's men seem to have been more culpable regarding
responsibility for the introduction of syphilis to the island about ten
months later. The French were blamed by the Tahitians, although
the latter called it the 'British disease', but there is an element of
uncertainty as to who actually was responsible. There had been
twenty venereal patients when the *Dolphin* left Plymouth, all
supposed to have been cured or sent home before she was clear of
the Straits of Magellan.

The unhappy Pinckney was considered suitable as an example.
Robertson told the captain. The charge – quite Cromwellian, if not

quite accurate – against Francis Pinckney was that he 'drew several cleats that were nailed with spike nails and forty-penny (four and a half-inch) ones, and sold them to the natives for mere baubles, which greatly hurted our other trade'. The cleats were those to which the main sheet – the rope at the lower corner of the mainsail – was belayed. After stealing the spikes, the reckless Pinckney had thrown the cleats overboard.

Wallis had the luckless fellow secured and all hands called on deck. After explaining the man's crime, and its complications – which must have caused some secret amusement – he ordered him to be whipped with nettles while he ran the gauntlet three times round the deck.

The 'nettles' consisted of three tarry rope yarns some three feet long, twisted up and knotted at the end. The usual procedure for the punishment of theft was that the man was triced up and given a dozen strokes with the 'Thieves' cat' (a particularly vicious cat-o'-nine-tails), by the boatswain's mate; then forced to walk slowly through a double line of men by the master-at arms and two of the ship's corporals, who kept him moving between the points of three swords, one before and two behind, while he was thrashed on the head, shoulders and back with 'nettles'. Thereafter he was taken to the ship's hospital to be rubbed with brine and cured.

The master placed the men in proper order with a 'nettle' in their hands. Several times he asked Pinckney if any of the rest were involved but continued to receive the answer 'No' which made the men very merciful. But, when ordered on the second round, the victim began to impeach some of them, hoping to be excused himself. Robertson told him it was now too late and sent him on the second round, when he got a good drubbing from his indignant shipmates. This saved him from the third round.

Robertson told the men that, if there were any similar complaints they might rely on a much more severe punishment and none would ever be allowed to go on liberty. They declared they would take greatest care that no such thing happened again; and thus was the ship preserved.

Wallis stated in his official report that he gave no more liberty.

The episode afforded a classic example of the scapegoat and a western analogy to the 'Canoe For Bearing Away Sins'. Here too the gods of the ocean had their offering, having been given the cleats.

* * *

Next morning at sunrise the traders and the now exonerated liberty-men were sent ashore. At eight Purea visited the ship and brought a good present of livestock, and Wallis ordered a gift to be given to her in return. Robertson took her and one of her principal attendants into the great cabin, where the captain ordered breakfast to be pre-pared and invited the Queen and the chief to sit down to tea and bread and butter. She was very merry.

Before he touched the food the chief rose to make a long speech, then, still talking, went to the quarter-gallery – the window stretch-ing across the stern – and looked out towards the sun. At last he sat down at Purea's left hand, took up a piece of soft bread and smelt it, and began to eat heartily. The officers gave him a knife and showed him how to spread the butter, but he, mistaking their meaning, laid the knife down, took up a little of the butter with the nails of his fore-fingers and smelt it, then threw it down on the floor, according to custom before eating, to make his offering to the gods. This put the unsympathetic Clarke out of humour. He snatched the butter away and ordered Wallis's servant to bring clean butter. His behaviour surprised the chief and put him off his food, made even the merry Purea look very grave, and embarrassed the captain. But the gentle-manly Wallis said nothing to 'Old Growl', and gave the Queen a present, which restored her good humour. Yet she neither ate nor drank.

After breakfast Robertson accompanied Purea round the ship between decks. She was highly pleased. He then took her into every cabin of the gun-room and gave her any trinket she seemed to like – a wine-glass, buttons and ear-rings. But she most fancied linen cloth – no doubt as being like finely-woven matting, to which some Polynesians attach much value, so that a fine mat becomes an heir-loom. He also gave her a very good ruffled shirt and showed her how to put it on. That trifling present, as he generously termed it, completely won her heart; he escorted her to the captain's cabin, where he left her in the highest spirits.

Wallis showed her all his curiosities. Purea looked upon him as the English king – an idea which the Spaniards were later to encourage, representing the English as a people who had no settled homes but wandered about living by robbery and violence – and was understood to wish him to sign a peace treaty to settle all differences between her people and his. This may in fact have been suggested by the liberty-men at some of their conferences with the Tahitians. But the captain, being still unwell and suffering moreover from a slight paralytic disorder in his hand, was unable to hold the pen, so excused himself until another occasion. He was not a man to sign treaties lightly.

★ ★ ★

Robertson noted that the Tahitians 'painted', as he called it, all the men's thighs black at the age of sixteen, and soon afterwards painted curious figures on their legs and arms. And the ladies seemed not more than twelve or thirteen when they underwent a similar operation. He supposed that they looked upon themselves as men and women at sixteen and twelve and that this was a sign of puberty. The girls, in fact, generally married at twelve or thirteen, the boys at fifteen or sixteen. Bougainville in due course remarked with Gallic humour that while European women painted their cheeks red, Tahitian women stained their loins and buttocks bright blue. Wallis, at the end of the notes in his manuscript journal, remarked that all men and women had 'their backsides marked black with striking a thing like a comb into their flesh and rubbing it with a paste made up of sutt and oyle (the soot was made of candle-nut) – those who are under twelve are not marked. Some people I saw had their legs marked in chequers. They seemed to be of greater note than the others'. These were the 'Painted Legs', the highest rank of *Arioi*.

The typical design of the tattooing on the buttocks of both men and women consisted of two lines the width of the hand or more running across the loins from hip to hip, meeting on the backbone. On these two lines all the others began and ended, curving or looping downwards, like dark-blue ribbons, ornamented with stars and sprigs: four broad looped lines on each buttock veiled most of the posterior.

When Robertson again went in the captain's cabin, Purea – perhaps having been prompted by the genial Wallis – took it into her head that he was tattooed, so wanted to see his legs, thighs and arms. Rather than disoblige her, he 'showed her all', which much surprised her. She would not believe that it was his skin until she felt it with her hands. Then she wished to see his chest. She was most surprised that it was covered with hair. 'She supposed I was a very strong man and certainly of Age altho not painted.' She began to feel his thighs and legs, to see if they were as strong as they seemed. He flexed his muscles, which made her look hard in his face and call out with admiration 'Oh! Oh! Oh!' She then asked the chief to feel his legs, which the master allowed; the chief was equally astonished.

The two Tahitians then talked at length and Purea took hold of the master to lift him, but he would not let her. She could not understand why she failed and astounded again called out 'Oh! Oh!' The chief signed to Robertson to lift Purea, which he did with one arm, carrying her round the cabin, certainly a remarkable feat of strength, for she may well have weighed two hundred pounds. This pleased her very much.

Robertson suspected from her subsequent behaviour that in this way Tahitian ladies tried out their men before they took them as lovers. Here he was mistaken. He also fancied, according to a note in his misplaced journal, that the Queen was showing signs of becoming interested in some of the gentlemen aboard (presumably himself) and 'seemed inclinable to improve the colour of her family'.

After so much exercise she was hungry. She made signs that she wished to go ashore, and Robertson informed the captain, who desired him to take the barge and see her to her residence, but not to stay there, as he and the lieutenants were ill. The master remarked that it was very surprising that all the principal officers were in such a bad state of health, while all the seamen had thoroughly recovered, except for one poor fellow who seemed to be in a decaying state ever since they left the Straits of Magellan.

★ ★ ★

As Robertson and Purea landed, hundreds of Tahitians were standing on the waterside to receive her. After they were carried over the river she took the master's hand and introduced him to the principal people, and made them shake hands with him and with the midshipman he had with him. He ordered six of the barge-men, armed, to come after them. He, Purea and the midshipman set out side by side for the guest-house, and the principal natives followed.

When in sight of the great house the people came out of it to greet them, and he and the midshipman shook hands with those whom she pointed out. Inside the house she made a long speech. A fine mat .was spread and all three sat down on it. Then she made another speech, the chief people standing round in a ring giving close attention. After this the members of the audience talked to one another with every appearance of satisfaction. It is possible that they were discussing a projected love affair between Purea and Robertson.

Just as the three were about to rise there entered an old, grave-looking woman, richly dressed. On seeing her, Purea made the white men sit down again and the old lady sat facing them on another mat. She and the Queen talked together, then the old woman moved close to the master and felt his legs and thighs and looked at his hairy chest. She, too, called out with surprise, 'Oh! Oh!' The Tahitians' bodies were usually fairly hairless, although their legends tell of hairy men. The old woman shook hands with Robertson and became jovial. She made signs that the two officers should stay and eat. But Robertson, being under orders to return on board, rose and made signs that he could not stay.

But before leaving he walked round the house to measure it with his broadsword; he estimated it to be thirty-six feet wide and not less than three hundred and twenty-one feet long. It was neatly built and the roof was supported in the middle with fourteen large pillars of wood, sixteen inches through, several very neatly carved.

While he was inspecting this palatial structure, an upstanding, brisk young man, of whom Purea took much notice, came up to them. He held out his hand, and Robertson shook it. He wanted to look at the broadsword, but the master was unwilling to hand it over. However, at a sign from Purea he did so, though he kept one of his pistols cocked in his hand.

The young fellow eyed the sword all over and felt its edge, then began to cut capers, typical of Polynesian dancing, with sharp, cutting clubs. It was no doubt a war dance, involving the slashing off of heads – such as the Samoans still dance on ceremonial occasions – and it made Robertson a little uneasy. He held out his hand to get the sword back, but the powerful young man only laughed at him and cut another caper. The master caught hold of his wrist and took the sword, not without some trouble, which made the Tahitian look a little surly. So Robertson gave him a stroke with the flat of the sword then swung round to make a stroke at a plantain tree growing close by. He had the luck to cut it through, which frightened the fellow so much that he promptly marched off, to the amusement of everyone, Purea and the old lady laughing very heartily.

Robertson now re-entered the house and saw three people beating up something which looked like fresh butter – probably fermented breadfruit paste (which was prepared in pits) and fresh breadfruit, which together were pounded into a sort of custard – and several others plucking fruit for dinner. He saw others carrying small pigs and fowls to a place a little way off, where smoke was rising. Then he went to take leave of the Queen and the old lady, whom he understood to be her mother. But they forced him to sit down and Purea cut him out a suit of *tapa* and wished him to throw off his own clothes, but he declined and put it on over his uniform. It was easily made. She cut off about ten feet of the piece of *tapa*, which was about five feet wide, and cut a hole in the middle, through which he put his head; then she tied it round his waist with a sash of much finer cloth. She wanted him to wear a second piece, but he refused and pointed to the midshipman, so she put it on him. It was a compliment to load people with cloth. She made a short speech to the natives, who seemed very happy, and she also gave the master another piece of cloth about sixteen yards long and three feet wide.

As by this time dinner was nearly ready, she insisted that the officers should stay to eat. When she found that Robertson was determined to go, she spoke to the old woman, who took hold of Robertson and tried to detain him. When she found she could not persuade him, she made very plain signs that he should have her daughter to sleep with. When this had not the desired effect, the hospitable old lady pointed out two very handsome young girls to Robertson and the midshipman with the same intention.

Robertson excused himself as best he could and grasped the Queen's and the old lady's hands to take his leave, giving them to understand that he would soon come back from England and sleep with Purea in his arms. This appeared to satisfy them, and the master parted from the old lady, who seemed well pleased. But Purea took hold of his arm and came with him.

Between the guest-house and the watering-place near the beach were several houses, full of the principal people of the island, who had, Robertson supposed, come to see the ship. The Queen made him call at every house, where he shook hands with the old people and joked with the young ones, as did the midshipman. The natives, seeing them both dressed in Tahitian fashion, were cheerful and happy, notwithstanding the deference they all paid to their Queen.

At the last house which they entered were the two prettiest girls Robertson ever saw in Tahiti. One was quite as fair as the average young Englishwoman. Had she been dressed in English fashion, no Englishman, he was convinced, would have thought she belonged elsewhere. He first shook hands with two fine jolly old people, apparently the girls' parents but both decidedly darker than they. They, of course, may have been their parents by adoption since Polynesians go in largely for adoption to compensate for gaps in the family circle. He then shook hands with the girls themselves, who were both fine brisk-spirited women. The fairer of the two, on seeing that Robertson took more notice of her than of the other, began to laugh, and he and she compared skins: hers was rather fairer and whiter than his.

He took so much notice of this girl that he almost forgot 'Her Majesty', who was conversing with the old people. But Purea, looking round and seeing the midshipman deeply engrossed with one young lady and the master enthralled with her fairer sister, was decidedly out of humour. She broke off her conversation with the old folk and said something to the girl to whom Robertson was talking which clearly upset her. Robertson, distressed to see his pretty young friend's discomfiture, took her in his arms to comfort her. Whereupon Purea grabbed his arm and gave the poor girl so furious a look that she was left on the point of fainting dead away.

Poor Robertson, knowing that it was his duty to please the Queen, did what he could to placate her. But she would enter no other house and led him to the side of the boat, where she saw him safely off to his ship.

CHAPTER XVII

*

FAREWELL TO TAHITI

ON THE following day Purea came on board the *Dolphin* bringing as a gift several large pigs for which, as usual, she would accept nothing in return, for she never stooped to barter.

While she was at breakfast in the great cabin, one of her attendants – thought by Wallis (who had been unable to find the least traces of religion in Tahiti) to be a priest – saw Dr Hutchinson fill the tea-pot by turning the cock of an urn which stood on the table. Having watched this attentively, he himself turned the tap and caught some water in his hand and, on being scalded, roared and danced about the cabin with ridiculous expressions of pain and astonishment. The other natives stood staring at him, amazed and slightly terrified. Hutchinson attended to him, but it was some time before he was easy.

Many Tahitians had scars, resulting apparently from severe wounds from stones and clubs, by which it was thought that they had efficient surgeons, as indeed they had in some respects. For their healers were capable even of trepanning, sometimes successfully fitting a piece of young coconut shell into a broken, living skull, as has been proved by examination of ancient skeletons.

While on shore a liberty-man ran a large splinter into his foot and his companions tried to remove it with a penknife. Having caused him much pain, they had to give up. Hau called to a native standing on the other side of the river, who waded across, looked at the foot, went to the beach, and taking up a shell broke it to a point with his teeth. With this instrument he laid open the place and extracted the splinter in a moment. As soon as he had called the other, Hau crossed the river, went a little way into the woods and returned with some gum, which he applied to the wound with a piece of his bark-cloth gown. The wound healed perfectly in two days. Dr Hutchinson procured some of the gum produced by the 'apple' tree, and used it very successfully for treating wounds.

When leaving the ship Purea invited Wallis to accompany her, and he took several officers and midshipmen with him. They went through the woods to the great house, Agitation, where she made them sit down and, taking off the captain's blue, gold-laced hat, she tied to it a tuft of feathers of various colours, such as, he said, he had seen nobody on shore wear but herself. Presumably he was thinking of Amo at the time of the attack on the ship. He considered the effect quite agreeable.

The Polynesians' taste in the arrangement of colours is excellent. Purple feathers from the whistling parakeet were worn by royalty. Red and yellow feathers, when worn by royalty, were thought to liken them to the gods. No doubt Wallis was thought to be god-descended, and, for people with such appreciation of fine manners as the Polynesians, the idea is not illogical, for the terrible relations which were to arise between European and coloured peoples in the nineteenth and twentieth centuries can be ascribed partly to the departure of fine manners.

Purea tied wreaths of plaited hair round her guests' necks and made them understand that both hair and workmanship were her own. She also gave them some curiously wrought mats.

The lines of braided hair – the Tahitians' most valued possession – were usually six or nine hairs thick and thirty or forty feet long. Thinner lines of hairs sometimes measured more than a mile, and a tremendous amount of time was spent by the women in winding them about their living hair in preparation for the dance.

In the cool of the evening Purea accompanied her guests to the beach and had some fruit and a sow big with young put into their boat. Wallis made signs that he would be leaving the island in seven days. She understood and signed that he should stay twenty days, go on a two days' journey into the country, bring back plenty of pigs and poultry and only then leave Tahiti. Wallis repeated his signs that he must go after a week, whereat she sat down on the beach, cried bitterly and was with difficulty pacified.

The gunner next morning sent off twenty hogs and quantities of fruit. The frigate's decks were now crammed with hogs and poultry, of which the captain allowed only the small ones to be killed. He was disappointed to find that neither species could, save with much trouble, be induced to eat anything but fruit, which made it necessary to kill them faster than had been intended. A boar and a sow were brought to England, where Wallis gave them to Mr Stephens, Secretary to the Admiralty. The sow died in farrowing and the breed – the Small White – is now extinct.

On the following day Wallis sent Hau another iron pot by the gunner together with some hatchets, billhooks and cloth. To Purea he sent two turkeys, two geese, three guinea-hens, a cat big with kitten, some china, looking-glasses, glass bottles, shirts, needles, thread, cloth, ribbons, peas, white kidney beans, sixteen sorts of garden seeds, a shovel, knives, scissors, billhooks, two iron pots and a few spoons. In return, Harrison brought off eighteen pigs and some fruit.

Shortly before sunset the captain went ashore with Clarke to the long house on the point. Wilkinson met his young beauty who brought him a fat pig, for which he paid her; but he took no notice of the previously desired signal. He told Robertson that he could not help thinking of the risk the native carpenter ran when she made him jump overboard at the mercy, as he thought, of ravenous sharks. Wallis's guard relieved one another regularly and got value, as it was called, for their nails.

★   ★   ★

Chancing to look that evening at an astronomical almanac, Robertson noticed that there was to be an eclipse of the sun on the 25th July, visible in Mexico and Peru. He therefore calculated that it would be visible here at about seven or eight o'clock the next morning. He told Wallis, who ordered him to fix the reflecting telescope, which had no dark glass; but the master found a dark glass in a small telescope, which he fitted to the largest telescope. Wallis told him to take the barge and observe the eclipse.

That same evening Wallis ordered Gore to take an armed party up the valley by the side of the river the following morning, to examine the soil and produce, trees and plants. When he and his party came to a mountain stream, they were to trace it to its source and look for minerals and ore. They were to make a fire if attacked, as a signal; not that that would have been of much use.

At sunrise Robertson prepared to observe the eclipse with the purser and a midshipman, George Pinnock. But as they were entering the boat, Clarke, up earlier than usual, stopped them.

'I am surprised,' said he, 'that you could take the barge without acquainting me.'

'It is the captain's orders that I should observe an eclipse of the sun which is due to happen shortly. If you stop me now, I must tell the captain, as the eclipse will be over before I get ashore,' replied Robertson.

'I know the captain's orders,' sneered Clarke as he ordered Gore with an armed party to get into the barge, cutter and launch alongside. Robertson, he said, could take the jolly boat if he wanted to look at the sun with an instrument he knew nothing about.

The master thanked him for his civility and ordered up the jolly boat's crew to shift the gear out of the barge. Even then Clarke found ways and means to detain them. Robertson said nothing more but got ashore with the purser and midshipman as fast as possible to the north end of the point. The partial eclipse, which lasted about sixty-nine minutes, had already started.

When it had nearly ended, Robertson told Pinnock to run and tell the captain that it was nearly over. Wallis was coming close along the beach in the barge, accompanied by Clarke.

The midshipman informed Wallis accordingly and Clarke snarled that he supposed the captain would arrive in time enough to see it ended, since it had not yet begun.

But the midshipman assured Wallis that he himself had been watching the eclipse for some time and that Robertson had sent word that, if the captain wanted to see it, he must make haste.

They all saw it, both with the large telescope and the common spy-glass. Wallis was highly satisfied and asked Robertson to be most exact in observing the end of it. The observation was, in fact, a success: the *Dolphin's* officers appear to have been highly efficient, and Captain Cook said later: 'To the credit of Captain Wallis and his officers, the longitude of Royal Bay (Matavai lagoon) was by them settled to within half a degree of the truth.' Nevertheless, more sneers and interference came from Clarke.

Just as the observation ended, Purea arrived with a chief. Robertson gave them a sight of the sun with the dark glass in the telescope, which surprised them very much. The master turned the telescope, without the dark glass in it, to the south-west point of the bay, and made the Queen and chief look through it at some natives about five miles away. Purea started back astonished and, directing her eyes as the shining instrument was pointed, stood some time motionless and silent. She looked through the glass again, then sought the objects in vain with her naked eye. As by turns they reappeared and vanished, her face and gestures expressed wonder and delight.

The chief was equally astonished and wished to have another look at the sun. The master set the telescope, but omitted to put in the dark glass and almost blinded the poor man. Robertson then inserted the dark glass and gazed at the sun, then stared the chief full in the face as if surprised at his not being able to look.

When the telescope had been removed, Wallis invited Purea and several chiefs now with her to go on board the *Dolphin*. Having in mind the security of the party he had sent up the valley, he felt sure that, while the Queen and the principal islanders were known to be in his power, no violence would be attempted against anyone belonging to the ship. He ordered a good dinner, but Purea would neither eat nor drink. On the other hand the chiefs ate heartily of whatever was set before them but would drink nothing but water.

The exploring party consisted of the mate, four midshipmen, the sergeant and twelve marines and twenty-four seamen, all armed; also four men loaded with ammunition and provisions, and four carrying hatchets and other articles for trade. Every man carried his day's allowance of brandy, and the hatchet-men had two small kegs of brandy, to be served out as ordered. Wallis always did things in style.

The explorers collected Hau from his house and followed the

course of the river in two groups, one marching on each side. The valley was of considerable width for the first two miles, with many thatched barn-like houses and walled gardens; it abounded in pigs, poultry and fruit trees. The soil was a rich, blackish loam. It should be remarked that, when Banks and Cook arrived on the scene a couple of years later, there had been, although they did not realise it at first, a war resulting in the overthrow of Purea and Amo. This war had led to a considerable reduction in the number of animals, which had been killed and carried off in great quantities. Even the vast house, Agitation, had been utterly destroyed, and no trace of it was left. This lay in the future; but it explains the shortage of pigs of which Cook and Banks complained, seeming to contradict the account given by the *Dolphin's* people.

Presently the gorge narrowed. As the ground rose abruptly on one side of the river, the men had to march on the other. Where the streams flowed limpidly from the hills, stone-lined channels irrigated plantations of fruit trees and gardens, walled-in with loose-piled rocks. Dark breadfruit and lofty 'apple' trees grew in rows on the slope of the hills; coconut palms and bananas, requiring more moisture, on the flat land. Under the trees, both on the sides and at the foot of the hills, was good grass but no undergrowth. The Tahitians' purpose in planting breadfruit also on the sides of the hills was to ensure a second crop from the uplands. It is possible that the breadfruit supply had been destroyed shortly before Cook's arrival. There had been nearly thirty varieties of the tree, and it seems strange that he should have found a shortage of the fruit. These varieties, bearing leaves that varied between nine inches and two feet, must have come about as a result of selective culture.

In the gardens was growing a herb which had never been brought to the market, and the natives were seen to eat it raw. It tasted like a West Indian spinach, but the leaf was different. The river's windings in the deep valley became innumerable. The hills on each side swelled into wooded mountains; vast crags towered overhead; the going became difficult. After travelling for about four miles along the gorge, the road for the last mile having been very bad, the party sat down to rest and have breakfast, in a very pleasant spot under a large 'apple' tree. Just as they were about to eat and to drink some brandy, a confused sound of many voices and a loud shouting alarmed them; seeing a multitude of men, women and children on the hill above them, they rose hastily and looked to their arms.

Hau motioned to them to sit still and went up to the natives, who became silent when he joined them and soon disappeared. They quickly returned, bringing a large roast pig, cooked breadfruit, yams and other provisions, which Hau distributed among the 'children of the glorious princess'. The mate gave the Tahitians nails, buttons and other things, with which they were delighted.

Gore said that he and his party proceeded along the valley as far as they could go, searching all the stream beds for traces of metal or ore, but found none.

The gorge actually extends inland for about twelve miles. There were houses for the first six miles, an indication of the density of the population at that date. Then the path frequently passed under rocky vaults, where people who were benighted often slept. Finally the river was banked by steep cliffs, from which fell a violent cascade, forming a beautiful pool, one of those exquisite pools of the volcanic islands of the South Seas. The rocks, nearly perpendicular and one hundred feet high, were exceedingly slippery; yet up these precipices a way was traced by a succession of long pieces of bark serving as a rope for a climber. The bark came from the *parau* – *hibiscus tiliaceus* – a large tree resembling an elm and bearing a yellow blossom. It was used for canoes, rafters and paddles; the inside bark made washing-mats for clothing, ropes and lines.

Hau began to tire and there was a mountain before them. Perhaps he did not wish to take these 'children of the glorious princess' right up the valley. He made signs that he would leave them and go home. He told the natives who had supplied the food to take the baggage, the fruit which remained and some coconut shells filled with water, and signed to the white men that they would follow them up the side of the mountain.

When he had gone the Tahitians gathered green boughs from trees, and with many ceremonies whose meaning the Europeans

The solitary tree – an *aetae* (Erythrina) – on Skirmish Hill. Sketched by Sydney Parkinson in 1769.

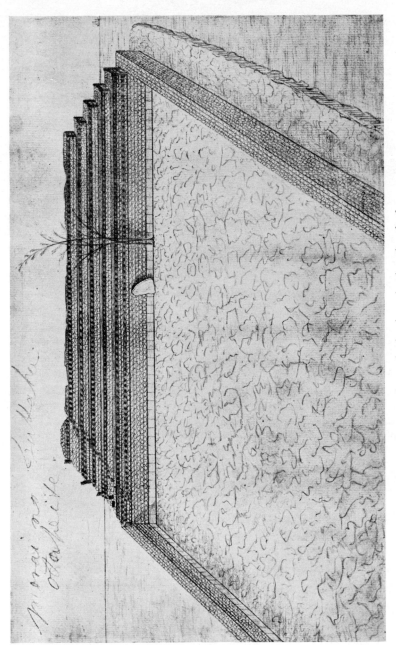

Robertson's *marai* from the landward side. Sketched in 1769.

did not know, laid them down before them. These were probably intended to be used to keep away the flies, but may have been symbols of delegated authority. They may have come from the *amai*, a close-grained wood, resembling mahogany, having a sweet smell and bearing a pod not unlike the scarlet bean. The tree was large, and its timber was used for canoes and the handles of tools. The deputy or the emissaries of a chief always carried a branch of it in his hand, to give authority to the message he delivered, for it was regarded as an emblem of truth; he that bore it was heard and received as if the chief himself were present.

The natives also now plucked *mati* berries with which they painted themselves red, as did the *Ariois;* the colour represented the blood of the sacred pig in which Oro dyed the league of men who sprang from him, in his effort for peace through free-love and dramatic entertainment, that they might 'enjoy their portion'. The tree, about the size of a cherry tree, clings to rocks on the moist sides of mountains. And they stained their garments with the yellow juice from the bark of a small tree, the *nono* – supposed to have been produced from ear wax.

The mate and his party began to climb the mountain while Hau was still in sight. Seeing that they were having difficulty in making their way through the dense undergrowth, the old man turned back and spoke to the Tahitians in a firm, loud tone, whereupon some twenty-five of the Tahitians went before the Europeans, cleared them a good path, refreshed them with water and fruit as they climbed and helped them over the most difficult places.

The ascent began at a point about six miles from where the party landed, and Gore reckoned the top of the mountain to be nearly a mile above the river which wound through the valley beneath. When in a very awkward spot he found a tree exactly like a fern, which he cut down and found the inside of it also like a fern, but even a section of it was too cumbersome to be carried.

On the summit of the mountain they sat down to rest and to eat and drink brandy. They had expected from here to command a view of the whole island. But they now saw before them wooded mountains so much higher that, in relation to them, they appeared

H

almost to be in a valley. These were the great central peaks of Tahiti.

The view in the direction of the ship was enchanting. The sides of the mountains were beautifully wooded and villages of thatched houses were interspersed everywhere on them. The valleys between them were even richer, the houses here stood thicker and the verdure was more luxuriant than up above. The white men saw very few huts above them, but smoke ascended in many places from between the highest mountains, and they thought that the loftiest parts of the island must be inhabited. The smoke, however, may have come from the fires of people working in the lonely and awe-inspiring interior, or from those of fugitives from sacrifice.

After a rest the 'children of the glorious princess' began to descend the mountain, attended by the painted Tahitians. They made towards the ship, but sometimes deviated a little to right and left when they passed any houses pleasantly situated. The inhabitants everywhere were ready to give them whatever they had. Sugar-cane grew wild, and ginger and turmeric – an ingredient of curry powder. The turmeric, in fact, grew like a weed, and the Tahitians extracted a yellow dye from it; and other Polynesians used it for food. These plants almost certainly were brought by their remote ancestors from Indonesia, together with breadfruit, pigs, fowls, candle-nuts and other things. The candle-nut, a large tree like the chestnut, bears a flat and very oily nut, something between a chestnut and a brazil. It would not burn well till scorched a little in the oven, when it was strung on the rib of a coconut leaf and afforded a tolerable light. The bark of the root of the tree yields a light-brown dye, and the trunk a good fuel.

No wild beast was seen, but a few wild hogs; nor any birds except parrots, parakeets (considered by the natives to be the shadows of royalty) and green doves (the shadows of the ghosts that haunted the woods), and by the river numerous ducks (the shadows of the sylvan elves). There are few duck now left, and presumably few sylvan elves. Every cultivated place flourished luxuriantly.

The mate planted peach, cherry and plum stones, the pips of limes, lemons and oranges, and a variety of garden seeds in the sort of situations where he had seen them growing in the West Indies. These foreign importations, including pineapples, Indian corn, tobacco and shaddocks, the last brought from Tonga by Captain Cook, seemed little valued by the islanders about thirty years later. They called the shaddock – a large citrus fruit – the foreign bread-fruit. But these plantings by the explorers Gore and Cook and others like Bligh, provided the basis for a considerable trade as soon as whaling began, the whalers buying such things as peaches and cabbages, which by the early nineteenth century had become quite common.

In the afternoon the party arrived at a delightful place, three miles from the *Dolphin*, where the local natives quickly cooked them two pigs and some fowls. There they remained until the cool of the evening, then made their way to the ship, having liberally rewarded their guides and the people who had provided so excellent a dinner. They behaved the whole day with decency and order, and separated from their Tahitian friends in perfect good temper.

★ ★ ★

When Gore's party came to the beach, Wallis put the Queen and her attendants into the boats to send them ashore. As Purea was going over the side of the ship she asked by signs if he was still determined to leave the island so soon. He made her understand that it was impossible for him to stay longer, whereupon she burst into a flood of tears which for a time rendered her speechless. As soon as her passion subsided she told him that she would come on board next day. 'And thus,' said Wallis, 'we parted.'

Next morning the traders were sent ashore, soon followed by Wallis, Clarke and the doctor. Meanwhile the master began to clear the ship for sea and had several sails bent, which had been unbent for repairs. A large double-canoe came from the south-west of the bay, with three of the fairest of the strong, well-made men whom Robertson had seen, paddled by eight of the red people. When they came alongside the fair men, who were very merry, seemed to want to come aboard, so Robertson signed for them to do so. But first they handed up three fine pigs weighing forty or fifty pounds each, then came up very cheerfully and shook hands on the quarter-deck. They appeared to be three brothers, about thirty, twenty-four and twenty years old. The seamen were ready to haul up the main-sail to bend it to the yard, so Robertson made signs to the brothers to assist. They pulled heartily until the sail was up to the yard; then the two youngest went up the shrouds and upon the yard and helped in bending the sail while the oldest stayed with the master, who paid him for his pigs. He seemed a sensible and intelligent sort of man.

Robertson asked the seamen if they had seen any of these brothers before; they said they had not. He tried to ascertain from the eldest where they lived. The man pointed to the south-west end of the bay, waved his hand farther and laughed, then made signs for Robertson to come and sleep at the place. The master tried to indicate that the ship would soon be going in that direction, when he would come to sleep at his house. That seemed to please the man. He called to his brothers in the shrouds, and made them come on to the quarter-deck and shake hands with Robertson, then told them to their delight that the ship was to come to their part of the island. At ten a.m. the barge returned with the captain and his companions, and the brothers were paddled away in their canoe towards the south-west. Purea also came aboard with a present of pigs and fowls, but soon went ashore.

The ship proceeded to complete her wood and water and was made ready for sea. More inhabitants came down to the beach from inland than had been seen before, many of superior rank. About three in the afternoon Purea arrived, handsomely dressed and followed by a large crowd. She crossed the river with her attendants and Hau and came on board with a gift of fruit, appearing very merry. But, the instant the captain indicated that he was to sail at sunrise, she was much concerned and made signs for him to stay ten days, telling him very earnestly that she would go into the country and bring plenty of pigs, fowls and fruit. (Here perhaps was an indication that the English were regarded as a people who just wandered about, getting what they could.) Wallis tried to express a proper sense of her kindness and bounty, but assured her that he would certainly sail next morning and emphasised his purpose by ordering the ship to be unmoored.

Purea then came down to nine, eight, seven, six and five days; and, when she found that he was still set to sail at sunrise, she cried for some minutes, then made numerous friendly signs to induce him to stay only two days longer. But Wallis could not agree. She burst into tears and wept in such a manner, Robertson said, that few men could have helped pitying her. Her reason for pressing them so hard to stay a few days longer he did not know; several officers suspected treachery and therefore agreed that it would be best to sail at sunrise.

Realising her precarious political position, Purea may have hoped to gain prestige by the captain's presence at the coronation of her small son, who donned the sacred girdle soon after the *Dolphin's* departure. Robertson, in any case, failed to understand the reason for his shipmates' uncharitable conjectures. He was convinced that this great lady had been their good friend ever since the first day she came on board the ship. Since then they had obtained nearly three times as much produce as they had before, and all the natives had been infinitely more trusting. They neither suspected they were being defrauded, nor had they attempted on their part to defraud. They had dealt fairly and honestly ever since; and the more the white men went among them, the happier they seemed to be. For days past the seamen had gone into the woods singly and had traded for all sorts of curiosities; and no man had ever made the least complaint of being swindled. And none of them had been molested, even when found by the natives with their girls well away from the guard.

Instead of harbouring treachery, Robertson said, the Queen shook hands with the officers and, when she found neither tears nor entreaties could persuade them to stay two days longer, made signs that she would spend the night on board that she might enjoy their company to the last. Her friendly plan was disapproved and she was made to understand that she must go ashore; but to please her they tried to indicate that they would soon return to her beautiful island.

She asked Wallis when he would return. He signified fifty days;

she made signs for thirty. The sign for fifty being continually repeated seemed to please her a little. She stayed on board the warship till night; then, with extreme difficulty, she was persuaded to go. All the officers gave her presents and she was told that the boat was ready. She threw herself down on the arms-chest, and wept a long time inconsolably. With extreme reluctance she then entered the barge, followed by her attendants and the old man. But the instant she was in the boat she again burst into tears. In Robertson's opinion, her grief proceeded from nothing but her unwillingness to lose their friendship and good company. When the barge put her ashore, she made a long speech to her people; the officer in the barge said that all seemed much concerned when she told them that the white men were really leaving in the morning.

Hau had often intimated that his son should accompany the ship, and the lad seemed willing. He had, however, now disappeared for two days. Wallis asked after him when he first missed him, and the old man made the captain understand that he had gone inland to see his friends but would return in time to sail. Wallis supposed that the father's courage failed him when the time drew near, and that he kept the boy in hiding till the ship was gone. That evening many large canoes came round the south-west point of the bay.

At break of day, Monday, 27th July, 1767, the *Dolphin* hove short to her anchor and the launch and cutter were sent for water. It was calm, and the anchor could not be weighed without a fresh breeze. When the boats got close to the watering-place, the 'children of the glorious princess' saw several hundred people on the beach. The spectacle made them unwilling to land as they had never before seen the natives come down there until the sun was up. They therefore suspected the Tahitians might be preparing to revenge the loss of their countrymen, killed when they tried to make a prize of the first ship.

The 'children' lay on their oars until they could see how the natives would behave. In a few minutes Purea came and made signs for them to land; but they would not until she ordered her people to the other side of the river. Then they went ashore, filled the casks and got them back into the boats. Purea gave the officer, Wilkinson, to understand that she had lain on the beach all night, with all the people whom he saw there, with the intention of seeing the white men once again before they sailed away.

She wept bitterly at seeing the ship move. And when Wilkinson stepped into the launch, having been carried to it, she wished to come off with him with her principal attendants. But he had strict orders from the captain not to allow any Tahitians on board. When he refused she ordered presents to be brought and had pigs and fruit put into the boat. She ordered a large double-canoe lying at some distance on the shore to be brought to her. She had probably been spending the night in it.

The boats came alongside the *Dolphin*. The seamen hoisted in the water-casks and took aboard the pigs, fowls and fruit, of which Purea had made a present. Her canoe was followed by sixteen others, and all came up to the frigate. She brought off yet more livestock. Wilkinson noted in his log-book for his own information that among the natives was 'one – the beautiful woman, all seeming very sorry for our departure'. His hand faltered when he wrote it.

The Queen came on board but, unable to speak, sat down and wept. After about an hour, a breeze sprang up. The *Dolphin's* anchor was weighed and sail was made. Finding it necessary to return into her canoe, Purea embraced the officers most affectionately, with many tears. All her attendants expressed grief at their departure.

Soon afterwards it fell calm and the seamen had to tow the ship up the lagoon with the boats. All the canoes returned to the war-ship, and Purea's canoe came up to the gun-room port, where her people made it fast. Again she shook hands with all the white men she could come near. Robertson said that she wept and cried with as much tenderness and affection as any wife or mother would do at parting with their husbands and children. Wallis recorded that she sat in the bow of her canoe, weeping inconsolably. He gave her many things which he thought would be useful, and some for ornament. She silently accepted them all but took little notice of anything.

Several of the large double-canoes had come from the south-west of the lagoon the previous night. In each of them, said Robertson, was a convenient place where a dozen people could sit under a canopy, not unlike the place where the gentlemen sat in the ornate City barges on the Thames, although not so finely decorated. In these large canoes were many families of jolly, fat, well-made people, much fairer than any he saw before, the two young ladies to whom the Queen introduced him excepted. They were dressed more neatly than any of the occupants of the other canoes. The servants who paddled these great canoes were copper-coloured, and their masters and mistresses appeared to have much power over them.

Robertson inquired of the trading party if they had seen these people before. They said 'no'. Neither had anyone on board the warship seen so many fair people at one time.

A venerable old man, to whom all the rest paid particular respect, was clothed better than the others; he wore a white turban and had a long grey beard. The fair people paid much attention to what he said and the servants seemed afraid when he spoke. But the people of Matavai Bay seemed not to understand him, and they all looked hard at him and kept clear of his canoe. Robertson saw his servants once paddle his canoe close to Purea's, when the old man was watching the seamen making sail. But the instant he observed his canoe foul of hers he spoke angrily to his servants and made them sheer off. That was the only respect he saw him show her, which made him suppose he was a high chief from a distance. He may have been Puni, the dreaded chief of Pora-Pora, and the fair people from the leeward islands Raiatea and Huahine, where the chiefly families were exceptionally fair.

Robertson had to take charge of the ship and carry her out to sea so could not take note of anything else except that both the men's and the women's ears were pierced though none had ear-rings. A few words which the old chief spoke Robertson wrote down, but being in a hurry he left the paper on the drumhead of the capstan, whence it was taken away or thrown overboard, so that the words and their meaning have been lost.

★   ★   ★

The *Dolphin* had laid in Matavai Harbour from the 24th June to the 27th July: nearly five weeks. Wallis named the bay Port Royal

Harbour, possibly after the famous harbour of Jamaica where the moon appears so exquisitely above the Blue Mountains.

By ten o'clock the ship was outside the reef; and, a fresh breeze springing up, the natives, and particularly the Queen, once more bade farewell, with such tenderness of affection and grief that, as Wallis said in the published account of the voyage, it filled both his heart and his eyes.

This and similar phrases introduced by his editor were to involve the gallant Wallis in a certain amount of criticism. Thus Horace Walpole, while blaming the editor, spoke of a new edition of Dido and Aeneas, adding that the new Dido did not even borrow the obscurity of a cave when she treated the travellers with the rites of Love as practised in Tahiti.

Some of the seamen, anticipating the mutineers of the *Bounty*, declared that they would stay here if they were sure of a ship home-ward bound in a few years' time. As for the Tahitians, they went up the hills and made farewell smoke-signals until the *Dolphin* and her company of human beings – no longer poor, distressed seamen – were out of sight, sailing to the west.

EPILOGUE

WRITING in 1891, the artist John La Farge said of Samoa that he felt 'a great wonder that no one had told me of a rustic Greece still alive somewhere, and still to be looked at. So that the old statues and frescoes were no conventionality – and the sailor, the missionary and the beachcomber were witnesses of things that they did not see, because they had not read'.

The old battle goes on. Those who recognise, even unconsciously, the classical influence in the South Seas are prepared to surrender to its charm, hook, line and sinker. For those with no knowledge of it or sympathy for it, the South Seas are 'all the bunk', and these people will rabidly attack the defenders of South Seas culture.

Strip the classical content from Herman Melville's *Typee*, and there is not much left. So Melville has been ferociously attacked for his *Typee* in a book recently published in the United States and England, and awarded the Anisfield-Wolf Award (with *Cry, the Beloved Country*) for the best work on racial relations published in its year. And one of La Farge's pictures of Samoa is misrepresented as an actual scene from *Typee* and attacked on that issue simply because the name Fayaway is attached to it, in a generic sense. La Farge makes this clear in his book. The fair Fayaway would never have been allowed alone in a Marquesan canoe, and a one-man canoe at that.

It seems strange that Dr Johnson should have been on the side of the Philistines, but so it was. The Admiralty commissioned Dr John Hawkesworth, a well-known journalist, to edit Byron's, Carteret's, Wallis's, and the first of Cook's voyages. At one period Hawkesworth used to dine weekly with Dr Johnson at the King's Head, a famous beef-steak house in Ivy Lane near St Paul's.

JOHNSON: These *Voyages* (pointing to the three large volumes of *Voyages to the South Sea*, which were just come out) *who* will read them through? A man had better work his way before the mast,

234

than read them through; they will be eaten by rats and mice, before they are read through. There can be little entertainment in such books; one set of Savages is like another.

BOSWELL: I do not think the people of Otaheite (Tahiti) can be reckoned Savages.

JOHNSON: Don't cant in defence of Savages.

BOSWELL: They have the art of navigation.

JOHNSON: A cat or a dog can swim.

BOSWELL: They carve very ingeniously.

JOHNSON: A cat can scratch, and a child with a nail can scratch.

Hawkesworth's compilation of the voyages to the South Seas again being mentioned, Johnson remarked: 'Sir, if you talk of it as a subject of commerce, it will be gainful; if as a book that is to increase human knowledge, I believe there will not be much of that. Hawkesworth can tell only what the voyagers have told him; and they have found very little, only one new animal, I think.'

BOSWELL: But many insects, Sir.

JOHNSON: Why, Sir, as to insects, Ray reckons of British insects twenty thousand species. They might have staid at home and discovered enough in that way . . .

BOSWELL: I am well assured that the people of Otaheite who have the bread tree, the fruit of which serves them for bread, laughed heartily when they were informed of the tedious process necessary with us to have bread; plowing, sowing, harrowing, reaping, threshing, grinding, baking.

JOHNSON: Why, Sir, all ignorant savages will laugh when they are told of the advantages of civilised life. Were you to tell men who live without houses how we pile brick upon brick, and rafter upon rafter, and that after a house is raised to a certain height, a man tumbles off a scaffold and breaks his neck; he would laugh heartily at our folly in building; but it does not follow that men are better without houses. No, Sir (holding up a slice of a good loaf), this is better than the bread tree.

Boswell goes on: 'I gave him an account of a conversation which had passed between me and Captain Cook, the day before, at dinner at Sir John Pringle's; and he was much pleased with the conscientious accuracy of that celebrated circumnavigator, who set me right as to many of the exaggerated accounts given by Dr Hawkesworth of his Voyage. I told him that while I was with the Captain, I catched the enthusiasm of curiosity and adventure, and felt a strong inclination to go with him on his next voyage.'

JOHNSON: Why, Sir, a man *does* feel so, till he considers how very little he can learn from such voyages.

BOSWELL: But one is carried away with the general grand and indistinct notion of *A Voyage Round the World*.

JOHNSON: Yes, Sir, but a man is to guard himself against taking a thing in general.

'I said I was certain that a great part of what we are told by travellers to the South Sea must be conjecture, because they had not enough of the language of those countries to understand so much as they have related. Objects falling under the observation of the senses might be clearly known; but every thing intellectual, every thing abstract – politicks, morals, and religion, must be darkly guessed. Dr Johnson was of the same opinion. He upon another occasion, when a friend mentioned to him several extraordinary facts, as communicated to him by the circumnavigators, slyly observed, "Sir, I never before knew how much I was respected by these gentlemen; they told *me* none of these things."

'He had been in company with Omai, a native of one of the South Sea Islands, after he had been some time in this country. He was struck by the elegance of his behaviour, and accounted for it thus: "Sir, he had passed his time, while in England, only in the best company; so that all he had acquired of our manners was genteel. As proof of this, Sir, Lord Mulgrave and he dined one day at Streatham; they sat with their backs to the light fronting me, so that I could not see distinctly; and there was so little of the savage in Omai, that I was afraid to speak to either, lest I should mistake one for the other."

'A gentleman expressed a wish to go and live three years at Otaheite, or New Zealand, in order to obtain a full acquaintance with people, so totally different from all that we have ever known, and be satisfied what pure nature can do for men.'

JOHNSON: What could you learn, Sir? What can savages tell, but what they themselves have seen? Of the past, or the invisible, they can tell nothing. The inhabitants of Otaheite and New Zealand are not in a state of pure nature; for it is plain they broke off from some other people. Had they grown out of the ground, you might have judged of a state of pure nature. Fanciful people may talk of a mythology being amongst them; but it must be invention. They have once had religion, which has been gradually debased. And what account of their religion can you suppose to be learnt from savages? Only consider, Sir, our own state: our religion is in a book; we have an order of men whose duty it is to teach it, we have one day in a week set apart for it, and this is in general pretty well observed: Yet ask the first ten gross men you meet, and hear what they can tell of their religion. . . .

Johnson continues: 'When we talk of pleasure, we mean sensual pleasure. When a man says he had pleasure with a woman, he does not mean conversation, but something of a very different nature. Philosophers tell you, that pleasure is *contrary* to happiness. Gross men prefer animal pleasure. So there are men who have preferred living among savages. Now what a wretch must he be, who is content with such conversation as can be had among savages! You may remember, an officer at Fort Augustus, who had served in America, told us of a woman whom they were obliged to *bind*, in order to get her back from savage life.'

BOSWELL: She must have been an animal, a beast.

JOHNSON: Sir, she was a speaking cat. . . . As to the sailor, when you look down from the quarter-deck to the space below, you see the utmost extremity of human misery: such crowding, such filth, such stench!

BOSWELL: Yet sailors are happy.

JOHNSON: They are happy as brutes are happy, with a piece of fresh meat, with the grossest sensuality. But, Sir, the profession of soldiers and sailors has the dignity of danger. Mankind reverence those who have got over fear, which is so general a weakness.

Here Mr (afterwards Sir William) Scott, who was of the company, interposed: But is not courage, mechanical, and to be acquired?

JOHNSON: Why yes, Sir, in a collective sense. Soldiers consider themselves only as part of a great machine.

SCOTT: We find people fond of being sailors.

JOHNSON: I cannot account for that, any more than I can account for other strange perversions of imagination.

* * *

The story of Captain Wallis's relations with the Tahitian chieftainess, Purea (better known in the England of the day as Queen Oberea), in the published record as edited by Hawkesworth, made Wallis the butt of London wits. But the facetious and sentimental interpolations of Dr Hawkesworth were mainly responsible for that result. He it was who introduced Wallis's tears, of which the captain made no mention in his manuscript journal. It was also he who, in Wallis's name, referred to Purea as 'my princess'. The captain had merely said – 'The Queen, I may call her', in his journal. The story of the voyage as edited by Hawkesworth had been read to the captain at the Admiralty, and he was given Hawkesworth's manuscript to peruse. As the reading at the Admiralty had been made in the presence of Lord Sandwich, the First Lord, Wallis may well have thought himself on safe ground in approving interpolations.

It was a strange fate for Wallis to travel thus down the ages. He was not entirely the polished and sentimental figure of the published voyage. But one would not wish it otherwise. Hawkesworth sensed the classical influence.

Horace Walpole wrote: Dr Hawkesworth is . . . provoking. An old black gentlewoman of forty carries Captain Wallis across a river when he was too weak to walk, and the man represents them as a new edition of Dido and Aeneas. Indeed, Dido the new does not even borrow the obscurity of a cave when she treats the travellers with the rites of Love, as practised in Otaheite.

In 1770 Wallis was appointed to H.M.S. *Torbay*, commissioned because of the tension created by the dispute with Spain about the Falkland Islands. Eventually he became an extra Commissioner in the Navy and died in 1795. He was not for long credited with the discovery of Tahiti. Its discovery was mistakenly attributed for about a hundred and twenty-five years to de Quiros, but was finally established in Wallis's favour, and so acknowledged by the Spaniards themselves.

Notwithstanding the abuse heaped upon him in his lifetime, and still subscribed to, for his editing of four voyages to the Pacific – which abuse, according to Fanny Burney, sent him into a decline and brought about his death – Hawkesworth in some respects did a good job as editor. He was one of the literary creators of the alluring Pacific Island legend, an honour which he shares with Bougainville and Forster, both men well versed in the classics and capable, like La Farge, of understanding what they saw. For this we – and Hollywood – are indebted to him; and for it in some measure the peculiar British Admiralty has to be thanked.

Robertson was given the rank of third lieutenant, the promotion dating from the beginning of the voyage, and fought at sea against the American colonists in the War of Independence. Before leaving the *Dolphin* he took a deputation of seamen to the Admiralty to receive the reply to their petition to the King for double pay, such as 'Foul Weather Jack' Byron's men had. If they failed to get the cash, at least they had experienced something new in the way of scenic beauty and sexual knowledge; perhaps the King and the Admiralty thought this a sufficient reward. They were told that if they would agree to serve on board guard-ships at various ports, suitable notice would be taken of them with respect to promotion. They found cold comfort in the reply and one of them showed his resentment by selling information regarding the voyage to a spy of the French and Spanish Embassies in London.

Little is known of Clarke beyond the fact that he was either dismissed or was too ill to go to sea again.

Furneaux and Gore were to become known through their association with Cook.

Purea finished poor and of little account, although she retained her royalty and her taste for young lovers to the end. Her last recorded words, to a British naval lieutenant, were, 'The king is frightened – you can have no hogs!' These should surely rank among famous last words. The wheel had come full cycle.

*　*　*

As for my qualifications for the task of writing this book: I have sailed before the mast in a top-sail schooner in the Pacific, one of the old wooden ships; have visited Tahiti; and have lived for long among Polynesians still in a fairly primitive state, for much of the time in their own houses.

The records for this work of reconstruction are remarkably complete.

In 1939 I was working on the book, as I had been for some time. While I was searching in the Public Record Office in London among unpublished journals of the early navigators to Tahiti, the late Major Hugh Carrington, of Christchurch, New Zealand, who had just finished writing his excellent *Life Of Captain Cook*, introduced himself. On learning what I was doing, he generously called my attention to the unpublished manuscript journal of George Robertson, the master of the *Dolphin*, as a document which might throw light on the character of the Tahitian named Tupaia. I was then searching in the journals of Cook's companions for information on this particular point. It was a rich find, and I forthwith devoted several weeks to making long extracts from Robertson's journal and various other manuscript journals of the *Dolphin's* voyage. I see that I wrote at the end of my final notebook – 'Copied in the Public Record Office, London, July and August, 1939. At the end, the records were being removed because of the prospect of war.'

Major Carrington subsequently produced an edition of Robertson's Journal for the Hakluyt Society, which was published in 1948. This work demands of the reader a fairly thorough knowledge of the discovery of Tahiti for full appreciation, although it contains valuable notes. The spelling is archaic; and inevitably it contains much redundant material from the point of view of the general reader. I should mention that my interpretation of Robertson's handwriting differs in places from Major Carrington's. For instance, where he reads – 'I saw Casey making out the plan of this Bay', I read – 'I was busey (busy) making out the plan of this Bay'. Major Carrington admitted in one of his notes that there was no one in the Ship's Muster Roll to whom the name of Casey can be made to apply, nor does 'Casey' appear elsewhere in the text of the *Journal*.

Robertson habitually made out the plans of bays. He refers to it himself; it was his job. Therefore I prefer my own interpretation, while I gratefully acknowledge that I have found the information in some of Major Carrington's notes very useful.

Later, I found in the Public Record Office an unpublished, and I think unclassified, *Journal* of Robertson's regarding the same voyage which I have been able to incorporate with advantage with the previous *Journal*. It is bound up by mistake with that of Captain Wallis. And there were the numerous log-books and journals of his shipmates in the Record Office. Before leaving the Pacific Captain Wallis took from the petty officers and seamen all their log-books and journals in the interests of official secrecy and for the information they might contain. Hence this book contains historical material which has never yet appeared in print.

The circumstances of the birth of the royal child in Tahiti, Queen Purea's relations with her husband, her lover, Tupaia, and mother, and the building of the great *marai* at Papara are given in various other records.

At all costs I wanted to avoid the detestable medium of fictional biography. It has been rightly said of it that 'it demands more credence from the reader than it is able to satisfy, because it hovers uncertainly between the presentation of fact and fantasy. The more sympathetic and searching it is in its fictional moments, the more wary the reader becomes, so that the author is never fully accepted'. In this book I have not (unless I have indicated the contrary) ascribed word or deed to Europeans or islanders which is not somewhere on record. I have introduced local colour here and there, as with naval customs; but the conversations are as recorded. I have usually quoted Robertson's brother officer Wilkinson in inverted commas, since he provides some valuable evidence never before published.

I have drawn on the Appendix to The Voyage of the 'Duff' – the record of the first English missionary voyage to the South Seas, published in 1799 – for passages concerning Tahitian customs and flora; and here I am able, I think, to clear up a certain amount of misunderstanding. The missionaries adapted this Appendix mainly from the second part of a manuscript copy of The Journal of James

Morrison, boatswain's mate of the *Bounty*, although they make scarcely any acknowledgement apart from vague references. They say: 'These papers have been drawn up from manuscripts attended with every mark of authenticity, and from conversations with a variety of persons who have been lately on the spot, and whose veracity is highly to be respected.' They also remark in the account of their voyage: 'An ingenious clergyman of Portsmouth kindly furnished Dr Haweis and Mr Greatheed with a manuscript vocabulary of the Otaheitean language, and an account of the country, which providentially he had preserved from the mutineers who were seized by the *Pandora*, and brought to Portsmouth for their trial, which was of unspeakable service to the missionaries, both for the help which it afforded them to learn before their arrival much of this unknown tongue, and also as giving the most inviting and encouraging description of the natives, and the cordial reception which they might expect.'

The Journal of James Morrison, from a manuscript copy in the possession of the Mitchel Library in Sydney, was first published in its entirety in 1935 by the Golden Cockerel Press. The editor says that from the first part 'other writers have made sundry quotations, but so far as I am aware no one has made any extract from the second part, which contains a detailed description of Tahiti and of the islanders' customs, social organisation and mode of life'. This second part, however, was, as I say, freely used by the missionaries in compiling their Appendix, as a detailed comparison of the two documents will show. Yet the editor of *The Journal of James Morrison* says, 'Nor does his work lose by comparison with the account of Tahiti which was compiled from the journals of the first English missionaries who visited the island, and included as an appendix to *A Missionary Voyage to the South Pacific Ocean, performed in the years 1796, 1797 and 1798 in the ship 'Duff'*. I must admit that it was some time before I myself saw the connection between the two documents. My information proves conclusively and finally the authenticity of *The Journal of James Morrison* and also establishes what happened to his missing vocabulary, which has been the subject of search.

I have occasionally quoted directly from Morrison. It was he who provided the bulk of the information on the early internal history of Tahiti, given by the missionaries in the 'Preliminary Discourse' to their book, of which I have made use.

From sundry references it is clear beyond doubt that the missionaries had access to the first part of *The Journal of James Morrison* – involving his adventures in Tahiti – in addition to the second part. Morrison undoubtedly left his mark on the Pacific, for he influenced the development of the missionary movement which decided, among other things, the fate of the dynastic wars in Tahiti. His influence, which must be felt to this day by the majority of people living in the central Pacific – for Tahiti was the centre of the missionary movement and the missionaries could scarcely have established themselves there without the anonymous help of Morrison – has not, so far as I know, received the slightest recognition. But this, I suppose, is not so very much out of the ordinary.

The facts regarding Queen Hototu, Queen Purea's insulting treatment of her own mother and niece, and the rise of the Teva family, are derived from *Reminiscences of the South Seas* published in 1913, a book written by the American painter, John La Farge. La Farge visited Tahiti in 1891 and stayed with Queen Marau. He was accompanied by the distinguished American historian Henry Adams, who covered the same ground and more in *The Memoirs of Ari'i Taimai*. La Farge states that he wrote down the legends largely in the Queen's actual words. He was most anxious to save them, and says that King Kalakaua of Hawaii had long wished to obtain them, but that Marau had been unwilling. Polynesians are apt to be very secretive in matters concerning genealogy, a peculiarity which Europeans find difficult to understand. When one tells them that Europeans have no objection to discussing their own genealogies, they will laugh and wriggle with a sort of horror, and say with bated breath that it is not so with them. I think it has something to do with land titles, or with a supposed totemistic origin. Anyway, there is some danger in the telling for the information might be used against them. Marau was known to Gauguin, who mentions her in *Noa Noa*. She was the great-great-great-niece of Purea; and Amo, Purea's husband, was her great-great-great-uncle. She was removed from her position for a time, for refusing to let Purea's great *marai* be used as a quarry.

I have been obliged to amend the spelling of some of the names, which, incidentally, brings to light the meaning of the warning given by the high priest Manea, regarding which La Farge said he was not clear. I have, in fact, corrected the spelling of Tahitian names wherever necessary.

The information regarding the *Arioi* Society is drawn from *Polynesian Researches* by the missionary W. Ellis, and from Captain Cook, Morrison and Orsmond. I might remark that descendants of other missionaries have accused the long-defunct Mr Ellis of having included their forefathers' writings and researches in his book without any acknowledgement, a characteristic of South Seas literature from the time of Defoe to the present century.

I have, of course, drawn on the writings of Carteret, Byron, Wallis and Cook, published in 1773 under the authority of the Admiralty, and on the Introduction of Dr John Hawkesworth, their contemporary editor. And I have checked my statements with Wallis's manuscript *Journal* in the Public Record Office.

With regard to Cook's first voyage, I have gone to Cook's verbatim account, in addition to that of Sir Joseph Banks, who accompanied him. Cook's *Journal*, edited by Captain W. J. L. Wharton, R.N., was first published in 1893 (*sic*). Banks's *Journal*, edited by Sir Joseph D. Hooker from the transcript in the British Museum, was first published, as a separate document, in 1896. Hawkesworth first combined the two stories, in Cook's name, in 1773.

I have referred to Bougainville's story of his own voyage, and have made reference to Cook's (Three) Voyages, published in 1842 by William Smith; also to George Forster's *A Voyage round the World, in his Britannic Majesty's Sloop 'Resolution', commanded by Captain James Cook, during the years 1772–1775.* This was published in 1777. Forster was a tutor of the famous Humboldt. His reference to the extraordinarily happy condition of Raiatea, as a result of the activities of a Society of free-lovers is worthy of note. He said that the *Ariois* so much resembled the happy indolent people whom

Ulysses found in Phæacia that they could apply the lines of Pope's *Homer* to themselves with peculiar propriety:

> *To dress, to dance, to sing, our sole delight,*
> *The feast or bath by day, and love by night.*

Unfortunately we know all too little about this astonishing experiment in the matter of eliminating war.

Some modern books which I have found useful are *The Exploration of the Pacific* by J. C. Beaglehole, 1934; *Pacific Horizons* by C. Lloyd, 1946; *The Life of Captain Cook* by H. Carrington, 1939; *Hawaiki* by S. Percy Smith; and Gauguin's *Noa Noa*. I have also derived information from the three volumes of the late B. G. Corney's English translations of numerous Spanish documents and the accounts of the early Spanish voyages to Tahiti, published by the Hakluyt Society in 1913 and entitled *The Quest and Occupation of Tahiti by Emissaries of Spain*.

I obtained some facts about naval customs of the period from a book on that subject by Mr John Masefield, and from *The British Fleet* by Commander C. N. Robinson, R.N., published in 1894. The author expressed the 'earnest hope' that his book might prove useful to the publicist and the student, and I have certainly found it so. I have consulted the *Dictionary of National Biography*.

A source of my information – particularly regarding *marai*, Back-to-back-wood-fetchers, peace ceremonies, and legends, in addition to a lot of minor matters – is *Ancient Tahiti* by Teuira Henry (Bernice P. Bishop Museum, Honolulu, Bulletin 48) published in 1928. This massive volume is based on material recorded by the Reverend J. M. Orsmond, one of the early missionaries, who arrived in Tahiti in 1817. Miss Henry was his grand-daughter. The manuscript of Mr Orsmond's book was lost by the French Government, to whom he had presented it for publication, but his grand-daughter, who died in Tahiti in 1915, undertook to reconstruct the work from the original papers. It is said of Mr Orsmond: 'Chief, priest, *arioi*, landowner and *manahune* – he knew them all, listened to what they had to say and recorded words, customs and legends while they were still fresh in memory.' Mr Orsmond (who had been an iconoclast in his time, but became more mellow afterwards) said: 'Feeling the great importance of crystallising Tahitian literature in all its original simplicity and style of rendering, wherein lies its greatest charm, I have carefully collected the records as they fell from the lips of priests and bards and other learned natives of both sexes, in doing which, with pencil and paper in hand, I have been struck with the beauty of the language and the richness of many of the words and figures of speech. This folklore I have carefully revised with the aid of the best native scholars of all classes.'

It is also said in one of the five prefaces to *Ancient Tahiti:* 'A debt is due to the old navigators and those who sailed with them, for their accounts are all that may be hoped for. . . . But the investigator in the Polynesian field who attempts to reconstruct the ancient life of Tahiti and the neighbouring islands must add two more names to the list, and acknowledge his deep indebtedness to the Rev. J. M. Orsmond and to his grand-daughter, Teuira Henry.'

This deep indebtedness I most gratefully acknowledge.

It has not seemed possible, however, to cover all the necessary information from such sources. The passage regarding the Polynesian method of signalling to advance, for instance, is my own, and comes within my personal knowledge; also a part of the passage regarding Polynesian massage and a good many similar comments.

I have to thank Dr J. W. Davidson, Ph.D., and Mr J. D. Freeman, a New Zealander, both of whom know the Pacific and its literature, and my brother, the Reverend E. J. Rowe, for reading the manuscript in an earlier stage and making various criticisms and suggestions which have been very helpful. I have particularly to thank Miss Elsa Brayley for reading the manuscript in its final stages and giving very valuable advice. I have referred to Sir Harry Luke, K.C.M.G., D.Litt., in the Foreword. I have also to express my indebtedness to the helpfulness and courtesy of the officials of the Public Record Office, in particular to Mr E. K. Timings, M.A.; the British Museum Library, particularly for permission to reproduce the valuable illustrations of this book; and the Municipal Libraries in Bristol (the Central Library) and Bath.

N. A. R.

May the land live!
The marai *is restored, it is weeded and*
become handsome.
The carved ornaments are renewed.
The altars are renewed.
The home of the gods is renewed.
The gods will all come, and gather in
the darkness.

Tahitian chant from *Ancient Tahiti*

BIBLIOGRAPHY

Adams, Henry (edited): *Memoirs of Ari'i Tamai*, Paris, privately printed, 1901.

Anson, Lord: *A Voyage Round the World in the Years 1740–4*, London, J. M. Dent, Everyman Edition, 1911.

Barrow, Sir John: *The Mutiny and Piratical Seizure of H.M.S. 'Bounty'*, Oxford University Press, 1914.

Beaglehole, J. C.: *The Exploration of the Pacific*, London, A. & C. Black, 1934.

Boswell, James. *The Life of Samuel Johnson*, London, J. M. Dent, Everyman Edition, 1928.

Bougainville, Count L. de: *A Voyage Round the World in the Years 1766–9*. Translated from the French by J. R. Forster. London, Nourse & Davies, 1772.

Burney, Fanny: *Early Diary*, London, G. Bell, 1907, and *Memoirs of Dr Burney*, London, Edward Moxon, 1832.

Carrington, Hugh: *Life of Captain Cook*, London, Sidgwick & Jackson, 1939.

(Edited) *A Journal by George Robertson*, London, The Hakluyt Society, 1948.

Cook, James: *The Voyages of Captain James Cook*, London, William Smith, 1842.

Corney, B. G. (edited): *The Quest and Occupation of Tahiti by Emissaries of Spain*, London, The Hakluyt Society, 1913.

Dalrymple, A.: *Letter from Mr Dalrymple to Dr Hawkesworth*, London, J. Nourse, 1773.

Darwin, Charles: *The Voyage of the Beagle*, London, J. M. Dent, Everyman Edition, 1906.

Diderot, Denis: *Supplément au voyage de Bougainville*, Paris, Editions de la Nouvelle Française, 1921.

Ellis, William: *Polynesian Researches*, London, Fisher, Son & Jackson, 1831.

Fairchild, H. N.: *The Noble Savage*, Oxford University Press, 1928.

Firth, Raymond, W.: *Primitive Polynesian Economy*, London, George Routledge, 1939.

Forster, Georg: *A Voyage Round the World in His Majesty's Sloop 'Resolution'*, 1772–5, London, B. White, 1777.

Furnas, J. C. *Anatomy of Paradise*, London, Gollancz, 1950.

Gauguin, Paul: *Noa, Noa*, New York, Nicolas L. Brown, 1920.

Guild, Caroline: *Rainbow in Tahiti*, New York, Doubleday, 1948.

Hawkesworth, John (edited): *Voyages for making Discoveries in the Southern Hemisphere*, London, Strahan & Cadell, 1773.

Henry, Teuira: *Ancient Tahiti*, Honolulu, Bernice P. Bishop Museum, Bulletin No. 48, 1928.

Holmes, Sir Maurice. *Introduction to the Bibliography of Captain James Cook*, London, Francis Edwards, 1936.

Hooker, Sir Joseph D. (edited): *Journal of Sir Joseph Banks*, London, Macmillan, 1896.

Kemp, Jonathan (edited): *Diderot, Interpreter of Nature*, London, Lawrence & Wishart, 1937.

La Farge, John: *Reminiscences of the South Seas*, London, Grant Richards, 1913.

Lee, Ida: *Captain Bligh's Second Voyage to the South Sea*, London, Longmans, Green, 1920.

Lloyd, Christopher: *Pacific Horizons*, London, George Allen & Unwin, 1946.

Loti, Pierre: *Le Mariage de Loti*, Paris, Calmann-Lévy, 1881.

Masefield, John: *Sea Life in Nelson's Time*, London, Methuen, 1905.

Melville, Herman: *Omoo and Typee*, London, J. M. Dent, Everyman Edition, 1907.

Missionary Voyage in the Southern Pacific Ocean, 1796–8, in the ship *Duff*: London, T. Chapman, 1799.

Morrison, James: *The Journal of James Morrison*, London, Golden Cockerel Press, 1935.

Murray, A. W.: *Forty Years' Mission Work in Polynesia and New Guinea*, London, James Nisbet, 1876.

Robinson, C. N.: *The British Fleet*, London, G. Bell, 1894.

Smith, S. Percy: *Hawaiki*, Christchurch, N.Z., Whitcombe & Tombs, 1920.

Stevenson, R. L.: *In the South Seas*, London, Chatto & Windus, 1890. *A Footnote to History*, London, Cassel, 1892.

Stoddard, Charles Warren: *Summer Cruising in the South Seas*, London, Chatto & Windus, 1905.

Thomson, Sir Basil (edited): *Voyage of H.M.S. 'Pandora'*, London, Francis Edwards, 1915.

Walpole, Horace: *Letters* (edited Toynbee), Oxford University Press, 1903–25.

Wharton, W. J. L. (edited): *Captain Cook's Journal* (Voyage of H.M.S. *Endeavour*), London, Stock, 1893.

Williams, John: *A Narrative of Missionary Enterprise in the South Sea Islands*, New York, Appleton, 1837.

Williamson, R. W.: *The Social and Political Systems of Central Polynesia*, Cambridge University Press, 1924.

Winter, John: *The voyage of M. John Winter into the South Sea by the Strait of Magellan, in consort with M. Francis Drake, begun in the year 1577. Edward Cliffe.* Hakluyt's Voyages, London, Maclehose & Jackson, 1903.

IN THE PUBLIC RECORD OFFICE, LONDON

Captain Wallis's manuscript Journal, Ad. 55/35.

Robertson's Journal and fifteen others in bundles, Ad. 51/4538–9, 4541–2–3–4.

Muster Roll of H.M.S. *Dolphin* and other official papers, Ad. 36/7580.

INDEX